Resacralizing the Other at the US-Mexico Border

This book focuses on the themes of border violence; racial criminalization; competing hermeneutics of the sacred; and State-sponsored modes of desacralizing black- and brown-bodied people, all in the context of the US-Mexico borderlands. It provides a much-needed substantive response to the State's use of sacralization to justify its acts of violence and offers new ways of theologizing the acceptance of the "other" in its place.

As a counter-hermeneutic of the sacred, the ultimate objective of the book is to offer an alternative epistemological, theoretical, and practical framework that resacralizes the other. Rejecting the State-driven agenda of othering border-crossers, it follows Gloria Anzaldúa's healing move to the sacred Other and creates a new hermeneutic of the sacred at the borderlands; one that resacralizes those deemed by the State as the nonsacred human other anywhere in the world.

This is an important and topical book that addresses one of the key issues of our time. As such, it will be of keen interest to any scholar of religious studies and liberation theology as well as religion's interaction with migration, race, and contemporary politics.

Gregory L. Cuéllar is Associate Professor of Old Testament at Austin Presbyterian Theological Seminary, USA. He is the author of *Voices of Marginality* (2008) and *Empire, the British Museum, and the Making of the Biblical Scholar in the Nineteenth Century: Archival Criticism* (2019).

Routledge New Critical Thinking in Religion, Theology and Biblical Studies

The *Routledge New Critical Thinking in Religion, Theology and Biblical Studies* series brings high quality research monograph publishing back into focus for authors, international libraries, and student, academic and research readers. This open-ended monograph series presents cutting-edge research from both established and new authors in the field. With specialist focus yet clear contextual presentation of contemporary research, books in the series take research into important new directions and open the field to new critical debate within the discipline, in areas of related study, and in key areas for contemporary society.

Laudato Si' and the Environment
Pope Francis' Green Encyclical
Robert McKim

Theology Without Walls
The Transreligious Imperative
Jerry L. Martin

A New Theist Response to the New Atheists
Edited by Joshua Rasmussen and Kevin Vallier

Biblical and Theological Visions of Resilience
Pastoral and Clinical Insights
Edited by Nathan H. White and Christopher C.H. Cook

The Fourth Pentecostal Wave in South Africa
A Critical Engagement
Solomon Kgatle

Resacralizing the Other at the US-Mexico Border
A Borderland Hermeneutic
Gregory L. Cuéllar

For more information about this series, please visit: www.routledge.com/religion/series/RCRITREL

Resacralizing the Other at the US-Mexico Border
A Borderland Hermeneutic

Gregory L. Cuéllar

LONDON AND NEW YORK

First published 2020
by Routledge
2 Park Square, Milton Park, Abingdon, Oxon OX14 4RN

and by Routledge
52 Vanderbilt Avenue, New York, NY 10017

Routledge is an imprint of the Taylor & Francis Group, an informa business

First issued in paperback 2021

© 2020 Gregory L. Cuéllar

The right of Gregory L. Cuéllar to be identified as author of this work has been asserted by him in accordance with sections 77 and 78 of the Copyright, Designs and Patents Act 1988.

All rights reserved. No part of this book may be reprinted or reproduced or utilised in any form or by any electronic, mechanical, or other means, now known or hereafter invented, including photocopying and recording, or in any information storage or retrieval system, without permission in writing from the publishers.

Trademark notice: Product or corporate names may be trademarks or registered trademarks, and are used only for identification and explanation without intent to infringe.

British Library Cataloguing-in-Publication Data
A catalogue record for this book is available from the British Library

Library of Congress Cataloging-in-Publication Data
A catalog record for this book has been requested

ISBN: 978-0-367-34833-5 (hbk)
ISBN: 978-1-03-208383-4 (pbk)
ISBN: 978-0-429-32824-4 (ebk)

Typeset in Sabon
by Apex CoVantage, LLC

To All Migrant Border Crossers

4   For they have no pain; their bodies are sound and sleek.
5   They are not in trouble as others are; they are not plagued like other people.
6   Therefore pride is their necklace; violence covers them like a garment.
7   Their eyes swell out with fatness; their hearts overflow with follies.
8   They scoff and speak with malice; loftily they threaten oppression.
9   They set their mouths against heaven, and their tongues range over the earth.

—Psalm 73:4–9, NRSV

Contents

List of figures viii
Acknowledgments ix

1 Introduction 1

2 Trespassing on the archive as the border-crossed other 27

3 The sacralizing performance of a counter archive 55

4 The desacralizing power of immigrant detention 81

5 Caring for the sacred Other 110

6 Afterword: humanitarian entrepreneurs of marketized migrant trauma 135

Index 159

Figures

1.1 On May 19, 1916, Mexican prisoners Melquíades Chapa and José Buenrostro posed in front of an altar with candles, flowers, a statue of Our Lady of Lourdes, and a crucifix. The photo was taken in the chapel of the newly built Cameron County Jail immediately before the two prisoners were led outside to the gallows. They were tried and convicted in Brownsville for the murder of A.L. Austin and his son Charles in the fall of 1915. Up until their hanging, reports indicate that both men maintained their innocence. (Photograph by Robert Runyon; Dolph Briscoe Center for American History.) 10

3.1 A 1915 picture postcard of Captain James Fox, Texas Ranger (left); a member of Fox's Ranger force (middle); Tom Tate, Cowboy/Special Ranger (right); and the bodies of four roped Mexican men: Jesús García, Mauricio García, Amado Muñoz, and Muñoz's brother. It was sold at public postcard stands in Brownsville, Texas, to intimidate ethnic Mexicans in the border region. (Photograph by Robert Runyon; Dolph Briscoe Center for American History.) 61

Acknowledgments

As a son of the Texas-Mexico borderlands, my initial ideas for this book trace back to my childhood. To the storytellers in my family who first nurtured my postcolonial imagination, I owe perhaps the most overdue acknowledgment. I can still recall the righteous indignation of my maternal grandmother, Maria Luisa Gonzalez Rios, when she spoke about the racial injustices of the King Ranch and *Los Rinches*. Growing up in South Texas, Mexican music was always in the background of everyday life. Whether at family gatherings or from my grandmother's crackling kitchen radio, my childhood was never lacking of Tejano and mariachi music. It is only now that I am really able to appreciate the influence my maternal grandfather, Francisco (Paco) Rios's, *corrido* singing had on my borderlands psyche early on in life. In writing about the biblical border *corridos*, I am indebted to my father, Daniel E. Cuéllar. Even well after his passing, I still listen to the albums he recorded with his two Mexican/Tejano Pentecostal Gospel bands, *Los Israelitas* and the Jerichos. While living in Victoria, Texas, his late-night guitar practicing in his bedroom was my lullaby. There were also the counter stories my uncle Derle Cuéllar told me about our Jewish heritage and the unjust loss of familial lands after 1848. Like so many "border-crossed" ethnic Mexicans/Tejanos, he is still fighting to recover them. To my mother, Delma Rios-Salazar, I owe a very great debt indeed. She was the first to teach me about the "other side" to Texas history, which for her was best found in Rodolfo Acuña's *Occupied American: The Chicano's Struggle Toward Liberation* (although as a ten-year-old, I would have preferred to stay home and play with my friends than go with my mother to her monthly LULAC Council 4319 meetings). The activist spirit of this book was nourished at these meetings. The scene of visionary Chicano/a community leaders around a table still inspires my political imagination and belief that through organized activism change is possible.

Thanks to Carlos Larralde for the many thought-provoking phone conversations about his uncle J.T. Canales and the atrocities of the Texas Rangers in the early twentieth century. Over the years of our friendship, he has elevated my archival awareness to new heights. Profound thanks are due to Daisy Machado. As a doctoral student at Brite Divinity School (Texas

Christian University), she was among the first to hone my thinking about borderlands religion. While director of the Borderlands Institute, she introduced me to a number of Latinx scholarly giants who have since shaped my understanding of the sacred and the US-Mexico border. They include Carlos Cardoza Orlandi, Ada Maria Isasi-Diaz, Orlando Espín, Jean-Pierre Ruiz, David Carrasco, Fernando Segovia, Otto Maduro, and Milagros Peña. Two radical historians have left their marks on this project in ways perhaps only they can see: José Angel Gutiérrez and his book *A Gringo Manual*, as well as David Montejano and his book *Anglos and Mexicans in the Making of Texas*. In my signed copies of these two books, José inscribed the words "¡*Viva la raza*!" and David inscribed "¡*Que viva la historia verdadera, vamos adelante*!" Their words continue to remind me to remain in the struggle for justice and equality in what many longtime ethnic Mexicans in South Texas consider to be occupied territory.

Many other people have helped me realize this book, either wittingly or unwittingly, and I am profoundly grateful to all of them: Néstor Rodríguez, Paul Barton, Daniel Ramírez, Efrain Agosto, Norma Pimentel, Joseph DeLeon, Lydia Hernández, Eli Fernández, and Caly Fernández. I was delighted to have an opportunity to test the ideas in this book at the Hispanic Summer Program (HSP). At the 2013 HSP and 2016 HSP, I offered a postgraduate master class titled "A Borderlands Reading of Deuteronomistic History (Joshua—Kings)." I am grateful to the students who bravely took this class. Their questions and classroom discussions have indeed shaped my sense of the sacred in the borderlands. The project also profited from the input of my cohort of the Wabash Teaching and Learning Workshop for Pre-Tenure Latino/a Religion Faculty in Theological Schools, Colleges, and Universities, and I would like to acknowledge them here: Santiago Piñón, Eduardo Fernández, S.J., Ana María Pineda, Miguel De La Torre, Elizabeth Conde-Frazier, Eric Barreto, Angel Santiago Vendrell, María Del Socorro Castañeda-Liles, Lourdes Rincón, Angela Tarángo, Adriana Nieto, Santiago Slabodsky, Sammy Alfaro, Déborah Junker, Cláudio Carvalhaes, Jacqueline Hidalgo, Paul Myhre (Wabash Center), Daniel Castelo, Christopher Tirres, and Oscar García Johnson. To the Wabash Center, I owe much debt. My 2013 Small Project Grant and 2016 Peer Mentoring Cluster Grant afforded me the opportunity to gather with coconspirators to discuss decentering pedagogies. Our meetings have proven invaluable to me as I conceived this book.

I have appreciated the opportunity to present parts of this manuscript at the 2010 Annual Meeting of the Society of Biblical Literature (SBL) and the 2015 International Meeting of SBL in Buenos Aires, Argentina. At both meetings, the audiences' comments and feedback were especially invaluable. Thanks to Jay Alanis for the multiple opportunities to present my ideas on border *corridos* in his course Mission in Latino Context at the Seminary of the Southwest. His passion for borderlands and the migrant border crosser has shaped my thinking in more ways than he knows. At these seminars, I was always motivated anew to write this book when students asked, "why didn't I learn this in school?" Other formative speaking engagements that refined my thinking for Chapter 2 include my 2015 lecture "Borderlands Hermeneutics" at The Center for the Study of Latin@ Theology and Ministry, McCormick Theological Seminary, and the 2013 lecture "A Borderlands Readings of the Bible" at the Interdisciplinary Dialogue, Perkins School of Theology (Southern Methodist University). A first version of Chapter 4 was prompted from a blog post I wrote for Centre for Migration, Policy, and Society (COMPAS) at the University of Oxford. The intellectual community that surrounded me while at COMPAS has left an indelible mark on my research, writing, teaching, and thinking.

Thanks go to my faculty colleagues at Austin Presbyterian Theological Seminary. My thinking about the borderlands has benefitted from their intellectual camaraderie. I would also like to acknowledge the archival assistance of Kristy Sorenson, without whom various sections of this book would have been impossible. Thanks to my superb graduate research assistants over the course of writing this project, Elizabeth Wallace, Julia Giddings, Sarah Shannon-Wildt, Hierald Osorto, Caitlin Parsons, and Usama Malik, who helped me work through various stages of the book in ways too meaningful to fully capture here. It has been a pleasure to work with Routledge. Thanks to Joshua Wells and R Yuga Harini for their generous patience and for seeing this book through to its final form.

There are two Latino colleagues whom I had in mind as readers for this book: my admired friend David A. Sánchez, and Luis D. León, whom I never formally met. During the final years of writing this, these two scholarly giants had sadly passed away. Much is due to my partner, Nohemi, who has nourished my soul with an unfailing love. To have you beside me on this journey of life has been a true joy and privilege. Also sustaining me in work and in life are our four loving daughters. They are what gets me up in the mornings.

Much of what Chapters 4, 5, and 6 are about stem from my volunteer work with *Arte de Lágrimas*: Refugee Artwork Project at the Humanitarian Respite Center in McAllen, Texas. *Arte de Lágrimas* is an art-based project that seeks to share the stories of asylum-seeking families, mainly those migrating from Central America, in an effort to raise awareness about their plight and treatment. From 2014 to 2016, I and a small team of graduate students partnered with Catholic Charities of the Rio Grande Valley to set up art-making stations at the Sacred Heart Catholic Church Relief Center and the Central Bus Station in McAllen, Texas. As the principal director of the project, I saw the biblical exilic tropes of homeland and journey as viable art-making tasks for the asylum-seeking children wanting ideas on what to draw. We witnessed how for each participating child artist, drawing pictures on the selected themes of journey and homeland helped them to construct a healing space in which their religious beliefs served to counter their traumatized memories of violence and victimization. To all the students, clergy, activists, and concerned citizens who participated in this project, I owe an immeasurable debt. To all of the asylum-seeking families we encountered during this volunteer experience, who showed me the face of the divine and taught me the meaning of the sacred, this book is in turn lovingly dedicated.

1 Introduction

Operating at the intersections of social bodies and ways of knowing is a plurality of hermeneutical regimes of the sacred. Not only do different regimes of hermeneutical approaches align themselves with particular social milieus, but they also give rise to varying economies of truth-making. Since the rise of the modern period, the reigning hermeneutical strategy in the Western world has designated the dispassionate eye of a disembodied interpreter as the master mode for understanding reality and human existence. As persuasive as this mode has been for Westerners, the sway of the sacred represents an equally influential optic for interpreting the meaning of life. For Western elite power structures, the high level of public authority ascribed to the sacred has attracted steady investments as a way to reproduce their power. For elite power structures to seize control of the sacred, they require a web of synchronized logics and an endless reservoir of economic wealth. With the will to conquer as its prerequisite, elite power turns to credentialing processes, modes of professionalization, institutions (state and religious), publishing markets, mass media outlets, and a network of agents like archivists, policing personnel, humanitarians, clergy, health care providers, lawyers, and educators. Here, the sacred loses its otherworldliness to become the exclusive world in which elite power is reproduced. By controlling the sacred, elite power moves to define the public meaning of the sacred and hence shape social reality. Here the intrinsic otherness associated with the realms of the sacred offer elite power not only harnessable public authority but also an othering weapon against certain people. Integral to this book is the latter benefit that comes to elite power from its investments in the sacred. The weaponization of the sacred in the form of an adverse othering mechanism is defined here as desacralizing power. In essence, this weaponizing dynamic entails the sacred being used to extract or deny that which is intrinsically sacred in all human beings. As revealed in this book's title, the clearest example of this form of desacralizing power can be seen operating against migrants, asylum seekers, and refugees at the US-Mexico border.

In the US-Mexico borderlands, the desacralizing power of the wealthy elite takes the form of bordering practices that insist on negating black- and brown-bodied people from any sacred worth. Although bordering in the

2 Introduction

US-Mexico borderlands registers on the social domain, its currency can be traced to elite power's investment in the sacred, which is an index point that has eluded social scientific analysis. As an agent of elite power, the sacred—specifically the sort with high public authority—defines what is familiar, alike, and yet separate. The separating function is a particular concern here in that it points to the sacred as a violent othering force used primarily against people. By designating certain people as the nonsacred other (hence the lowercase "o"), this othering force erupts as an eradicating agent onto their spaces, ways of knowing, and archives. In the US-Mexico borderlands, this desacralizing scheme can be seen most clearly in the names elite power gives to black- and brown-bodied migrant border crossers—"illegal immigrant," "criminal alien," "drug dealer," "gang member," "Mexican rapist," or "Muslim terrorist." In this way, turning to elite power's investment in the sacred offers a fuller assessment of the length its othering ambitions are aiming to go. Here, my notion of the sacred refers less to a particular religious tradition than to the public elevation of a belief system or an economy of truth-making to a divine status. In a general sense, the sacred involves a consensus of thought and yet its specific attachment to a divine realm renders such thought an impenetrable social force. Though presented in this book in the singular form, I understand the sacred as referring to economies of truth-making and currencies of public authority that have the capacity to exonerate violent social actions of elite power. In this way, the sacred can take many forms—monuments, institutions, social practices, spatial arrangements, and people—and yet together have the capacity to defend, justify, exonerate, and legitimate the most gruesome and tortuous acts of state-sanctioned violence. Hence, the aim here is not to define the sacred in a prescriptive sense, but rather to show investments in notions of the sacred either as a legitimating force for elite power or a source of empowerment for the subjugated Other. Of primary concern in the former domain is how elite power has harnessed the sacred to legitimate bordering practices at the US-Mexico border that not only render migrants, asylum seekers, and refuges socially dispossessed, but even more devastatingly allow for their total eradication.

In view of the demographic that elite power is targeting in the border region, its wielding of the sacred seeks to effect various forms of material change—an aim contingent to concentrated wealth—through sacralized acts of violence that range from militarized border security to migrant family separations to mass incarceration to mass deportation. Through investments in the sacred, conventions like public good and public safety are given a sacral character, not so much in keeping with ethics but as a way to legitimate acts of violence against those deemed the nonsacred human other.[1] The boundaries of this sacralized violence are coterminous with the public currency of the sacred in which elite power has invested. Among the reaped benefits for elite power is the growing intensity of its sacralized violence against its designated human other, as in the current expansion of the immigration detention industrial complex.[2]

Currently in the US-Mexico borderlands, the sacred of white American evangelical Christianity has proven to be a worthwhile domain of investment for political elites—yielding high concentrations of sacralized violence against black- and brown-bodied people. Under the control of colonizing power, this evangelical version of the sacred offers a theology that sacralizes government structures while also demonizing those who oppose them regardless of their governing nature.[3] Hence, the contours drawn here of the sacred seek to alert the skeptical scientific critic—particularly those indifferent to all things transcendental, spiritual, religious, or metaphysical—as well as the humanitarian critic to an urgent nodal point that, if left unexamined, can have devastating social consequences. Central to this book is the sacred that elite political power enlists to sacralize the violence it performs against its designated human other in the US-Mexico borderlands. This follows first the existence of the sacred as an authoritative domain of truth-making for many in US society; for without this, elite power has little incentive to invest in it. In view of elite power's twofold mission, its reproduction and the eradication of its designated nonsacred human other, this book also offers an intervening hermeneutic of the sacred that invests in ways of knowing that come from the people targeted for eradication in the US-Mexico borderlands. These are not only the racially criminalized people in the border region, but more pertinent here, they are those casted as a threat to what elite power has deemed sacred, such as public safety, heritage, citizenship, national sovereignty, state archives, and the Western scientific gaze. With the threat set at the level of the sacred, the actions taken to defend elite power are also understood as sacred and as such opens the way for eradicating forms of violence.

Under elite power's current version of the sacred, those targeted for eradication in the US-Mexico borderland are the black- and brown-bodied migrant border crossers who carry what Aviva Chomsky describes as "the border with them."[4] For the State, the border represents a key investment in the sacred, for it sustains the sacral character of citizenship, sovereignty, public good, heritage, and archive. Sacralized as a symbol of sovereignty, the State moves to sacralize all border security activities, such that they constitute a sacred duty. This sets up border crossings by non-citizens as an affront to the State's sacred apparatus, and as such they are seen to incarnate trespass—transgression—contravention.

Terms like "security," "sacrifice," and "safety" are amply deployed within the political discourse to sustain the sanctity of the border within the public sphere. With renewed sanctity, border crossers continue to warrant eradicating forms of violence by the State. Here their transgression of the sacred border leads not just to their racial criminalization but more importantly to their desacralization, which is a process that intensifies the offense as to require the total eradication of migrant border crossers. Much like political discourse, this eradicating violence also reinforces the sanctity of the border for elite power, thereby ensuring the permanency of this form of violence at the US-Mexico border. Although xenophobic mentalities and racializing logics contribute in part to this violence, its longevity in the border region stems largely from the legitimating power of the State's sacred apparatus.

In the US-Mexico borderlands, the border also points to the conquest of social bodies and as such constitutes an abiding postcolonial wound. As expressed in the post-1848 Texas-Mexican saying (*dicho*): "we didn't cross the border; the border crossed us."[5] Here, the border coincides not just with Anglo-American imperialism but also with the investments made in the sacred that in turn became the catalyst for conquest. Under the same racially criminalizing logic that targets contemporary migrant border crossers, those "border-crossed" (conquered Mexican nationals of what is now the US Southwest) also incarnate the border—marking instead their colonization and generational postcolonial trauma. Among the investments in the sacred that elite power made to sacralize Anglo-American imperialism was a Reformed Protestant idea of Manifest Destiny.[6] As expressed by John Louis O'Sullivan, the originator of this sacralized imperialist doctrine:

> Why, were other reasoning wanting, in favor of now elevating this question of the reception of Texas into the Union . . . for the avowed object of thwarting our policy and hampering our power, limiting our greatness and checking the fulfillment of our manifest destiny to overspread the continent allotted by Providence for the free development of our yearly multiplying millions.[7]

When traced to the sacred, Anglo-American imperialism registers as a desacralizing power that legitimized the conquest of Mexico's northern territories and rendered infinite the postcolonial wound of those initially conquered and their offspring. The version of the sacred that O'Sullivan offered elite power was uniquely suited for the most veracious desires of the Anglo-American male imaginary. Drawing on the Calvinistic theological concept of "Providence," the Protestant God has made manifest—through their civilizational achievements and monuments of progress—the divinely sanctioned destiny of Anglo-Americans to rule the Western hemisphere.[8] As O'Sullivan puts it, "The Anglo-Saxon foot is already on its [California] borders. Already the advance guard of the irresistible army of Anglo-Saxon emigration has begun to pour down upon it, armed with the plough and the rifle, and marking its trail with schools and colleges, courts and representative halls, mills and meeting-house."[9] Different from the currency of non-theologically based ideologies, the sacred offers empire-building regimes an authoritative economy of truth-making that commands an entrancing permanence. For the conquered, Manifest Destiny made permanent a vandalizing and insatiable wound that withers all sense of human worth, squashes out ancestral memory, and deprives us of the fundamental right that all earthlings have—which is the right to exist. Yet for the conquerors, the sacred that underwrote Manifest Destiny created an efficacious framework through which Anglo-American notions of racial superiority and imperial ambitions could be aligned with divine will. In O'Sullivan's view, this "manifest design of Providence" was "the inevitable fulfillment of the general law which is rolling our population westward."[10] In a quite calculated way, the investments made in Manifest Destiny instantiated long-term material domination for Anglo-Americans through the sacralization of their heritage and racial type as well as their acts of violence against the non-Anglo other. When tracing the sacred within the unfolding of Anglo-American imperialism, violence assumes a sacral character, while at the same time the non-Anglo other is desacralized. With each act of violence, the sacred that underpins it increases in authority, which in turn allows for the repetition of violence and, by extension, the reproduction of Anglo-American dominance. For the US-Mexico borderlands, the sacralized violence that proceeded from Manifest Destiny was the Mexican-American War of 1846–1848.[11] In a victory sermon delivered to the US military in Mexico City at the end of the Mexican-American War, US Army chaplain Rev. John McCarty declared these words:

> let us realize that He [God] has not preserved and brought us here to "revel in the Halls of Montezuma," but to serve Him and do our duty; especially by turning our success and our consequent influence over this people into the means of enlightening their religious ignorance and raising them from the degradation to which they are reduced. And this by extending the light and the blessings of our purer faith; so that by our Christian influence and example and by the intercourse between us they may imbibe something of our free spirit and throw off the shackles of military and spiritual despotism.[12]

The time and place of this sermon's delivery mark the importance of the sacred for elite power. As a military chaplain, Rev. McCarty represented the sacred while at the same time functioned as an agent of the State. In other words, he was the embodiment of the State's investment in the sacred; and, through his words, elite power sought legitimation for the war and the conquest of Mexico. His sermon, as understood from this genre of speech, not only defined the violence but also sacralized it. Echoing the core claims set out in Manifest Destiny, McCarty sacralizes the violence with notions of Anglo-American Protestant superiority. In his phrases "our duty," "our purer faith," "our Christian influence," and "our free spirit," McCarty harnesses the sacred to create a lasting dichotomy between the superior Anglo-American and the inferior Mexican. For McCarty, their inferiority begins in the realm of the sacred, which as he states involves "religious ignorance" and "spiritual despotism." Although casted as socially inferior, the sacred in this instance functions to desacralize Mexicans, thereby linking their social improvement to those proven to have divine favor—Anglo-Americans. Rendered the nonsacred other, McCarty sets up ethnic Mexican culture, society, and religion as objects for eradicating violence. This is where the sacred offers elite power an impenetrable legitimating logic or theology by calibrating their inferiority to the religious and spiritual. At the same time, his use of the sacred sacralizes Anglo-American superiority and hence their ensuing colonization of Mexicans. Here the sacred exonerates violence, or in McCarty's words "to serve Him [God] and do our duty." As an agent of the State, McCarty's sermon contributed to the longevity of elite power by assigning its acts of war and conquest to divine favor.

In harnessing the sacred, Rev. McCarty's sermon had in view the permanent subjugation of Mexicans to Anglo-Americans. In his sermon, he desacralizes ethnic Mexicans by casting them as unenlightened, ignorant, inferior, and morally bankrupt. As he states:

> the Mexicans most need for their improvement, a purer exhibition of the Gospel of Christ (which toleration and the light of the scriptures would eventually give them,) may it be ours to secure by all proper means the toleration of Protestants, so clearly their right and which we know from experience in other countries would exert an enlightening and purifying influence on the church of this country.[13]

Rev. McCarty urges a distinction between the sacred of Anglo-Americans (Protestantism) and the sacred of Mexican nationals (Catholicism) in ways that invalidate the latter as intrinsically inferior and cast the former as the natural superior. The emphasis on this distinction established an integral component to Rev. McCarty's desacralization of ethnic Mexicans in that it began not with their innate criminality but, more importantly, with what he saw as an inferior version of the sacred. Under his theology, it was only from an Anglo-American Protestant version of the sacred that ethnic Mexicans could improve their social and cultural debasement.

By foregrounding the sacred here, this book locates Anglo-American imperialism within an underexamined nodal point of elite power that begins not with social pathologies but with investments in specific domains of the sacred (e.g. Protestantism, military chaplaincy, the sermon, and the Christian scriptures, to name a few). Turning our critical gaze to the sacred brings into clearer view a more radical social force that ends not just with the othering of ethnic Mexicans. These domains of the sacred function as fulcrums to forms of othering that have as their ultimate end the eradication of ethnic Mexican culture, society, and religion. It is this particular end and its incontestable legitimation that makes the sacred a worthwhile investment for colonizing power. The sacred sets the threshold of elite power's ambitions to the realms of divine favor, thereby creating othering practices that do more than dehumanize—they desacralize the totality of personhood.

Linking the violence that elite power deploys against its designated nonsacred other to notions of divine favor has in view forms of control that are totalizing, infinite, and devastating. Indeed, these investments in the sacred reflect much more permanent objectives of domination that involve the utter erasure of elite power's nonsacred other from any earthly trace. This may appear as an overestimation of the effectual social force of sacred, preferring instead to assign the manufacturing of violence solely to the operations of government systems, ideological movements, or economic structures. These are indeed important indexes to the reproduction of elite power and its manufacturing of violence; however, what this book argues is that the sacred affords elite power a transcending and yet arbitrary power that forecloses on democratic processes and an ethic of equality. The sacred under colonizing power facilitates the highest forms of domination through legitimated forms of violence that are grotesque, gruesome, tortuous, and eradicating.

In the 1848 Treaty of Guadalupe Hidalgo, which officially marked the end of the United States' war with Mexico, the rules for Anglo-American colonization—covering territorial boundaries, citizenship, property, and trade—are listed under the following opening statement: "In the name of Almighty God."[14] What some may consider a benign reference to the divine marks an unfailing investment in the sacred that conceptually is akin to Rev. McCarty's sacralized vision of Anglo-American colonization. In fact, the reference to "Almighty God" appears twice in the Treaty, both preceding the twenty-three articles that define the conditions of Mexico's subjugation to the United States:

> The President of the United States has appointed Nicholas P. Trist, a citizen of the United States, and the President of the Mexican Republic has appointed Don Luis Gonzaga Cuevas, Don Bernardo Couto, and Don Miguel Atristain, citizens of the said Republic; Who, after a reciprocal communication of their respective full powers, have, **under the protection of Almighty God**, the author of peace, arranged, agreed upon, and signed the following: Treaty of Peace, Friendship, Limits, and Settlement between the United States of America and the Mexican Republic.[15]

This investment in the sacred not only sacralizes the Treaty but the colonizing activities it stipulates. Here, elite Anglo-American power benefits from the sacralizing force that the sacred affords, for it renders permanent social relations, power dynamics, and eradicating violence. Ultimately, by setting the threshold of colonization to the realm of the divine, the sacred enables a permanence to a social reality that ensures the reproduction of elite power.

Among the colonizing actions stipulated in Article V of the Treaty was the creation of the official territorial boundary between the US and Mexico. As it states:

> The boundary line between the two Republics shall commence in the Gulf of Mexico, three leagues from land, opposite the mouth of the Rio Grande, otherwise called Rio Bravo del Norte, or Opposite the mouth

of its deepest branch, if it should have more than one branch emptying directly into the sea; from thence up the middle of that river, following the deepest channel, where it has more than one, to the point where it strikes the southern boundary of New Mexico; thence, westwardly, along the whole southern boundary of New Mexico (which runs north of the town called Paso) to its western termination; thence, northward, along the western line of New Mexico, until it intersects the first branch of the river Gila; (or if it should not intersect any branch of that river, then to the point on the said line nearest to such branch, and thence in a direct line to the same); thence down the middle of the said branch and of the said river, until it empties into the Rio Colorado; thence across the Rio Colorado, following the division line between Upper and Lower California, to the Pacific Ocean.[16]

In harnessing the sacred at the beginning of the Treaty, elite power assigns a sacralizing function to the border for Anglo-Americans. "Under the protection of Almighty God," the Treaty first sacralizes the creation of the US's southern border with Mexico. Under the sacred, the coordinates of the border—from the Gulf of Mexico to the Pacific Ocean—are made to appear natural and indisputable. As a sacred border, it in turn serves to instantiate divine favor on Anglo-American imperialism and society. Conversely, this sacralized border also allows Anglo-Americans to permanently desacralize ethnic Mexicans as the inferior other. Herein lies the power of the sacred in that by sacralizing Anglo-American imperialism in the Treaty, the border under Article V also sacralizes. It not only sacralizes the victors of the Mexican-American War but also their ensuing colonizing activities in the region. Under the sacred, the border legitimates Anglo-American domination while also exonerating them from acts of violence against the desacralized Mexican other. Such an arrangement bespeaks a persistent dynamic that is still in operation in the current age, the desacralized other are those south of the border and those sacralized remain the Anglo majority in US society.

Rather than dismiss the sacred as lacking the impetus for reproducing colonizing power, this book takes seriously the prominent role it has played in justifying Anglo-American imperialism. Its continual use in political discourse reflects more than a Western conventional form; instead it maps a hermeneutical investment in the sacred that sets the threshold for elite power's ambitions beyond earthly reach. Within such an imaginary, the sacred turns lethal, grotesque, gruesome, and traumatizing, precisely because of how it allows for the manufacturing and performance of violence to be construed as part of divine will. By expanding the field of social agency to an otherworldly level, elite power is able to foreclose on democratic-based logics and sanction tyrannical-acts of violence like conquest and colonization. In addition to expanding the target zone for violence, investments in the sacred by colonizing power have in view the perpetual use of violence in tandem with its uncontestable justification. Hence the repetition and placement of the phrase "Almighty God" in the Treaty of Guadalupe Hidalgo functions not as a noble religious gesture, but actually as a hermeneutical investment in the sacred that sanctioned the colossal acquisition of nearly half of Mexico's northern territory and thereby birthed the US-Mexico borderlands.

By the twentieth century, Anglo-American imperialism morphed into state power and as such the cycle of sacralized violence shifted from brute military conquest to the orderly policing of a desacralized Mexican other. Under this mode of elite power, the sacred is reified in a state apparatus of procedures, protocols, programs, and processes. Yet the goal of colossal domination remains the same, for again this result underlies why elite power invests in the sacred. The mega-action of its sacralized violence is therefore at the quotidian level and hence infinitely multiplied—using systems, technologies, standards of operation, networks of affiliation, architecture, and credentialing. The way this book conceptualizes this iteration of sacralized violence under state power can be visualized in the 1916 photograph shown here (Figure 1.1).

Behind the guise of the sacred (altar) stands an agent of the State with a gloating smile; while in front of it stands the racially criminalized Mexican other ("bandit"). As visualized here, the sacred reflects a hermeneutical investment of not those captured but the captors. Despite its Catholic iconography, its design, placement, and hence function are under Anglo-American control. In this eerie photo, state-sanctioned violence against the incarcerated Mexican other is sacralized. The sacred casts the captors as magnanimous, which in turn exonerates them from the grotesque spectacle of their hanging in the public square. To function on behalf of the Mexican other assumes their livelihood and longevity; instead it is the perpetuation of state power that the sacred is commissioned to accomplish. Though the sacred represented in the photograph may appear accommodating to the religious needs of the captured, the assemblage of violence surrounding it mark other intentions for the sacred of which involve the eradication of the Mexican other. When viewed from the context of state power, the sacred is the cause of wound rather than a source of healing for the captured Mexican other. For through the sacred, elite power is reinforced, affirmed, and legitimated; yet for the desacralized Mexican other, the sacred is the conduit of scarring and flesh-eating violence that, in the end, renders them nonexistent.

This brief assessment of elite power's investments in the sacred (Manifest Destiny, McCarty's sermon, Treaty of Guadalupe Hidalgo, and the photo) both before and after the creation of the US-Mexico border only serves as a preamble to a much more complex phenomenon than suggested here. Yet in terms of the aims of this book, these initial investments in the sacred point us to an underestimated threshold of elite Anglo-American power. By harnessing the sacred, this group of elite power was able to align their claims of superiority and acts of conquest with divine favor. Through religiously affiliated state agents, Anglo-Americans sacralized themselves and their colonizing activities. As part of its legitimating benefits, commanding the

Figure 1.1 On May 19, 1916, Mexican prisoners Melquíades Chapa and José Buenrostro posed in front of an altar with candles, flowers, a statue of Our Lady of Lourdes, and a crucifix. The photo was taken in the chapel of the newly built Cameron County Jail immediately before the two prisoners were led outside to the gallows. They were tried and convicted in Brownsville for the murder of A.L. Austin and his son Charles in the fall of 1915. Up until their hanging, reports indicate that both men maintained their innocence.

Source: Photograph by Robert Runyon; Dolph Briscoe Center for American History.[17]

sacred also allowed Anglo-Americans to desacralize ethnic Mexicans. This mode of the sacred marks another type of threshold for elite power and its manufacturing of violence. In Rev. McCarty's sermon, the violence of colonization is framed as a sacred duty; in the Treaty of Guadalupe Hidalgo, the violence of creating a border is an act authorized under "Almighty God"; and in the photograph, the sacred sacralizes the public hanging of two Mexican nationals. Just as the sacred allows elite power to imagine its existence in terms of divine favor and hence the infinite, the sacred also offers elite power desacralization as a justified mode of violence that is equally favored by the divine and thus infinitely devastating to the ethnic Mexican other.

An Anzaldúaian pivot to the sacred Other

I, too, as an eighth generation "border-crossed" ethnic Mexican from South Texas, carry the postcolonial wounds of Manifest Destiny and its insidious offspring of sacralized state-sanctioned colonization. Yet, another way I think about my "border-crossed" condition is to harness it as an intervening hermeneutic of the sacred that redresses the desacralized social bodies—or alternatively, those designated as the "transgressors" and "aliens"[18]—at the US-Mexico border. These dark-skinned bodies are what Gloria Anzaldúa calls "*los atravesados*" (the crossed people); they are "the squint eyed, the perverse, the queer, the troublesome, the mongrel, the mulato, the half-breed, the half dead; in short, those who cross over, pass over, or go through the confines of the 'normal.'"[19] For these aggregates of desacralized others, the border "*es una herida abierta*" (is an open wound), making it—both literally and figuratively—a place that is "vague," "undetermined," "prohibited," and "forbidden."[20] Though what represents a site of trauma for the dark-skinned other, specifically with respect to present-day migrant border crossers, is also where "the only 'legitimate' inhabitants are those in power, the whites and those who align themselves with whites"—that is, a power structure which privileges Anglo-Americans first and foremost, but also grants provisional access to light-skinned Hispanics.[21]

Attending to the fragmenting wounds of racism and colonialism (*sustos*) is central to Anzaldúa's epistemological pivot to the sacred Other, dealing as she does with the Other as queer, dark-skinned, and oppressed people and the sacred as their inherent spiritual/psychic capacities (*la facultad*).[22] Also for her, the Other is sacred in that otherness points not to an enemy of the State, but instead points to the "supernatural world—the subtle world, the 'other' world"[23]—that is, a spiritual world with *other* ways of being (*nepantla/nepantlera*, shapeshifting, Queer Spirit, spiritual *mestizaje*),[24] *other* ways of knowing (double-knowing, *conocimiento*, the reptilian eye),[25] and *other* ways of truth-making (spiritual activism, border *arte*).[26] In contrast to elite power—in which the Other, otherness, and othering constitute the nonsacred—Anzaldúa renders otherness the starting point of the sacred. The outcome is othering as a mode of sacralization that seeks to honor human differences rather than dominate them through exclusion or homogenization. As gleaned from Anzaldúa's notions of healing and spirituality, the sacred as Other marks the blueprint to this book's proposed borderland hermeneutic. Anzaldúa's conceptualization of the sacred Other not only offers us a hermeneutic of the sacred that attends to postcolonial trauma, but it also dismantles elite power's desacralization of otherness. Rather than creating otherness as an empire-building strategy, can it function instead as a healing strategy of radical inclusion of a multiplicity of differences? Is otherness natural to our humanity and as such is it intrinsically sacred? If so, is not elite power then operating contrary to this intrinsic sacredness of all humans by manufacturing unnatural forms of otherness through homogenizing social systems (nation-states, sovereignty, citizenship)? At issue here is the Other, otherness, and othering as desacralizing weapons of elite power to create a world of trauma.

Recognizing, exploring, interrogating, and agitating the fragmenting wounds of racism and colonialism assume a spiritual/sacred role that involves creative processes (art, writing, reading),[27] imaginings (*ensueños*),[28] "other" epistemologies,[29] and dialogue/*conocimiento*, thereby reconstituting otherness as a concept for healing and not a reproducing strategy of elite power.[30] This spiritual activist work of attending to these fragmenting wounds done to the body, mind, and spirit is not limited to an intellectual exercise of reading against the grain of the archives of imperial violence, as modeled in the scientific prose of postcolonial theory; rather, to be a sacred work, the wounded Other must engage the personal and collective traumas fearlessly as a way of "taking back the scattered energy and soul loss wrought by woundings."[31] Central to this book are the embodied wounds of postcolonial trauma, which, as Anzaldúa teaches us, torment brown-bodied people in the US-Mexico borderlands. For those of us bearing these wounds, attending to the archive without a critical view of elite power's investments in the sacred only allows for provisional healing. By turning our gaze to the sacred, Anzaldúa admits to the weaponization of the sacred by elite power to colonize the mind, as with the Christian church and biblical interpretation.[32] Thus redressing the wounds of colonization involves a thorough critique of the manuscript content in the archive, but also the sacral character of the archive.[33] Here the archive functions as an integral component to elite power's hermeneutic of the sacred, for it produces a version of history that sacralizes colonizing power. In the spirit of Anzaldúa's postcolonial pivot to the sacred, my wounds as a border-crossed son of the borderlands draw me to the discourse of the sacred in the archive (Manifest Destiny, McCarty's sermon, Treaty of Guadalupe Hidalgo, and the photograph [see Figure 1.1]) as well as the archive itself as sacred. Although my postcolonial wounds motivate my critique of the archive, Anzaldúa reminds me of how the sacred is both a cause of my inherited wounds and yet a source of healing. In terms of the former dynamic, I implicate the archive as playing a key role in fostering my inferiority complex as an ethnic Mexican; hence the sacred I pursue comprises of archive as text and archive as place, procedures of access and acquisition methods. Yet in interrogating the sacred in the archive, Anzaldúa would also not have me stay here in redressing my postcolonial wounds. Indeed, her notions of the sacred Other invite those of us wounded by colonization to other ways of knowing that lie outside of the sacralized world of state archives.

The activist impulse underwriting Anzaldúa's borderland hermeneutic of the sacred compels the wounded Other to decolonize consciousness first by sacralizing all that is otherness in them.[34] At the same time, the ways in which colonial violence has registered on the US-Mexico border bring into focus particular contours of sacralized elite power that Anzaldúa in turn desacralizes as "the Gringo world," "Anglo terrorism," "Anglo vigilante groups," or in poetic verse, as "the anglo buzzing around her [her mother] like a mosquito, landing on her, digging in, sucking."[35] In sacralizing the wounded Other, which includes "the females, the homosexuals of all races, the darkskinned, the outcast, the persecuted, the marginalized, the foreign,"[36] she likens their postcolonial wounds to the dismembered female body of *Coyolxauhqui*, the Aztec goddess of the moon.[37] The sacral character of "the trauma of colonial abuses fragmenting our psyches"[38] in Anzaldúa's epistemology serves to resacralize the colonized—darkskinned—female—queer— border-crossing Other, which deems them worthy of healing and complex wholeness (the latter tied to her notion of the *Coyolxauhqui* imperative).[39] To confront these sacred wounds, she states that "you have to plunge your hands into the mess, plunge your hands in *la masa*, into embodied practical material spiritual political acts."[40] Plunging into the wounded-self (*la masa*) functions as a sacralizing act that for Anzaldúa leads to healing. In this way the wounded-self is Other and hence intrinsically sacred; and yet the wounded-self also constitutes a sacralized archive of pains, abuses, hurts, and betrayals, all of which deserves redress. Take for instance these plummeting poetic words by Anzaldúa, as she sacralizes her own dismemberment:

>1,950 mile-long open wound
>>dividing a *pueblo*, a culture,
>>running down the length of my body
>>staking fence rods in my flesh,
>>splits me   splits me
>>*me raja   me raja*

The border as an open wound captures the untreated rawness of this wound. This chronic wound is described in terms of mileage and as such constitutes a geographical wound on the very landscape itself. From geography, this border wound extends to the personhood of the colonized people themselves, in her words "dividing a *pueblo*, a culture." Ultimately, this chronic wound moves from a marked landscape to a divided culture to a split body. Such are the wounds of postcolonial trauma, for they bespeak acts of conquest (border mileage), colonization (border dividing), and dispossession (border embodied). As Anzaldúa describes this condition, "we were jerked out by the roots, truncated, disemboweled, dispossessed, and separated from our identity and our history."[41] Through the sacralizing medium of poetry, Anzaldúa plunges into these fragmenting wounds, thereby resacralizing that which elite power has desacralized in order to legitimate its reproduction. Rather than normalize the border, her poetic plunging allows her to confront the disfigurement that the border has done to her land, people, and personhood. In this sacralizing process, she reminds herself that the border is an open wound and hence needs mending. Anzaldúa's plunging process mirrors in a figurative way Melquíades Chapa's and José Buenrostro's pose in the photograph before their public hanging by elite Anglo-American power (see Figure 1.1); in it, they stare directly at their captor (a white male photographer) and his intended Anglo-American audience with a confident gaze, defiant smirk, and more importantly their backs facing the version of the sacred that the State has constructed to legitimate their deaths and thereby reproduce Anglo-American dominance in the US-Mexico borderlands. This posture—which for me illustrates in symbolic form Anzaldúa's plunging pivot to the sacred wounds—maps the conceptual and theoretical itineraries this book seeks to establish in constructing a borderland hermeneutic of the sacred that resacralizes present-day migrant border crossers. Here, to face the postcolonial wounds is to confront candidly and defiantly the captor/colonizer/racist inflicting these wounds on behalf of elite power's investments in the sacred. In other words, what Anzaldúa and symbolically the photograph teach us is that the sacred is not an abstract concept but rather takes the form of human agents (captor/colonizer/racist) who are commissioned by elite power to inflict lasting wounds on land, communities, and bodies in the name of the sacred. Hence, turning to face the agents who manufacture and administer elite power's version of the sacred (as in the photograph) is consistent with Anzaldúa's sacralizing exercise of plunging into the "the mess" or "*la masa.*" Within this approach to colonizing power, the captor/colonizer/racist comes to the fore as devoid of sanctity because his violent acts are understood for what they really are— massacre and genocide. This type of defiant and subversive posture ascribes sacred worth to the wounds themselves—in part because they constitute a form of otherness to the self. As a sacralizing strategy, the healing that Anzaldúa has in view can be framed as a form of counter desacralization of elite power's version of the sacred. This type of mending of postcolonial wounds renounces the authority of elite power's version of the sacred over the self while also naming elite power's sacred apparatus (border security, citizenship, sovereignty) for what it really is—eradicating violence.

The wounds of Western objectivity and institutionalized religion

Understood from Anzaldúa's diagnosis of colonialism's wounds is how the US-Mexico border exists as an abiding open wound of Manifest Destiny/

Anglo-American imperialism. Yet, in terms of its subsequent operations of wounding the sacred Other, her decolonizing gaze (which I consider to be a form of desacralization) turns to Western systems of thought, processes of meaning-making, and institutionalized forms of knowledge. More specifically, Anzaldúa identifies "white rationality" as that which bonds these wounding agents of colonizing power together in the US-Mexico borderlands. In what represents a "higher" mode of consciousness for the colonizer, its most concrete expression is—as Anzaldúa indicates—Western objectivity.[42] In describing the colonization of her inner psychic senses (the sacred Other) as a *mestiza* Chicana queer from the Texas-Mexico border, Anzaldúa recounts the following:

> I allowed white rationality to tell me that the existence of the "other world" was mere pagan superstition. I accepted their reality, the "official" reality of the rational, reasoning mode which is connected with external reality, the upper world, and is considered the most developed consciousness—the consciousness of duality.[43]

For Anzaldúa, white rationality/Western objectivity operates as a fragmenting strategy of what it has deemed as the "savage mind," displacing non-Western constructions of reality and desacralizing indigenous ways of truth-making. Sacralized by white elite power as the higher, more developed mode of consciousness, Anzaldúa desacralizes it with these words: "in trying to become 'objective,' Western culture made 'objects' of things and people when it distanced itself from them, thereby losing 'touch' with them. This dichotomy is the root of all violence." [44] The sway of objectivity for the Western mind has its roots in the early modern period, and yet its rise to sacred status can be linked to Western scientific thought. As Anzaldúa argues, this mode of truth-making in which all "things and people" are objectified is the root of all violence. There is not only the violence of dichotomizing the self but also the violence that this optic engenders when combined with a racial logic. For the desacralized dark-skinned other, the objectification that white rationality imposes translates into their subjugation and ultimate eradication.

In turning to the wounded sacred Other at the US-Mexico border, this book takes seriously Anzaldúa's damning assessment of white rationality/Western objectivity and yet also nuances the violence it produces when combined with a white supremacist racial logic. Where this tandem appears to work at its optimum—specifically as it pertains to wounding the dark-skinned other—is within the praxis of Western science. Implicated here are optic-centric modes of scientific inspection in diagnosing black- and brown-bodied people so as to ensure their lower worth as human beings at the US-Mexico border. Indeed, Anzaldúa acknowledges Western science as a major vehicle for the propagation of Western objectivity, writing in her seven stages of *conocimiento*, "you doubt that traditional western science is the best knowledge system, the only true, impartial arbiter of reality. You question its definition of progress, whose manifest destiny imperializes other peoples' energies and snuffs out their realities and hopes of a better life."[45] By a sleight of the hand, Western science coupled with a criminalizing racial logic receives its immunity from the belief that human inspectors can divest themselves from all sociality. Not only does this system colonize the mind of the dark-skinned other in ways that leads them to embrace a self-effacing version of "truth"; it also, as Anzaldúa discerns, desacralizes the sacred/spirit that comprises the self. In her critique of Western science, she writes that "this system and its hierarchies affect people's lives in concrete and devastating ways and justify a sliding scale of human worth used to keep humankind divided. It condones the mind theft, spirit murder, exploitation, and genocide *de los otros* [of the other]."[46] This book heeds Anzaldúa's prognosis of Western science, calling into question its accuracy as a hermeneutic for human care—particularly when the humans are dark-skinned—and yet also follows her pivot to "other" forms of knowledge like "curanderismo and Toltec nagualism" as a way to foster different modes of human care.[47]

Alongside Western science sits institutionalized religion as an agent of white rationality/Western objectivity, and therefore it is also an inflictor of wounds for the dark-skinned queer other. As with Western objectivity, Anzaldúa also views institutionalized religion—specifically the Catholic and Protestant Churches in the West—as advancing a consciousness of duality. In her words, "the Catholic and Protestant religions encourage fear and distrust of life and of the body; they encourage a split between the body and the spirit and totally ignore the soul; they encourage us to kill off parts of ourselves."[48] Whether the soul, sexuality, or spirituality, institutionalized religion severs the self from the self, leaving behind dismemberment, dislocation, and debilitating wounds. Anzaldúa argues in her *Interviews* that all institutionalized religions "impoverish life, beauty, and pleasure" (desacralization) and "always side with those in power."[49] For this book, the latter relationship is of pressing concern, for it points back to a core argument about how elite power like the State invests in the sacred to reproduce itself. As Anzaldúa keenly describes, "to me religion has always upheld the status quo, it makes institutions rigid and dogmatic."[50] Within the context of the US-Mexico borderlands, the Western Christian Church (Catholic and Protestant) serves as a primary example in Anzaldúa's acute critique of institutionalized religions. For her, both Catholic and Protestant religions have proven to be profitable allies to imperial power (Spanish and Anglo-American) such that they legitimated "the oppression and genocide of the Indians."[51] The current investments that the State has made in the sacred continue to show US Protestantism, more specifically white evangelicalism,[52] as a worthwhile ally in legitimating the oppression and eradication of dark-skinned border crossers. Through the State's othering strategies, dark-skinned border crossers are racially criminalized and as such white evangelicalism provides divine coverage over the State and its border security operations of detention and deportation. From this alliance, the white evangelical church affirms the sanctity of US sovereignty while also foreclosing on modes of human care that inspire total liberation from a self-effacing system of control. The fear that this current iteration of institutionalized religion engenders is still life, as Anzaldúa teaches us; yet, with the added nuance that this fear gives life to the State and hence takes away the lives of the dark-skinned border crossing other, who are the enemies of the State.

Healing otherness with otherness

The proposed borderland hermeneutic begins with the Anzaldúaian notion that what colonizing power has deemed the nonsacred queer other—either through white supremacy, Western objectivity, or institutionalized religion—conversely constitutes a healing economy of the sacred. This counterintuitive pivot to the sacred Other lies central to the praxis that this book seeks to initiate—a praxis of healing through a borderland hermeneutic of the sacred that sacralizes those desacralized by the State at the US-Mexico border. In view of Anzaldúa's appraisal of suffering in the border region, among the most vulnerable populations are refugee border crossers. As she describes, "living in a no-man's-borderland, caught between resistance and deportation, the illegal refugees are some of the poorest and the most exploited of any people in the U.S."[53] To follow Anzaldúa's activist approach to healing requires that we begin with the woundings of the most vulnerable Other at the US-Mexico border. This master site of wound grounds her activism not in a universally applicable humanitarianism, but rather in a borderlands *curanderismo* that is dedicated to the care and healing of migrant/asylum-seeking/refugee border crossers.[54] Although healing and care are spiritually resourced, their aim is to transform the border crossers' material suffering by attending in activist ways to the specific place of their wounds. In the current age, the border continues to serve as the master site of wound for black- and brown-bodied people, migrants, asylum-seekers, and refugees.[55] The persistence of this wound at the border attests to Anzaldúa's diagnosis of the US-Mexico border as an open wound that is constantly hemorrhaging. Hence healing this wound is inextricably linked to an activist awareness of the border—its history, meaning, and function. To accomplish this healing praxis, Anzaldúa states that "you must fall headlong into that wounding—attend to what the body is feeling, be its dismemberment and disintegration."[56] Falling headlong into the wounds of current asylum-seeking migrant border crossers, the activist encounters those who Anzaldúa describes as "faceless, nameless, invisible, taunted with 'Hey *cucaracho* (cockroach)'"—that is, the ones bearing the full brunt of the State's sacralized violence. Arguably for those hemorrhaging today at the US-Mexico border, their options for embodied liberation are acutely tenuous, often accelerated through forced scarcity to the breaking point of life. Again, Anzaldúa's diagnosis reverberates here, "as refugees in a homeland that does not want them, many find a welcome hand holding out only suffering, pain, and ignoble death."[57]

Under the State's hermeneutic of the sacred, black- and brown-bodied border crossers emerge as the ultimate nonsacred other. Such an assessment accounts for the State's investments in the sacred not only to resource its othering mechanisms but to ensure their threshold of results match the eternal ambitions of the State. Capturing this dynamic is the term "desacralization," which sets the horizons of healing more accurately not just to their social exclusion but to their complete eradication. In following Anzaldúa's activist itinerary for healing, we are shown how the wounds of the State's desacralization can be converted into an otherness that heals—largely because otherness defines what the State has rejected in order to reproduce itself. Immersed in the State's designated otherness, we discover "other" epistemologies, other ways of truth-making, other worldviews, other myths and spiritual traditions, particularly those demonized by colonizing power. This counterintuitive strategy rejects the pull of the State on black- and brown-bodied people to live only within its standards of measurement, systems of truth-making, and modes of human care—to use Anzaldúa's words, "the anglo world sucks you toward an assimilated, homogenized, whitewashed identity."[58] With the sacred as Other, otherness serves as a resacralizing force for those homogenized into white society by the State's sacred apparatus. Resacralizing the Other, as argued in this book, deals with the border as a sacralized site of the State that functions to desacralize migrant border crossers, as to render them an undesirable other and hence warranting eradication. Hence there is the undoing of the State's othering that is integral to my proposed re-sacralization of the Other; but more importantly there is also the reclaiming of otherness as a way of knowing and in the Anzaldúa sense as a way to healing postcolonial wounds.

The otherness that is a mechanism of the State's investments in the sacred reflects ambitions that involve monopolizing life on earth at the expense of those desacralized. The alternative to this dispensation requires, as Anzaldúa suggests, a pivot to the State's nonsacred other as the only life-giving source for meaning and healing. Rejecting the State's economy of the sacred may lead to increased suffering for the Other; though by not doing so, the alternative is the acceptance of a desacralizing othering that in the end reproduces colonizing power. Consider these urgent words by Anzaldúa:

> Let's all stop importing Greek myths and the Western Cartesian split point of view and root ourselves in the mythological soil and soul of this continent. White America has only attended to the body of the earth in order to exploit it, never to succor it or to be nurtured in it. Instead of surreptitiously ripping off the vital energy of people of color and putting it to commercial use, whites could allow themselves to share and exchange and learn from us in a respectful way.[59]

The notion that healing can be achieved by turning to the State's nonsacred other admits to an epistemological shift in which recognizing the woundings of otherness yields ways of being and knowing that desacralize the State's sacred apparatus. This harnessing of the wounds maps not just the pathology of colonizing power—as to not become it—but more critically the contours of an Other way of being in the world. Rendered here as resacralizing the Other, Anzaldúa describes this process:

> Rupture and psychic fragmentation lead to dialogue with the wound. This dialogue, in turn, opens imaginings, and images awaken an awareness of something greater than our individual wounds, enabling us to imagine ways of going through nepantla's disorientations to achieve wholeness and interconnect to others on the planet.[60]

Though the State's human other is stripped of all sanctity, not all is lost; for as Anzaldúa teaches us, those othered by the State possess alternative forms of sacralization that are based on otherness itself.[61] The driving premise here relates to how the State's otherness constitutes a source of sacralization for activists and humanitarians providing human care to migrants, asylum seekers, and refugees at the US-Mexico border. Anzaldúa points the way to the State's otherness with these words, "I use cultural figures to intervene in, make change, and thus heal colonialism's wounds. I delve into my own mythical heritage and spiritual traditions, such as curanderismo and Toltec nagualism, and link them to spirituality, spiritual activism, mestiza consciousness, and the role of nepantla and nepantleras."[62] By sacralizing the State's otherness, the central aim of this book is to move migrant care away from the State's desacralizing logic to instead the migrants' otherness, which include other ways of knowing and other modes of truth-making.

Charting a borderland hermeneutic of the sacred

As important as Anzaldúa's pivot to the sacred Other is to the conceptual and activist aims of this book, the next steps from this starting position depart from her work, in large part because some of her wounds are not my wounds as a "border-crossed" cisgender heterosexual Chicano from the Rio Grande Valley. The postcolonial wounds I bear move me instead to flesh out a borderland hermeneutic of the sacred that stems from my own shamed condition as a Chicano male living in a "Gringo world." I, too, fit Anzaldúa's grievous diagnosis of the Chicano male's postcolonial condition:

> In the Gringo world, the Chicano suffers from excessive humility and self-effacement, shame of self and self-deprecation. Around Latinos he suffers from a sense of language inadequacy and its accompanying discomfort; with Native Americans he suffers from a racial amnesia which ignores our common blood, and from guilt because the Spanish part of

him took their land and oppressed them. He has an excessive compensatory hubris when around Mexicans from the other side. It overlays a deep sense of racial shame.[63]

From this emasculated position, this book turns to Chapter 2, "Trespassing on the Archive as the Border-Crossed Other." Undergirding this chapter is a didactic mission in which I model a decolonizing maneuver that begins with the State's master archive. As part of the State's investments in the sacred, its master archive is ascribed a high level of sanctity, for in it are its stories of origin, myths of superiority, meta-narratives of chosenness, and monuments of triumphs over its designated human other.

In the Texas-Mexico borderlands, the sacred status of the State's master archive has made it an effective desacralizing weapon against ethnic Mexicans on both sides of the border. From the State's master archive, notions of ethnic Mexican criminality, indolence, and inferiority have a guaranteed permanence in the political discourse (here the threshold of permanence is commensurate with the master archive's sanctity). Hence, as a next move in my proposed borderland hermeneutic, Chapter 2 aims to trespass on the State's master archive in order to desacralize the violence that it sanctions against ethnic Mexicans in the US-Mexico border region. As a "border-crossed" ethnic Mexican other, to enter the State's archive is to trespass on it largely because the narratives held up as sacred to the State cast me as an enemy of the State. Moreover, trespass also points to a strategy that involves upending the State's archive for the sole purpose of resacralizing the ethnic Mexican Other at the US-Mexico border. The sacred story of the State's master archive that I trespass on lies at the intersection of the 1899 Laredo smallpox epidemic, Anglo-American medical inspection, and the Texas Rangers. Here, this chapter seeks to desacralize a historical nodal point dense with sacredness in the State's master archive, as a way to model a decolonizing maneuver that resacralizes the archive's designated nonsacred other. By turning first to the State's master archive, my proposed borderland hermeneutic admits to its abiding power in sacralized state violence against ethnic Mexicans at the US-Mexico border. Yet the selected nodal point within the master archive also attends to desacralization of this violence by showing how ideals like Anglo-American scientific inspection function as a lethal mode of human care when combined with a criminalizing racial logic.

From trespassing on the master archive, the third chapter, "The Sacralizing Performance of a Counter Archive," turns to the archive of border *corridos* as the next step in my proposed borderland hermeneutic. Although silenced in the meta-narratives of dominant US society, ethnic Mexican border culture possesses counter archives like the border *corridos*, which rely on an alternative borderland hermeneutic of the sacred. Born out of border conflict between Mexicans and Anglos, the border *corridos* represent a performed archive of storytelling that recasts Mexican male identity not as criminal but rather as superior to Anglo male identity. As a counter archive, the border *corridos* map an artistic process for coping with postcolonial male trauma alongside thwarting the desacralizing assaults of the State's master archive. From here, the discussion turns to an offspring of the border *corrido* genre, which I call Bible border *corridos*. Similar to the ways in which early border *corridos* drew subversively from the iconic currency of the Texas Rangers to embolden the ethnic Mexican male imagination, the Bible border *corridos* harness the sacredness of the Bible to elevate and affirm the sacred worth of Bible-believing Mexicans. By presenting the Bible through the performative framework of the border *corrido* genre, they infuse the counter archive with sacred status that in turn is conferred to Bible-believing Mexicans on both sides of the US-Mexico border. This process points to a sacralizing strategy in which a counter archive interfaces with sacred text and religious faith to elevate to an eternal level the human worth of a desacralized population.

From archives to border crossers, the fourth chapter of the book shifts to the mass expansion of immigrant detention. Entitled "The Desacralizing Power of Immigrant Detention," this chapter presents the fourth step to my proposed borderland hermeneutic, which involves an activist interrogation of the State's use of the sacred to legitimate its desacralization of border crossers. I argue that just as a political-ideological discourse (e.g. Manifest Destiny) actualized a physical border on the Mexican landscape, it requires an activist hermeneutic to transform the borderlands into an inclusive terrain that sacralizes border crossers. A worthwhile site of activist interrogation is at the nexus of privately run immigrant family detention centers in South Texas and their provision of religious care services. Herein lies an acute situation for the activist and humanitarians providing healing care to migrant border crossers—one that involves carceral control, albeit in incremental and subtle doses, over mind, body, soul, and spirit of immigrant parents and their children. Here, religious care services—like chaplaincy—in privately run immigrant family detention centers interface between President Trump's sacralized public safety ("Make America Safe Again!") and immigrant religious care needs. Because this juncture is framed by issues related to faith, the sacred, spiritual well-being, and emancipation, detained immigrant families are vulnerable to genocidal annihilation as the imagined outcome of Trump's sacralized public safety.

In the fifth chapter, "Caring for the Sacred Other," I present the healing care of migrant border crossers as the fifth strategy to my proposed borderland hermeneutic. Such a move admits to the State's desacralization of migrant border crossers within the sacred domains of human care. Hence, as a response, my proposed borderland hermeneutic turns to borderlands *curanderismo* (from the Spanish verb *curar*, which means "to heal" or "to cure") as an epistemological source for constructing a sacralizing praxis of healing care for migrant border crossers. Endowed with a different valuing system, I argue that borderlands *curanderismo* begins with a generous valuation of all life forms and their contexts of origin, resulting in a sacralizing approach to the pained and wounded human Other. By calibrating my proposed borderland hermeneutic to a *curandera* valuing system, the aim here is to replace the commoditizing approach of the current human care regime with a vernacular borderlands vision of healing care that elevates the intrinsic sacredness of all migrant border crossers.

In the end, the mission of this book is not to offer an all-encompassing hermeneutic to the postcolonial condition, but rather to attend in healing ways to the recurring wounds of postcoloniality (open wound) at the US-Mexico border. My aims here are intensely personal, in the sense these are my wounds too, and yet activist-driven because of the eradicating ambitions of elite power in the border region. Although I am indebted to Anzaldúa for her wisdom on the sacred otherness of wounds and how this framing of them lead the way to healing, these wounds are also personal; therefore, when harnessed to create a borderland hermeneutic, the results can never claim universal status. If there is any contribution worth recognizing from this book, it would be its appraisal of the sacred as a viable source for reproducing elite power. Finally, a word about what this book is not. First of all, notions of the sacred in this book only seek to initiate a different kind of discussion about the operations of elite power rather than exhaust it. At times subsuming the reproduction of elite power under notions of the sacred can appear overly simplistic and void of specificity. Such a risk should compel readers to consider this book in conjunction with the rest of the literature in critical theory and postcolonial theory. Indeed the exigencies of the current era require that all people wounded by empire contribute to a thorough dissection of elite power from a range of epistemological positions. My only argument in this book, however, is that by not taking "the sacred" seriously—either as catalyst in the reproduction of elite power or as an alternative epistemology—activist and humanitarian efforts in the border region risk being instrumentalized by elite power or rendered irrelevant to migrant border crossers.

Notes

1 Helene Cooper and Thomas Gibbons-Neff, "They're Trained for War: Now American Troops Are Headed to the U.S. Border," *The New York Times*, October 30, 2018; Leif Reigstad, "Trump's Deployment of Troops to the Border: What You Need to Know," *Texas Monthly*, April 5, 2018.
2 Geneva Sands, "Trump Administration to Allow Longer Detention of Migrant Families," *CNN*, August 22, 2019, www.cnn.com/2019/08/21/politics/immigration-family-detention-flores/index.html; Michael D. Shear and Zolan Kanno-Youngs, "Migrant Families Would Face Indefinite Detention Under New Trump Rule," *The New York Times*, August 21, 2019, www.nytimes.com/2019/08/21/us/politics/flores-migrant-family-detention.html; Noah Lanard, "ICE Just Quietly Opened Three New Detention Centers, Flouting Congress' Limits," *Mother Jones*, July 9, 2019, www.motherjones.com/politics/2019/07/ice-just-quietly-opened-three-new-detention-centers-flouting-congress-limits/.

3 Carol Kuruvilla, "Evangelicals Keep Misusing the Same Bible Verses to Give Trump a Pass," *HuffPost*, June 20, 2018, www.huffpost.com/entry/evangelicals-keep-misusing-the-same-bible-verses-to-give-trump-a-pass_n_5b297b7fe4b0a4dc9921e6e8; Tara Isabella Burton, "The Racist History of the Bible Verse the White House Uses to Justify Separating Families," *Vox*, June 15, 2018, www.vox.com/2018/6/15/17467818/bible-verse-white-house-immigration-racism-romans-13; Julie Zauzmer and Keith McMillan, "Sessions Cites Bible Passage Used to Defend Slavery in Defense of Separating Immigrant Families," *The Washington Post*, June 15, 2018, www.washingtonpost.com/news/acts-of-faith/wp/2018/06/14/jeff-sessions-points-to-the-bible-in-defense-of-separating-immigrant-families/; E. J. Dionne Jr., "Trump Is Weaponizing Evangelicals' Mistrust: And He's Succeeding," *The Washington Post*, August 21, 2019, www.washingtonpost.com/opinions/trump-is-weaponizing-evangelicals-mistrust-and-hes-succeeding/2019/08/21/e2df0d5e-c436-11e9-9986-1fb3e4397be4_story.html.
4 Aviva Chomsky, *Undocumented: How Immigration Became Illegal* (Boston: Beacon Press, 2014), 54.
5 Mathew C. Gutmann, Félix V. Rodríguez, Lynn Stephen, and Patricia Zavella, eds., *Perspectives on Las Américas: A Reader in Culture, History, & Representation* (Malden, MA: Blackwell Publishing, 2003), 10.
6 John C. Pinheiro, *Missionaries of Republicanism: A Religious History of the Mexican-American War* (Oxford: Oxford University Press, 2014), 65–66.
7 John L. O'Sullivan, "Annexation," *The United States Democratic Review* 17, no. 1 (July–August 1845): 5.
8 Reginald Horsman, *Race and Manifest Destiny: The Origins of American Racial Anglo-Saxonism* (Cambridge, MA: Harvard University Press, 1981), 82; Richard A. Bailey, *Race and Redemption in Puritan New England* (Oxford: Oxford University Press, 2011), 30; Pinheiro, *Missionaries of Republicanism*, 130.
9 O'Sullivan, "Annexation," 9.
10 Ibid., 7.
11 Pinheiro, *Missionaries of Republicanism*, 2, 61.
12 John McCarty, *Thanksgiving Sermon: Preached in the National Palace, City of Mexico, on Sunday, October Third, A.D. 1847* (Mexico: The Office of American Star, 1847), 13.
13 Ibid.
14 *Treaty of Peace, Friendship, Limits, and Settlement, Between the United States of America and the Mexican Republic* (Washington, DC: US Congress, 1848), 3.
15 Ibid.
16 Ibid., 7.
17 The Robert Runyon Photograph Collection, RUN00139, *The Dolph Briscoe Center for American History*, The University of Texas at Austin, http://runyon.lib.utexas.edu/n2c?urn:utlol:runyon.00139.
18 Gloria Anzaldúa, *Borderlands/La Frontera: The New Mestiza*, 2nd ed. (San Francisco: Aunt Lute Books, 1999), 24–25.
19 Ibid.
20 Ibid.
21 Ibid., 25.
22 Gloria Anzaldúa, *Light in the Dark/Luz en lo Oscuro: Rewriting Identity, Spirituality, Reality* (Durham, NC: Duke University Press, 2015), 87, 88, 90; Anzaldúa, *Borderlands/La Frontera*, 60–61; Gloria Anzaldúa, *Interviews/Entrevistas* (New York: Routledge, 2000), 123.
23 Anzaldúa, *Interviews/Entrevistas*, 41.
24 Gloria Anzaldúa, *The Gloria Anzaldúa Reader* (Durham, NC: Duke University Press, 2009), 230; Anzaldúa, *Light in the Dark/Luz en lo Oscuro*, 119–20.

25 Anzaldúa, *Light in the Dark/Luz en lo Oscuro*, 127–28, 151.
26 Ibid., 44, 154.
27 Ibid., 44.
28 Ibid., 34–35.
29 Ibid., 44.
30 Ibid., 89–90.
31 Ibid., 89.
32 Anzaldúa, *Light in the Dark/Luz en lo Oscuro*, 121–22; Anzaldúa, *Interviews/Entrevistas*, 95–96.
33 Antoinette Burton, ed., *Archive Stories: Facts, Fictions, and the Writing of History* (Durham, NC: Duke University Press, 2005), 5.
34 Anzaldúa, *Interviews/Entrevistas*, 41.
35 Anzaldúa, *Borderlands/La Frontera*, 30, 83, 105, 138.
36 Ibid., 60.
37 Anzaldúa, *Light in the Dark/Luz en lo Oscuro*, 89.
38 Ibid., 90.
39 Anzaldúa, *The Gloria Anzaldúa Reader*, 292, 296, 312, 320.
40 Anzaldúa, *Light in the Dark/Luz en lo Oscuro*, 90.
41 Anzaldúa, *Borderlands/La Frontera*, 29–30.
42 Ibid., 59.
43 Ibid., 58–59.
44 Ibid., 59.
45 Anzaldúa, *Light in the Dark/Luz en lo Oscuro*, 140.
46 Ibid., 118.
47 Ibid., 44.
48 Anzaldúa, *Borderlands/La Frontera*, 59.
49 Anzaldúa, *Interviews/Entrevistas*, 95–96.
50 Ibid., 95.
51 Ibid., 97.
52 Michael Gerson, "Some White Evangelicals Are Difficult to Recognize as Christians at All," *The Washington Post*, August 15, 2019, www.washingtonpost.com/opinions/how-we-christians-order-our-outrage-says-a-lot-about-us/2019/08/15/a5a0c2e2-bf91-11e9-a5c6-1e74f7ec4a93_story.html?noredirect=on; Jason Koon, "White Evangelicals Have Won Political Influence: But at What Cost?" *Sojourners*, July 18, 2019, https://sojo.net/articles/white-evangelicals-have-won-political-influence-what-cost; Martin Longman, "White Evangelicals Like Having a Bully-in-Chief," *Washington Monthly*, August 13, 2019, https://washingtonmonthly.com/2019/08/13/white-evangelicals-like-having-a-bully-in-chief/; Michael Boorstein and Julie Zauzmer, "Why Many White Evangelicals Are Not Protesting Family Separations on the U.S. Border," *The Washington Post*, June 18, 2018, www.washingtonpost.com/news/acts-of-faith/wp/2018/06/18/why-many-white-evangelical-christians-are-not-protesting-family-separations-on-the-u-s-border/.
53 Anzaldúa, *Borderlands/La Frontera*, 12.
54 Anzaldúa, *Light in the Dark/Luz en lo Oscuro*, 133.
55 Kirk Semple, "'I Didn't Want Them to Go': Salvadoran Family Grieves for Father and Daughter Who Drowned," *The New York Times*, June 28, 2019, www.nytimes.com/2019/06/28/world/americas/rio-grande-drowning-father-daughter.html; Peter Orsi and Amy Guthrie, "Disturbing: Photo of Drowned Father and Daughter Highlights Migrants' Tragic Struggles," *HuffPost*, June 25, 2019, www.huffpost.com/entry/photo-drowned-father-daughter-migrants-struggles_n_5d129258e4b04f059e4b2222; The Times Editorial Board, "Editorial: As the El Paso Massacre Showed Once Again, White Supremacy Is the Poison in Our Well," *Los Angeles Times*, August 6, 2019, www.latimes.com/opinion/story/2019-08-06/massacre-el-paso-white-supremacy-trump; Adam Serwer, "A Crime by Any Name," *The Atlantic*, July 3, 2019, www.theatlantic.

com/ideas/archive/2019/07/border-facilities/593239/; Manny Fernandez, "A New Migrant Surge at the Border, This One From Central Africa," *The New York Times*, June 16, 2019, www.nytimes.com/2019/06/16/us/border-africans-congo-maine.html.
56 Anzaldúa, *Light in the Dark/Luz en lo Oscuro*, 89.
57 Anzaldúa, *Borderlands/La Frontera*, 12.
58 Anzaldúa, *Light in the Dark/Luz en lo Oscuro*, 126.
59 Anzaldúa, *Borderlands/La Frontera*, 68.
60 Anzaldúa, *Light in the Dark/Luz en lo Oscuro*, 89–90.
61 Ibid., 120.
62 Ibid., 44.
63 Anzaldúa, *Borderlands/La Frontera*, 105.

Bibliography

Anzaldúa, Gloria. *Borderlands/La Frontera: The New Mestiza*. 2nd ed. San Francisco: Aunt Lute Books, 1999.
———. *The Gloria Anzaldúa Reader*. Durham, NC: Duke University Press, 2009.
———. *Interviews/Entrevistas*. New York: Routledge, 2000.
———. *Light in the Dark/Luz en lo Oscuro: Rewriting Identity, Spirituality, Reality*. Durham, NC: Duke University Press, 2015.
Bailey, Richard A. *Race and Redemption in Puritan New England*. Oxford: Oxford University Press, 2011.
Boorstein, Michael, and Julie Zauzmer. "Why Many White Evangelicals Are Not Protesting Family Separations on the U.S. Border." *The Washington Post*, June 18, 2018. www.washingtonpost.com/news/acts-of-faith/wp/2018/06/18/why-many-white-evangelical-christians-are-not-protesting-family-separations-on-the-u-s-border/.
Burton, Antoinette, ed. *Archive Stories: Facts, Fictions, and the Writing of History*. Durham, NC: Duke University Press, 2005.
Burton, Tara Isabella. "The Racist History of the Bible Verse the White House Uses to Justify Separating Families." *Vox*, June 15, 2018. www.vox.com/2018/6/15/17467818/bible-verse-white-house-immigration-racism-romans-13.
Chomsky, Aviva. *Undocumented: How Immigration Became Illegal*. Boston: Beacon Press, 2014.
Cooper, Helene, and Thomas Gibbons-Neff. "They're Trained for War: Now American Troops Are Headed to the U.S. Border." *The New York Times*, October 30, 2018.
Dionne, E. J., Jr. "Trump Is Weaponizing Evangelicals' Mistrust: And He's Succeeding." *The Washington Post*, August 21, 2019. www.washingtonpost.com/opinions/trump-is-weaponizing-evangelicals-mistrust-and-hes-succeeding/2019/08/21/e2df0d5e-c436-11e9-9986-1fb3e4397be4_story.html.
Fernandez, Manny. "A New Migrant Surge at the Border, This One from Central Africa." *The New York Times*, June 16, 2019. www.nytimes.com/2019/06/16/us/border-africans-congo-maine.html.
Gerson, Michael. "Some White Evangelicals Are Difficult to Recognize as Christians at All." *The Washington Post*, August 15, 2019. www.washingtonpost.com/opinions/how-we-christians-order-our-outrage-says-a-lot-about-us/2019/08/15/a5a0c2e2-bf91-11e9-a5c6-1e74f7ec4a93_story.html?noredirect=on.
Gutmann, Mathew C., Félix V. Rodríguez, Lynn Stephen, and Patricia Zavella, eds. *Perspectives on Las Américas: A Reader in Culture, History, & Representation*. Malden, MA: Blackwell Publishing, 2003.

Horsman, Reginald. *Race and Manifest Destiny: The Origins of American Racial Anglo-Saxonism*. Cambridge, MA: Harvard University Press, 1981.

Koon, Jason. "White Evangelicals Have Won Political Influence: But at What Cost?" *Sojourners*, July 18, 2019. https://sojo.net/articles/white-evangelicals-have-won-political-influence-what-cost.

Kuruvilla, Carol. "Evangelicals Keep Misusing the Same Bible Verses to Give Trump a Pass." *HuffPost*, June 20, 2018. www.huffpost.com/entry/evangelicals-keep-misusing-the-same-bible-verses-to-give-trump-a-pass_n_5b297b7fe4b0a4dc9921e6e8.

Lanard, Noah. "ICE Just Quietly Opened Three New Detention Centers, Flouting Congress' Limits." *Mother Jones*, July 9, 2019. www.motherjones.com/politics/2019/07/ice-just-quietly-opened-three-new-detention-centers-flouting-congress-limits/.

Longman, Martin. "White Evangelicals Like Having a Bully-in-Chief." *Washington Monthly*, August 13, 2019. https://washingtonmonthly.com/2019/08/13/white-evangelicals-like-having-a-bully-in-chief/.

McCarty, John. *Thanksgiving Sermon: Preached in the National Palace, City of Mexico, on Sunday, October Third, A.D. 1847*. Mexico: The Office of American Star, 1847.

Orsi, Peter, and Amy Guthrie. "Disturbing: Photo of Drowned Father and Daughter Highlights Migrants' Tragic Struggles." *HuffPost*, June 25, 2019. www.huffpost.com/entry/photo-drowned-father-daughter-migrants-struggles_n_5d129258e4b04f059e4b2222.

O'Sullivan, John L. "Annexation." *The United States Democratic Review* 17, no. 1 (July–August 1845): 5–10.

Pinheiro, John C. *Missionaries of Republicanism: A Religious History of the Mexican-American War*. Oxford: Oxford University Press, 2014.

Reigstad, Leif. "Trump's Deployment of Troops to the Border: What You Need to Know." *Texas Monthly*, April 5, 2018.

The Robert Runyon Photograph Collection. *The Dolph Briscoe Center for American History*. The University of Texas at Austin. http://runyon.lib.utexas.edu/n2c?urn:utlol:runyon.00139.

Sands, Geneva. "Trump Administration to Allow Longer Detention of Migrant Families." *CNN*, August 22, 2019. www.cnn.com/2019/08/21/politics/immigration-family-detention-flores/index.html.

Semple, Kirk. "'I Didn't Want Them to Go': Salvadoran Family Grieves for Father and Daughter Who Drowned." *The New York Times*, June 28, 2019. www.nytimes.com/2019/06/28/world/americas/rio-grande-drowning-father-daughter.html.

Serwer, Adam. "A Crime by Any Name." *The Atlantic*, July 3, 2019. www.theatlantic.com/ideas/archive/2019/07/border-facilities/593239/.

Shear, Michael D., and Zolan Kanno-Youngs. "Migrant Families Would Face Indefinite Detention Under New Trump Rule." *The New York Times*, August 21, 2019. www.nytimes.com/2019/08/21/us/politics/flores-migrant-family-detention.html.

The Times Editorial Board. "Editorial: As the El Paso Massacre Showed Once Again, White Supremacy Is the Poison in Our Well." *Los Angeles Times*, August 6, 2019. www.latimes.com/opinion/story/2019-08-06/massacre-el-paso-white-supremacy-trump.

Treaty of Peace, Friendship, Limits, and Settlement, Between the United States of America and the Mexican Republic. Washington, DC: US Congress, 1848.

Zauzmer, Julie, and Keith McMillan. "Sessions Cites Bible Passage Used to Defend Slavery in Defense of Separating Immigrant Families." *The Washington Post*, June 15, 2018. www.washingtonpost.com/news/acts-of-faith/wp/2018/06/14/jeff-sessions-points-to-the-bible-in-defense-of-separating-immigrant-families/.

2 Trespassing on the archive as the border-crossed other

The task I take up as a "border-crossed" reader involves subverting master-narratives or what I term trespassing on the archive, largely because those "border-crossed" have been desacralized by them. As revealed in empire studies, master-narratives that wield power within a body politic often seek the authoritative status of universality.[1] In the Western context, from the seventeenth century onward, modern scientific knowledge (objectivity) serves as a master sense[2] or what Michel Foucault calls "the sense by which we perceive extent and establish proof."[3]

For the disciplines that appeal to Western scientific ways of knowing, visual observation is deemed the normative strategy for achieving truth claims. Hence, whether it is inspecting the human body for disease or reading sacred manuscripts for their original intent, objectifying what or who is seen represents a central goal for Western scientific ways of knowing. Though disciplinary boundaries in the West labor hard to show themselves as specialized and distinct fields of knowledge, those disciplines rooted in scientific objectivity are resolutely optical-centric. In short, what I am trying to hint at here is less the practical relation between visibility and scientific thought than the sway of scientific inspection as a master-narrative through the privileging of visibility and rendering tangible that which is seen. As a biblical scholar, I have both resisted and complied with this master-narrative duo. Paradoxically, being "border-crossed," I have also been constrained, racialized, and disembodied by Western scientific ways of knowing. In the end, I become—as Foucault describes—the principle of my own subjection.[4] In using Western scientific objectivity, I am not only taught to affirm sight as the master sense for defining truth, but I also enable this mode of truth-making to be used against me as a border-crossed person. In this way, I have become both someone who objectifies (biblical scholar) and is objectified (border-crossed). This dynamic operates under the illusion that scientific observers can enter an unbiased and pristine state, separate from their social location, cultural formation, and political convictions. Moreover, because scientific objectivity is conflated with the highest forms of civilizational progress, this way of knowing has accrued sacred authority in Western modern society. This in turn has rendered scientific objectivity a viable resource for elite power in that it can control social bodies, first through their objectification and second through the sacred status of scientific sight.

In an effort to pull away from the truth-making systems that objectify me, I turn to my "border-crossed" condition not only because it is a source of hermeneutical emancipation but also because, as Américo Paredes suggests, the "border-crossed" Texas-Mexican must attend to the places and times that have a hold on our social selves.[5] This combined with Anzaldúa's plunging notion of the border as her wound, the history of violence and injustice in the US-Mexico borderlands require continual attention and redress, largely because these wounds are transferred to subsequent border-crossed generations. Among the violent scenes of the past in which the master-narrative of Western scientific knowledge and a racializing optic converge violently on Texas-Mexicans in the borderlands was the 1899 smallpox epidemic in Laredo, Texas. Rather than offer a bird's-eye view of state-sanctioned atrocities in the border region, this chapter plunges into a specific border wound—attending to a convergence of sacralized state violence, Western scientific gaze, and the desacralization of ethnic Mexicans. Also at issue here is the State's sacred archive, like Texas Ranger lore, as a site that renders this wound perpetually open and hence unhealed. As someone trained to use scientific objectivity and ascribe it sacred status, this chapter plunges, in the Anzaldúaian sense, into a historical instance in which this mode of truth-making reveals its lethal potential when piloted by a criminalizing racial logic. On the other side, as a border-crossed son of the borderlands, the archived lore of the Texas Rangers combined with its sacred status have also kept the wounds of border-crossed people bloody and raw.[6] Mending the multiple wounds that the Texas Rangers have inflicted on ethnic Mexicans in the US-Mexico borderlands requires a trespassing on this sacralized archive in order to expose their eradicating violence.

Anglo-American scientific inspection

By the late nineteenth century, physicians of the Texas State Medical Association (TSMA) were committed to elevating the scientificity of the medical care profession. In his 1898 presidential address at the TSMA's thirtieth annual session, Dr. Bacon Saunders of Fort Worth, Texas, declared that "the science of medicine is now and must ever be a system of accurately observed and faithfully recorded truths."[7] This view coincided with general US medical practice in the late nineteenth century in which the human body was visually inspected for symptoms followed by a diagnosis through a process of exclusions.[8] Interestingly, Saunders likened the task of the physician to a minister exegeting the Bible, stating, "he studies the text in the original, looks up the meaning of every word and phrase in the Greek, Latin and Hebrew lexicons; finds the opinions of all the commentators; investigates the questions involved in the light of history, both sacred and profane."[9] For Saunders, visual inspection functioned as a universal tool of scientific inquiry, and therefore could be used interchangeably in both medical care and biblical exegesis to make a truth claim. In this regard, the affective force of scientific inspection is rooted in the Western notion that the tandem of seeing and objects can yield an unbiased truth claim. Here scientific truth is commensurate with the degree of objectivity that the inspector's eyes are able to achieve. Attaining perfect impartiality assumes that the scientific inspector can shift into a disembodied state that is detached from all cultural entanglements and socializing processes. Hence, what is casted as objectivity actually constitutes an illusionary state of the inspector's socialized self. In this way, scientific inspection functions not as a pristine mode of truth-making but rather as a permanently subjective tool that under the right conditions can be socially destructive.

Although visibility in the Western scientific sense links the domain of medical care to the domain of biblical exegesis, Saunders's analogy also implies an overarching hermeneutic of the sacred in which scientific inspection of the body and the Bible rise to the level of a sacred duty. Like the biblical text, the human body represents a domain of the sacred that scientific medicine is charged to diagnose and ultimately heal. By correlating the body to the Bible, Saunders not only renders the body a sacred object, but also by association sacralizes the medical care profession. As a sacred endeavor, which is made possible through the sacralization of the body, the command of sight, and the scientificity of medical inspection, an ideal instrument ensues for colonizing elite power. In essence, with the diagnosis of the body, medical inspectors are able to determine the body's social reality. In this system of truth-making, inspected social bodies accept their diagnosis as truth in part because of the convincing force of sight. For elite Anglo-American power in the nineteenth century, the sacred status of medical inspection was harnessed as an advantageous instrument for controlling social bodies.

Following Saunders's address was a speech on the state of the medical profession by the TSMA's selected orator, Dr. I.N. Suttle of Corsicana, Texas. In distinguishing the medical profession as a scientific enterprise, he made the following observation: "a profession like ours that is invested with the power of unequaled beneficence, that disdains all mystery, all prestige of authority, and all superstitious veneration for traditional dogmas, that asks for confidence on the sure basis of scientific knowledge."[10] Underlying his notion of "sure basis" is the convincing force of scientific inspection in solidifying truth claims about the body within the medical care profession. In his view, this was what made the medical care profession a sacred endeavor or in his words, "the gift of heaven open to the good of all mankind."[11] The sacralization of the medical care profession was not unique to Saunders and Suttle, but rather coincided with how the American Medical Association (AMA) portrayed physicians as ministers. In its *Code of Ethics* under the section "Duties of the physician to their patients," the AMA states that "Physicians should, therefore, minister to the sick with due impressions of the importance of their office."[12] Here the AMA's notion of minister has in view this term's religious connotations. As stipulated in its ethical code, "the physician should be the minister of hope and comfort to the sick," which represents the physician's "sacred duty."[13] By conflating the medical profession with the religious domain, the AMA doubly sacralizes scientific inspection. Here, physicians assume a priestly function in which their sacred duty is to objectively diagnose bodies for infirmities and disease. The religiosity of the medical profession is not spiritual in nature but rather linked to the sacred status of its healing mission and the belief that physicians' diagnoses are untainted by their biases, values, and convictions. In nineteenth-century Texas, however, the investments made to this sacralized domain by elite Anglo-American power weaponized the priestly function of the medical profession by combining it with a scientific racial logic. Among the benefits of this sacred tandem (medical inspection and scientific racism) in the Texas-Mexico border was how they enabled an unfavorable diagnosis of black and brown bodies as to ensure their subjugation to Anglo-Americans.

The master-narrative of Texas reminds us that the implied ideal practitioner of scientific inspection was the Anglo-American male. This entanglement with Anglo-American masculinity rendered the medical scientific care of the body a site of control for the same population dominating US property ownership, business, wealth, politics, education, legal system, and military, to name a few.[14] In this context, the sacred domain of medical care converges with the social ideal in US society that results in the reproduction of Anglo-American values, norms, and beliefs. In other words, to diagnose the pained body through the eyes of Anglo-American medical men, particularly those socialized to believe they were racially superior to all other bodies, meant to align scientific inspection with the power structures that ensured Anglo-American social, political, and economic dominance. On the other hand, such entanglements also marked the destructive confluence of a white supremacist racial logic, science, the sacred, and the care of the body in that together they legitimated violence against ethnic Mexicans in the Texas-Mexico borderlands. Indeed, the sacred status of this convergence with Anglo-American society gave way to eradicating forms of violence, such that the diagnosis of brown bodies led to their bodies being mangled, burned, lynched, and unburied.[15]

Casting ethnic Mexicans as the undesirable other

The United States' decision to annex Texas was ratified in 1845 as a result of a resolution passing in the US Senate during a convention in Austin, Texas, on March 1 and on July 4. Included in the annexation agreement was the United States' claim to the disputed territory lying between the Nueces River and the Río Grande. In 1845, war ensued with Mexico after US troops marched to claim the Río Grande as the official US/Texas-Mexico territorial boundary.¹⁶ In just two years after the war, the US acquired nearly one million square miles of Mexico's northern territories, which consisted of the present-day states of California, New Mexico, northern Arizona, Nevada, Utah, Colorado, Kansas, Oklahoma, and Wyoming. With the signing of the Treaty of Guadalupe-Hidalgo in 1848, which is sacralized with its opening words "In the name of Almighty God," the US-Mexico boundary was drawn from the Gulf of Mexico westward along the Río Grande to a point just above El Paso del Norte, Chihuahua, and through the Sonoran Desert onto the Pacific just below San Diego, California.¹⁷ An appeal to the biblical notion of the "chosen people" and Anglo-American providential destiny provided initial impetus for extending the boundaries of US sovereignty. Under this religious inflection of US imperialism, the Río Grande was viewed as the divinely preordained boundary between US/Texas and Mexico.¹⁸ Sacralized as such, the river became a bordering weapon for the protection of a divinely chosen society against a people group racialized as "a mongrel race of Spaniards and Indians."¹⁹

Since the inception of US society, notions of "life, liberty and the pursuit of happiness" have had the Anglo-American male property owner as the standard-bearer of these inalienable rights.²⁰ In Saidiya Hartman's words:

> the implied citizen of the Constitution and subject of "we the people" was the white male. Citizenship presupposed the equality of abstract and disembodied persons, and this abstraction disguised the privileges of white men. The presumed whiteness and maleness of the citizen transpose the particular into the universal, thus enabling white men to enjoy the privileges of abstraction and a noncorporeal universality.²¹

Prior to Anglo-American expansion into Mexican territory, chattel slavery had long served as the primary social incubator for the construction of white male dominance in US society. Yet for ethnic Mexicans, their operative racial order was a system of mixed racial types constructed during the Spanish colonial period. Under Spanish colonial rule, privilege and citizenship was measured, for the most part, according to a hierarchically structured grid of miscegenation, notions of nobility, Catholic-Christian faith, and purity of blood.²² Inserting brownness to the abiding US black-white racial binary, particularly as it pertained to reproducing Anglo-American social dominance, required the systematic vilification and desacralization of ethnic Mexicans.

A prominent domain for advancing vilifying racial constructions of ethnic Mexicans was the US publishing market, in particular the popular genre of Texas historiography.²³ During the years between Texas' first Anglo-American settlement and its annexation to the United States, the popularity of Texas history books was not only linked to their affirmation of Anglo-American ideals like individualism and progress but also for their stigmatization of ethnic Mexicans.[24] Generally regarded as the first Anglo-American Texas historian, Mary Austin Holley, in her 1836 book *Texas*, distinguishes ethnic Mexicans as "very ignorant and degraded, and generally speaking, timid, irresolute . . . commonly very indolent, of loose morals, and if not infidels of which there are many, involved in the grossest superstition."[25] In these words, Holley's desacralization of ethnic Mexicans begins with the belittlement of their mental capacities moving then to their moral and religious depravity. Moreover, assumed in Holley's racializing assessment is the sacralized status of Anglo-Americans as the standard bearer of mental capacities, morals, and religion.

Solicited to write a history of Texas, Henry Stuart Foote, a member of the Mississippi House of Representatives, wrote these words in his 1841 book *Texas and the Texans: Or, Advance of the Anglo-Americans to the South-West*: "the Mexican population are as evidently deficient in all those high faculties of soul and understanding, which can alone confer the sublime capability of self-government."[26] Like Holly, Foote's desacralization of ethnic Mexicans ranges from the mental to spiritual. Latent in Foote's description presupposes Anglo-American superiority in intelligence, religion, and hence self-government. In this way, his desacralization functions multi-directionally, for in desacralizing ethnic Mexican personhood, he in turn sacralizes Anglo-American superiority.

Even more unsettling was the instrumental role of Anglo-American clergy and missionaries in writing histories that desacralized ethnic Mexican personhood. The Reverend A.B. Lawrence, a Presbyterian minister and editor of *New Orleans Presbyterian*, visited Texas. Here, he wrote a volume primarily intended as an immigrant guidebook for fellow Anglo-Americans.[27] Titled *Texas in 1840: Emigrant's Guide to the New Republic*, Lawrence described ethnic Mexicans as follows:

> In point of character for intelligence, vigor or enterprise, the Mexicans are far inferior to Anglo-Americans, or any class of Europeans. For the most part they are small in stature and of feeble frame . . . they are destitute of high moral qualities requisite to produce elevation or energy of character, or even to preserve them from degrading vices. Hence in general their morals are low and debased in every respect. And licentiousness is scarcely thought worthy of rebuke.[28]

Here again, the historian begins his desacralization of ethnic Mexicans with a low ranking of their mental capacities. Rather than imply Anglo-Americans as the standard bearers of intelligence, Lawrence states explicitly, "the Mexicans are far inferior to Anglo-Americans." His diagnosis of ethnic Mexican inferiority extends from mental capacities to physique to morals to character. Starkly similar to how white superiority was facilitated by a collective antipathy to blackness, showing ethnic Mexican personhood as mentally, culturally, and morally bankrupt served to expand Anglo-American domination in the newly conquered Mexican territories.[29]

Before coming to Brownsville, Texas, as a Protestant missionary, Melinda Rankin wrote a short history of Texas with the aim "to enlist Christian sympathy and co-operation in aid of evangelizing a country which is destined, evidently, to exert an important influence over other contiguous country."[30] Although she claims to give an impartial account of Texas history, Rankin frequently makes desacralizing distinctions between Anglo-American Protestantism and Mexican religious/moral character. In her chapter on Texas social institutions, Rankin correlates the moral improvement of Mexicans with their exposure to Anglo-American Protestants:

> Let Texas stand beside Mexico, highly evangelized, and the contrast would serve to show the superiority of the Protestant over the Catholic religion; the tendency of which would be to constrain the degraded Mexicans to yield to the influence of that system of faith, which might elevate them to the like happy condition. . . . Their proximity renders it apparent, that the moral condition of the one will evidently affect the other. The bale effects of Mexican influence must be counteracted and overcome, and Christians must buckle on anew their armor in the prosecution of a work.[31]

Rankin's sacralization of Anglo-American Protestant superiority begins with its geographical location of Texas and then extends to its people and their Protestant witness. Rankin's tripartite sacralization of land, people, and religion constitute a religious border between Anglo-American Protestants and Mexican Catholics. The aim is to ensure the constraint of "the degraded Mexicans." Deemed an inferior people, Rankin viewed ethnic Mexicans as a religious and moral threat to Anglo-American Protestant society. For her, "the superiority of the Protestant over the Catholic religion" legitimates Anglo-Americans' domination of ethnic Mexicans, as she states, "the bale effects of Mexican influence must be counteracted and overcome." Apart from protecting Anglo-American Texans from inferior Mexicans, their domination should result in the moral elevation of Mexicans. This framing of Anglo-American domination as a necessary action for the religious and moral improvement of ethnic Mexicans also appears in McCarty's 1847 sermon. As he states, "that witnessing our superiority not only as soldiers, but as Christian men, they may honor our land, not only as free, enlightened and prosperous, but as blessed by superior means of Christian knowledge and piety, which are the foundations for all."[32] Lastly, Rankin draws on military language in defining Anglo-American religious domination, stating: "Christians must buckle on anew their armor in the prosecution of a work."[33] For both McCarty and Rankin, sacralizing the superiority of Anglo-American Protestants not only opened the way for their domination, but also their sacralization made possible the use of physical violence as its primary mode.

The sacralization of Anglo-American Protestantism set the threshold for relations with ethnic Mexicans at domination, some of which included the use of state-sanctioned violence. They had achieved an elite form of the divine and chosen as such; they also set their relations with ethnic Mexicans as permanently superior. In the previous historical samples, the sacralization of Anglo-American Protestant superiority extends to both land and people. In this way, the border between Texas and Mexico was assigned a religious function such that it became the dividing line between a superior and inferior religion. This division contributed to the antagonism and conflict that marked social relations between Anglo-Americans and ethnic Mexicans in Texas in the nineteenth century.

By the late nineteenth century, published anti-Mexican racial constructions served to underwrite Anglo-American notions of the public good in the Texas-Mexico borderlands region. As viewed in the previous sample, historians first sacralized Anglo-American superiority—from their intelligence to their morals to their religion to, finally, their society—and as such ensured their domination. In this literature, Mexicans north and south of the border were cast as the utmost threat to Anglo-American public safety, health, and morals. For the colonized ethnic Mexican population in the north, their debasement as the "indolent," "destitute," "degraded," "bale" other in popular Texas histories created a social reality of cultural, religious, and physical eradication. As the antithesis to the Anglo-American social ideal (white male Protestant), their lives were destined for permanent exclusion from resources, wealth, credentials, property, and rights.

Securing the border from migrating disease

At the beginning of 1899, there were a growing number of residents in the border town of Laredo, Texas, who were infected with the highly contagious and fatal disease of variola, or smallpox. On January 12, 1899, the brief article "Laredo Smallpox" appeared on the front page of the *Austin Daily Statesman* and reported that "in all there have been about forty cases, wholly amongst the ignorant Mexicans, who make no report of the disease until it has been well developed. Americans are not alarmed as the disease is a common one amongst the Mexicans."[34] From the outset of the smallpox outbreak in Laredo, the public and political discourse defaulted to an insidious binary logic in which good health was linked to Anglo-Americans and disease was intrinsic to ethnic Mexicans. As Hartman argues, in nineteenth-century US society "the linking of whiteness with purity, neatness, and health accedes to a politics of contagion that eventually serves to justify segregation and license the racist strategies of the state in securing the health of the social body." In the US-Mexico border, equating viral disease with ethnic Mexicans resulted in targeted policing practices that sought to prevent viral diseases from migrating north. Those charged with this task were a network of state agents such as customs officers, quarantine officers, assistant surgeons, sanitary inspectors, and military and police personnel. For instance, Lea Hume, Assistant Surgeon of the United States Marine Hospital Service (USMHS) in Eagle Pass, Texas, had charge of scouting by horseback communities north and south of the border in order to identify people infected with smallpox or other contagious diseases. In his public health report to the US Surgeon General on February 18, 1899, he provides the following observation on C.P. Diaz Mexico (modern day Piedras Negras) across the river from Eagle Pass: "In all I covered some 250 miles, but found no contagious disease, though I suspected smallpox at Mokal, Mexico (20 miles from here on the Rio Grande River), and for that reason established a guard on the American side of the river at that place."[35] Hume's medical intuitions rendered suspect Mexicans as the host of migrating disease, hence resulting in heightened border security "on the American side." In reporting the number of smallpox cases, Hume identifies three in C.P. Diaz and yet states that "it is very likely that there are numerous other cases of smallpox in C.P. Diaz which are not known, these cases being among the lower class of Mexicans."[36] For Hume, viral disease had a migration path of south to north and its ultimate source was the Mexican poor. It is important to note how Hume's conflation of viral disease with the Mexican poor in the US-Mexico borderlands translated into tangible border security practices in which brown-bodied border crossers were accused, examined, vaccinated, and quarantined. As reported by E. Alexander, Sanitary Inspector from El Paso, Texas, on March 1, 1899:

> Thousands of excursionists from all parts of the United States came into Mexico, through the inducement of very low railroad rates. These people not only visit the different numerous churches, etc., but generally go around in the huts of the lowest of the low, no doubt very often visit houses where cases of small-pox exist, and carry the germs in their clothing to Maine and Oregon, endangering the unprotected at such places.[37]

By declaring the Mexican poor as the host of contagious disease, the ensuing practice was, as Hume reports, "a strict watch ... continually kept on C.P. Diaz and all people coming from Mexico are thoroughly examined."[38] Revealed in Hume's medical inspection of ethnic Mexican bodies was the presupposition that they were the source of disease. Herein lies another facet to the desacralization of ethnic Mexicans by Anglo-Americans, for in addition to their moral depravity and mental ignorance, they bred viral disease. Such a framework skewed medical inspection to the extent that border security operations targeted the Mexican poor. Both the State and Hume's credentials as a physician solidified the authority of his border reports on the spread of smallpox to the broader public. These reports not only harnessed the dominant beliefs about ethnic Mexican inferiority in Anglo-American society, but they also made official the notion that ethnic Mexicans were the source of infectious disease. Further boosting their public authority was their inclusion in the state archive, for here the archive afforded these reports longevity of influence in the public sphere.

In Hume's second report on February 25, 1899, his diagnosis of the Mexican poor as the host and transmitter of viral disease resulted in increased border security:

> I have one Marine-Hospital Service guard stationed on the Rio Grande just opposite the Mexican town of Mokal, this guard patrolling the river for a distance of 10 miles, and allowing no one to cross the fords in his territory. The customs inspectors of Eagle Pass and Del Rio are aiding me in keeping out the disease, and I feel sure that no case will get to this side. Every person coming into the United States is thoroughly examined, and everything is being done to prevent the entrance of smallpox, or any other contagious disease.[39]

Hume's medical inspections assigned a disease control function to border security. Their diagnosis of smallpox was a mobilizing agent for border guards and customs officers. In this way, their patrolling and inspections at the border now included "keeping out the disease." The fear of disease combined with Hume's biased inspection reinforced the south-facing policing gaze of border security. Along with their standard role of protecting US society from "indolent" and "degraded" Mexicans was now a disease control function that heightened their anti-Mexican sentiments. In Hume's words, "the Rio Grande is continually watched, I having stationed 1 Marine-Hospital Service guard at Upson, Tex., with instructions to watch all the fords and allow no suspicious characters to cross to this side."[40] From Hume's medical inspections, the diagnosis of disease yielded an itinerary of its source and activated a bordering gaze that is arguably still in use today. As part of the State's sacred apparatus, medical inspections sacralized Anglo-American public health by locating the source of viral disease in the ethnic Mexican body. Commensurate with the sacred status of white male medical inspections was the heightened border security that they prompted at the US-Mexico border. Conversely, the sacralization of Anglo-American public health allowed for further desacralization of ethnic Mexicans. In addition to their inferior mental state and destitute morality was an infected and diseased body, all of which prepared the way for their eradication.

The elite politics of contagion

On February 26, 1899, Dr. H.J. Hamilton, Assistant Surgeon of the USMHS in Laredo, identified in his public health report a total of 376 smallpox cases and 83 deaths, which according to Hamilton pointed to the fact that "the Mexicans do not employ, nor will they permit, a physician to take charge and treat them properly."[41] Attentive to Hamilton's reports was Laredo Mayor Louis Christen and city council members who, as a response, commissioned city hall security guards to serve as municipal health inspectors.[42] The science was simple: inspect ethnic Mexicans, in particular the lower class since they had been deemed more likely to reject modern scientific medical practice. Among the targeted residents for health inspection and in-house quarantine was the working-class Texas-Mexican population residing in the Zacate Creek neighborhood near Laredo's major factory district.[43] Designating this disease as a problem of the Mexican poor legitimated the policing of the Zacate Creek neighborhood in ways that were invasive and dehumanizing.[44] As John Mckiernan-González observes, the city's response to the smallpox outbreak involved both elite Anglos and middle-class Mexican-Americans who "relied on civic-minded and intrusive performance of middle-class respectability."[45] Containing the spread of smallpox meant recruiting citizens who had accepted state-approved medical practice as not only intrinsic to the public good but also imperative to addressing the health risk posed by the diseased Mexican poor.

The desacralized status of the ethnic Mexican residents of Zacate Creek was reflected in the local press coverage as well as in the militant measures used to inspect this demographic, such as forced entry, stripped-naked, and mandated vaccination.[46] In addition, local authorities had ordered the closure of all schools, churches, and plazas, which severed these residents from vital social and religious networks.[47] Yet even with these targeted policing measures, prominent citizens—mainly elite Anglo-Americans and middle-class Mexican-Americans—sought to intensify the city's public health strategies as the spread of smallpox cases began to reach Laredo's business district. By March 4, 1899, Assistant Surgeon Hamilton had tallied in his public health report fifty-nine new smallpox cases and nineteen deaths.[48] Dissatisfied with the city's response to Laredo's Mexican problem were, as described by the *Austin Daily Statesman*, "the most prominent citizens." Confident in their collective authority, they sent a signed telegram to Dr. W.F. Blunt, State Health Officer, which according to the *Austin Daily Statesman* read: "smallpox situation serious, in our opinion the local authorities are unable and incompetent to handle same, come at once and assume charge."[49] In response, Dr. Blunt sent a letter to Governor Joseph D. Sayers on March 9, 1899, stating, "in view of the fact that the smallpox situation in Webb county, has not improved, but rather grown worse, in fact, practically beyond the control of the authorities in said county; and the disease is scattered all through the business and resident parts of the city of Laredo, so much so, that it is not safe for people to visit there, or for traveling salesmen to go there."[50] Here, Blunt's assessment coincides with Hume's diagnosis of the disease, with its source being the ethnic Mexican body. Moreover the bordering security that accompanied

Blunt's diagnosis extended to the movement of Mexican bodies north of the US-Mexico border. As Blunt described, "in view of the further fact that just at this time, there is an annual exodus of Mexicans from south Texas to the central part of the state, to engage in farm labor, and there is so much danger of their scattering the disease over the state."[51] In the same way Hume's medical inspections introduced disease control to border security, Blunt equates seasonal labor-based migration of Texas-Mexicans with the spread of smallpox. Although residents of the US, under the gaze of Anglo-American medical inspectors their Mexican ethnicity rendered their bodies suspect of infectious disease, regardless of where they were located. Converging here in the desacralization of ethnic Mexican bodies is the State's disease control apparatus, racist medical inspectors, border security, and superior notions of Anglo-American public health. Here the State adds disease to the litany of Mexican defects—moral lack, ignorance, religious despotism—that Anglo-American society had propagated in sermons, histories, folklore, monuments, and state archives. Yet in many ways, the sacral character of the medical profession afforded the othering mechanisms already operating in Anglo-American society a clearer path to subjugating ethnic Mexican bodies. With the diagnosis of disease, the State had license to intervene with violence, either by excluding ethnic Mexicans through heightened border security or inhibiting their migration through quarantining strategies. In terms of the latter measure, Blunt proposed to Governor Sayers that a quarantine be established against Webb county and the city of Laredo.[52] In a telegram, Governor Sayers asked Dr. Blunt to have Dr. J.M. McKnight, State Health Officer at Laredo, quickly confirm "the situation and number of cases on hand," to which Dr. McKnight gave this telegraphed response: "there are at least one hundred and fifty cases now situation very serious."[53] As reported on March 13, 1899, in the *Austin Daily Statesman*, the quarantine was a "blow to the business of the city," and as a result "a large number of prominent citizens met the city council the city and county officials in the market hall . . . to devise means to cope with the epidemic."[54] Even though their public assembly was in violation of a city ordinance, their privileged status as prominent citizens entitled them to higher levels of political influence. As the press described, these citizens were "red hot" and demanded that "vigorous steps will be taken at once to stamp out the disease."[55]

On the evening of March 13, 1899, local officials and the board of health devised a more aggressive public health plan of forced vaccination and confinement in a detention camp. Replacing the previous enlistment of volunteer medical inspectors were five physicians, who with medical assistants and police officers engaged in house-to-house health inspections.[56] Chairman Quintin Villegas, who was a Spaniard by birth,[57] and Secretary J.O. Nicholson of the Laredo Business Men's Club served as official spokesmen for the disgruntled elite male citizenry. Villegas and Nicholson had appealed directly to Governor Sayers for state intervention, thereby undercutting the established chain of command. In a telegram sent March 14, 1899, they wrote, "at a meeting of citizens held yesterday it was resolved that the Governor be requested to take charge of the smallpox situation immediately on account of inability of local authorities to control spread of disease."[58] On the same day, Governor Sayers had telegraphed the US Surgeon General, stating concernedly, "will you do me the great favor to immediately see the Secretary of War and obtain from him the loan of about five hundred tents to be used in isolating those who have the disease. The state will take charge. Please act promptly."[59] On March 15, 1899, Dr. Blunt informed Governor Sayers of the situation in a letter:

> There are about 500 cases of smallpox in the city of Laredo and the county of Webb and whereas, the citizens of Laredo have appealed to me for assistance, assuring me that they have no money with which they can operate in caring for the sick already on hand, and to stop the further spread of the disease in the city and the county and whereas, the disease prevails among the poorer classes of Mexicans who are helpless and must be cared for by someone.[60]

Blunt recommended that the state make an immediate appropriation of $2,000 to assist the city of Laredo in "stamping out the scourge of smallpox now prevailing in the city."[61] Notice the progression of ideas in Blunt's assessment, from his diagnosis of "the disease" to "the poorer classes of Mexicans" to then his plan of action, "stamping out the scourge of smallpox." Here, his medical reasoning imagines the use of force as part of the State's disease control strategies. As revealed below, medical inspection of ethnic Mexican bodies initiates state-sanctioned violence as the primary mode of care.

With the Texas House of Representatives in regular session, Governor Sayers was given the floor in order to address the entire Texas Legislature about conditions in Laredo and ask for Dr. Blunt's requested amount. As a result, the committee on Public Health and Vital Statistics was charged with drafting a senate bill, which they entitled "An Act to make appropriation of two thousand dollars to assist the local authorities at Laredo, Webb county, Texas in suppressing and abating the epidemic of smallpox now raging in that city."[62] With the disease medically linked to the Mexican poor, the resulting legislation sanctions "suppressing" and "abating" as the modes of care. As a product of Anglo-American medical inspections, this legislation has in view the location and movement of Mexican bodies, for again they are the primary bodies that medical inspectors have diagnosed as the source of the disease.

On March 15, 1899, the senate bill was passed, thereby instituting its prescribed modes of care. Essential to this narrative was how elite male society instrumentalized scientific inspection to exert control over the location and movements of Laredo's Mexican poor. The ease with which Anglo-American medical diagnosis translated into heightened border security and legalized detention of ethnic Mexican bodies attests to the sacral authority of scientific inspection, particularly when the experts were Anglo-American men. On the afternoon of March 16, 1899, Dr. Blunt arrived at Laredo to assume command of the State's public health operation. Rather than in-house quarantine, he planned for the infected Mexican poor to be placed in a provisional hospital at the old Davis Oaden & Co. hide house and a house of detention, or "pest house," at an old woolen mill building near the Zacate Creek neighborhood.[63] In addition to mandatory detention, he also enforced compulsory vaccinations in Laredo, which as he declared in a telegram sent on March 17 to Governor Sayers, "I am vaccinating everybody."[64]

The Zacate Creek protest

On March 18, several residents of the Zacate Creek neighborhood began distributing copies of a Spanish petition against the enforcement of the state's disease control practices such as house fumigation, compulsory vaccination, and involuntary detention.[65] The petition was translated from Spanish and printed in the *Laredo Times* with the title "Protest against Forcible Vaccination."[66] In its opening statement, Zacate Creek protestors not only objected to the universal injection of the smallpox vaccine but also "conferring absolute power on the doctors and sanitary inspectors to profane home and perpetrate all kinds of abuses against the persons."[67] Contrary to Anglo-American stereotypes regarding ethnic Mexican ignorance and debased morality, the ethnic Mexicans of Zacate Creek showed the resolve to confront elite power. Their protest attests to their will to resist their desacralization ("profane home") by sacralized Anglo-American medical inspectors. It also confirms the violent nature of the State's sanctioned modes of care, the origin of which can be traced to Blunt's medical reports and passed legislation. The Zacate Creek protesters also had a keen sense that the State was racially targeting them, stating "instead of commencing vaccination in precinct no. 4 or in no. 1 or with the people at the Heights, it began at the Arroyo-Zacate with Mexico-Texas population against whom it appears all rigor is used and who must pay all the misfortunes which befall Laredo."[68] Their formal protest evidences the unjust social effects of Hume's and Blunt's racist diagnosis of the disease. By linking the source of smallpox to the Mexican poor, Anglo-American medical inspectors had license to profane, abuse, and subjugate ethnic Mexican bodies. Indeed, these words, "it appears all rigor is used and who must pay all the misfortunes," attest to the intensity of the State's desacralizing violence against the ethnic Mexican protestors of Zacate Creek. Yet in view of the State's sacred apparatus, these words do not exhaust the depths this violence was destined to reach. For since the Mexican-American War, the State's version of the sacred set the threshold of violence against ethnic Mexicans to a state of eradication.

The Zacate Creek protesters listed three major grievances against the State's public health operations in Laredo. The first involved desacralizing modes of medical inspection whereby the doctor and accompanying police were "profaning the home, and compelling our children, our wives and our mothers to expose to them their persons . . . that they may laugh at the expense of the families."[69] While the protestors did not reject the smallpox vaccination as a viable medical solution, they ardently opposed the violent modes that public health inspectors were using to administer it. For the Zacate Creek residents, state desacralization had invaded the sanctuary of the private and converted it into a profane site of bodily violation.[70] The protesters notion of "profaning the home" renders the medical inspections a rape scene in which they penetrate the home, dominate the bodies in it by stripping them naked, and then laugh at them. As they indicate, their desacralization was spatial (home), familial (children, wives, mother), and corporeal (expose). As the protesters keenly decried, "to administer vaccination to all persons at any time, and under any conditions is to send the Mexico-Texas people to the graveyard."[71] Rather than the universal application of the vaccine, the protestors demanded more sensitivity from medical inspectors as to the individual contexts of each household. Their critique marked the harmful symptoms of a racially inflected mode of medical inspection in which the aim was less about contextualized care than preservation of elite society through domination. In their words, "it is an infamous crime to traffic with the health, the life, with the honor and with the peace of families for political purposes."[72] The Zacate Creek protesters confirmed from lived experience the violent contours of Anglo-American scientific/medical inspection. When assembled together from a sacred apparatus of white supremacist logic, state power, and Western scientificity, its mission is, as they describe, politicized for purposes other than human care. For them, human care translated into criminal acts of desacralization that targeted the health, life, honor, and peace of Texas-Mexican families of Zacate Creek.

Subtending the grievances of the residents of Zacate Creek was a borderland hermeneutic of the sacred that contrasted starkly from the State's sacred apparatus. In the latter, medical inspections sacralized Anglo-American public health by casting it not as the source of disease but rather the source of wholeness, hygiene, and sanitation. Through a white supremacist racial logic, these medical inspections were in turn weaponized to desacralize lower class ethnic Mexicans as to ensure Anglo-American superiority. As gleaned from the Zacate Creek protesters, they envisioned a form of medical care that treated people equally, rather than according to social status or ethnic background. Different from the object-centered approach of scientific/medical inspection, they imagined a human care approach that sacralizes rather than profanes the lived context of people. Indeed, their idea of public health was not a shaming of the body but rather the body's healing through contextualized care. Here home, kinships, and bodies were sacralized in that they were treated as worthy of health, life, honor, and peace.

Arming public health with Texas Rangers

The demands of the Zacate Creek protestors were immediately construed as a threat to the State's notions of proper citizenship, which involved submitting to public health inspections. Unlike the protest results of Laredo's prominent citizens, the Zacate Creek protest led to increased policing of homes and bodies in this ethnic Mexican neighborhood. After receiving a copy of their protest, J.M. Rodriguez, Webb County Judge, wrote to Governor Sayers, stating that there was "a protest from citizens of Mexican origin which is incendiary and liable to bring out serious results."[73] On March 19, Dr. Blunt sent an urgent telegram to Governor Sayers, indicating "cannot enforce quarantine regulations without using force many infected refuse to submit to being (to be) sent to hospital and detention camp without such measures the disease cannot be suppressed shall I use such means as are necessary to enforce?"[74] Immediately Governor Sayers telegraphed the Secretary of War for the temporary use of the Tenth Cavalry division, which was an African-American unit stationed nearby at Fort McIntosh (i.e. Buffalo Soldiers), until the arrival of the Texas Rangers.[75] Meanwhile, Dr. Blunt telegraphed Governor Sayers again, stating "will use every precaution and prudence Ft McIntosh troop been placed at my disposal think public knowledge of this will be sufficient and do not expect any bloodshed."[76] Blunt's move to militarize disease control, such that bloodshed was a possible outcome, marks the threshold of violence that his desacralization of ethnic Mexicans had provisioned. From a simple telegram, his medical inspections were reinforced with weapons of war. The scene was set for black- and brown-bodied carnage between two desacralized people groups, African-American Buffalo Soldiers and the ethnic Mexicans of Zacate Creek. And those privileging from their carnage were their Anglo-American masters, for they were the primary manufacturers of this violence.

Apart from the Buffalo Soldiers, Dr. Blunt also had at his disposal the Texas Rangers to enforce his medical inspections of the Zacate Creek residents. The Texas Rangers were much different from the African-American Tenth Calvary division in that they had emerged as a white male paramilitary unit during the US-Mexican War and later functioned as the military police of occupation.[77] Within nineteenth-century Anglo-American society, the Texas Rangers' heroic status was linked to their role in purging Texas of "Mexican bandits" and ensuring Anglo-American ranchers ownership of land. David Montejano explains that "the Rangers were not merely suppressing seditious Mexican bandits; in the large picture, they played the critical part in paving the way for the newcomer farmers."[78] Armed with a handgun, Winchester rifle, and cartridge belt, the Texas Rangers secured the settlement of Anglo-American opportunists often with inhumane brutality.[79] Indeed, their legacy of brutal violence with ethnic Mexicans would prove vital to Blunt's militarized health inspections in the Zacate Creek neighborhood.

Before the twentieth century, the Texas Rangers operated under two specialized divisions, the Frontier Battalion and the Special Ranger Force.[80] Their warrior-hero status in Texas emerged in the aftermath of the wanton use of violence they had directed toward American Indians and ethnic Mexicans on both sides of the US-Mexico border.[81] Their deployment to Laredo, however, had expanded their policing duties in the border region to include the State's disease control operations. Intrinsic to this state police force was not the provision of care for ethnic Mexicans, but rather they were trained and commissioned primarily to terrorize, persecute, and, if need be, massacre ethnic Mexicans, particularly when they interfered with Anglo-American domination. For the Texas Rangers in the nineteenth century, the ideal ethnic Mexican body was a dead one. Apart from protecting Anglo-American property, their mission in Laredo had in view the protection of Anglo-American public health from what the State had diagnosed as diseased ethnic Mexican bodies. Though the Texas Rangers needed little convincing of ethnic Mexicans' inferiority, adding to this the State's diagnosis only intensified their antagonism and killer instincts. They were indeed the State's ideal manufacturers of eradicating violence, particularly the kind that targeted ethnic Mexicans. Now assigned to the State's disease control operation, the Texas Rangers did not reinforce notions of human care in Blunt's medical inspections, but rather weaponized them to terrorize and eradicate the ethnic Mexican residents of Zacate Creek.

On March 19, 1899, Captain John Rogers and Private A.Y. Old of Company E, which was a Texas Rangers Frontier Battalion stationed in Cotulla, Texas, arrived in Laredo to assist Dr. Blunt in moving Zacate Creek residents from their houses to the "pest-house" or detention camp. As stated in the following police report by Sergeant C. Dubose of Company E:

> The streets were crowded with excited Mexicans who manifested a disposition to Riot, the first patient was moved over the protest of the inmates of the house. City Marshal Barthlow by order of Dr. Blunt broke open the door in order to get the patient and convey some to Pest-House. Later in the day the Mexicans organized and made demonstration against the life of City Marshal Barthlow and his assistants by attacking them with guns and stones resulting in the wounding of Policeman Idar.[82]

Newspapers across the US reported the conflict with titles like "Furious Mexicans: Mob of 500 or 600 Attack American Health Officer" (*Morning Oregonian*), "Mexicans Resist Heath Officers in a Texas Town" (*Denver Evening Post*), "Mob of Mexicans Attack the Health Officer in Laredo Texas" (*The Daily Picayune*, Louisiana) or "A Clash with Mexicans: 500 Armed-Men Interfere with Americans at Laredo, Texas in Removing Smallpox Patients" (*The New York Times*). These reports cast the scene as Mexican aggression and violence against Americans, thereby reinforcing

Anglo-American stereotypes of Mexican criminality and moral lack. According to these reports, Zacate Creek residents gathered on East Matamoros Street protesting the forced removals when nearly twenty shots were fired, resulting in multiple arrests. Immediately after, five hundred or six hundred armed Zacate Creek residents were mobilized to defend the neighborhood from any further public health inspections. As a result, Dr. Blunt temporarily suspended the forced removals until the arrival of the Texas Rangers. In his telegram to Governor Sayers, Blunt reported that "The War Department telegraphed authority to use troops at Fort McIntosh. The Mexicans are much excited and a fight is probable when the regulars arrive."[83]

On March 20, Captain Rogers and Private A.Y. Old of Company E along with Special Ranger Thomas Ragland, Sheriff Ortiz, and two deputies went to execute search warrants in certain houses where weapons were stored as part of the Zacate Creek neighborhood resistance.[84] When state and city police arrived to the home of Agapito Herrera, a former Laredo policeman, they encountered him and three other armed Texas-Mexicans who, soon after, attempted to escape from the rear of Herrera's house. Two were obtained, but one avoided capture and began firing on Captain Rogers. Meanwhile Herrera, who was armed, ran for safety at a vacant house across the street. According to Dubose's police report, "Agapito Herrera and others appeared in the street armed with Winchesters Herrera fired on Capt. Rogers at the same time Capt. Rogers fired on him. Capt. Rogers was shot through the right shoulder by Herrera and Herrera was shot through the right breast. Private Old shot Herrera twice in the head killing him instantly."[85] Wounded in the conflict was Agapito Herrera's sister, Refugia Herrera, who had fired at the Texas Rangers from the window of a nearby vacant house.[86] Santiago Grimeldo was also seriously wounded in the conflict. He was shot in the abdomen. With Agapito Herrera's dead body lying on the street, the residents retreated into their houses. Outnumbered, Texas Rangers Old and Ragland left the street and as claimed in the police report "they were stoned by a throng of women as they turned into the next street but no shots were fired."[87] Dr. Blunt immediately detached several other Texas Rangers to the street corner south of where the body of Agapito Herrera lay. When they arrived, his body was surrounded by Zacate Creek residents. Those armed immediately began firing on the Texas Rangers, who also returned fire. The police report stated that "house corners and trees poured a steady fire upon the Rangers who kept advancing and firing at the Mexicans the fight lasted something over 30 minutes and was a decided victory for the Rangers none of whom were injured in this fight."[88] The Texas Rangers' claim of victory was premised on the preservation of white male lives. As for the Zacate Creek neighborhood resistance, among the wounded were Margarito Herrera, Candido Garcia, and Antonio Pacheco.

Matters intensified with the arrival of the Tenth Calvary, who as reported by Sergeant Dubose, "were of great service to Rangers officers and citizens."[89] Also, a force of twenty-five Texas Rangers were sworn in and charged with guard duty at the "pest-house."[90] Under the command of Captain Ayers, the African-American Tenth Calvary came to the Zacate Creek neighborhood fully armed with one hundred rounds of ammunition. Domingo Castello, a neighborhood leader, tried to talk to a cavalryman but was promptly knocked down with the butt of a carbine, which shortly after resulted in his death.[91] As one press report described, "a gatling gun and an ambulance corps accompanied the cavalrymen, and affairs took on a decidedly martial appearance."[92] On March 23, Dr. H.J. Hamilton of the USMHS reported that "the state quarantine officer has all smallpox isolated; . . . All quiet."[93]

This bloodshed of ethnic Mexicans in the Zacate Creek neighborhood points to the eradicating violence that the State's sacred apparatus afforded to Anglo-American scientific/medical inspection in the US-Mexico borderlands. Sacralized Anglo-American public health assigned the source of infectious disease to the State's desacralized other, who in the nineteenth century was the ethnic Mexican poor. Under the legitimating cover of medical science, the State's desacralization of ethnic Mexicans at the border was made official in health inspection reports, which then led to the legalization of terrorizing and brutal forms of human care. Armed with a state police force trained to kill ethnic Mexicans, Anglo-American scientific inspection was weaponized to eradicate the ethnic Mexican residents of Zacate Creek.

The eradicating violence that the Texas Rangers manufactured in the border region was legitimized under the State's sacred apparatus (US Manifest Destiny/Anglo-American Protestant superiority/border-sovereignty-citizenship). With the Zacate Creek incident, their policing services were broadened to protecting Anglo-American public health not only from Mexican banditry but now from Mexican contagion. Rather than submit to this ruling hermeneutic of the sacred, the Texas-Mexican protestors of Zacate Creek were left with no other option but violent resistance. Instead of subjecting their bodies to desacralizing health inspections and its shaming violence, these residents sacrificed their bodies in defense of their version of the sacred. Even before they had expressed their grievances about the profaning health inspections to the local press, other agents of the State's sacred apparatus had already destined them for eradication (see McCarty's sermon and early Anglo-American Texas histories). Their use of violence, therefore, was less a reflection of their innate criminality, as reported in the press, than the abandonment of the State. Throughout the border region the Texas Rangers had earned the reputation for being a violent state police force that terrorized ethnic Mexicans.[94] Hence, it is no wonder that their arrival to the Zacate Creek neighborhood signaled to its Texas-Mexican residents the State's violent intentions. The Texas Rangers functioned as the executioners of the State's sacralized threshold of violence, for they specialized in Mexican carnage. In the face of their eradication, the Texas-Mexican residents of Zacate Creek chose to take up arms and defend their lives. To not do so would have meant submitting to the State's desacralizing claims about their personhood. In many ways, their recourse to violence mirrors these words by Frantz Fanon:

> The underprivileged and starving peasant is the exploited who very soon discovers that only violence pays. For him there is no compromise, no possibility of concession. Colonization or decolonization: it is simply a power struggle. The exploited realize that their liberation implies using every means available, and force is the first.[95]

Turning to violence as a response to the State's desacralizing medical inspections were actions that ran counter to the prevailing Anglo-American stereotypes regarding ethnic Mexican inferiority. In this instance, the Texas-Mexican residents showed the resolve and courage to resist their eradication. Indeed, their borderland hermeneutic of the sacred made provisions for the use of violence not as an instrument for domination, as revealed in the State's sacred apparatus, but more specifically as a viable option for resisting what the State's desacralization had destined for them.

Conclusion

In trespassing on the State's archive of the 1899 smallpox epidemic in Laredo, Western scientific inspection comes to the fore as a reproducing force for elite Anglo-American power and a deadly weapon for the ethnic Mexican other. When assembled with a white supremacist logic and state power, this "objective" approach can have genocidal consequences. When inspecting the body, a white supremacist version of scientific inspection inevitably defaults to a hermeneutic of the sacred that desacralizes black- and brown-bodied people. Here these bodies are rendered objects for domination and, as in the case above, eradication.

With the militarization of the State's disease control operations in the Zacate Creek neighborhood, African-Americans were weaponized by and yet subjugated to elite Anglo-American power. As co-manufactures of violence against ethnic Mexicans, the Buffalo Soldiers acted as a colonizer and yet as black bodies in the Jim Crow South, their service to the State's sacred apparatus primarily benefitted Anglo-American society. Pertinent here is Saidiya Hartman's line of questioning:

> Irony riddled the event of emancipation. How does one narrate a story of freedom when confronted with the discrepant legacy of emancipation and the decidedly circumscribed avenues available to the freed? What does autonomy mean in the context of coercion, hunger, and uncertainty? Is the unavoidable double bind of emancipation an illusory freedom and a travestied liberation?[96]

In the end, what this chapter has sought to problematize is scientific inspection as a sacralized mode for truth-making in Western society. If predisposed toward white supremacist logic, then scientific inspection of the body will inescapably produce truth claims that legitimate this logic. Indeed, the Zacate Creek residents attested to the cruel consequences of this type of scientific inspection. Using white supremacist logic, the State diagnosed their bodies for capture, not care. For in the eyes of the State's medical inspectors, the ethnic Mexican body was innately corrupt, weak, ignorant, diseased, and debased, which was a predisposition that not even Western scientific objectivity could dislodge.

For a borderland hermeneutic, this indictment of Western scientific inspection is crucial to understanding its current use by the State in desacralizing border crossers.[97] As important as trespassing on the State's archive is to redress the desacralization of the Mexican other, a borderland hermeneutic must also connect the archive to the current assemblage of scientific inspection in the US-Mexico borderlands. Being suspicious of the archive as a desacralizing force—enough to trespass on it—implies unresolved traumas as well as an awareness of a pathology of state-sanctioned violence against the sacred human Other.

Notes

1 Michael Hardt and Antonio Negri, *Empire* (Cambridge, MA: Harvard University Press, 2001), 47; Jack A. Goldstone and John F. Haldon, "Ancient States, Empires, and Exploitation: Problems and Perspectives," in *Dynamics of Ancient Empire*, eds. Ian Morris and Walter Scheidel (Oxford: Oxford University Press, 2009), 17; Alejandro Colás, *Empire* (Cambridge: Polity Press, 2007), 119; Ann Laura Stoler, *Haunted by Empire: Geographies of Intimacy in North American History* (Durham, NC: Duke University Press, 2006), 1–22.
2 Jay Martin, "Scopic Regimes of Modernity," in *Vision and Visuality*, ed. Hal Foster (Seattle: Bay Press, 1999), 3.
3 Michel Foucault, *The Order of Things: An Archaeology of the Human Sciences* (London: Routledge, 1994), 132–33.
4 Michel Foucault, *Discipline and Punish: The Birth of the Prison*, trans. Alan Sheridan (New York: Random House, 1995), 202–3.
5 Ramón Saldívar, *The Borderlands of Culture: Américo Paredes and the Transnational Imaginary* (Durham, NC: Duke University Press, 2006), 8.
6 Daniel Blue Tyx, "Who Writes History? The Fight to Commemorate a Massacre by the Texas Rangers," *The Texas Observer*, November 26, 2018, www.texasobserver.org/who-writes-history-the-fight-to-commemorate-a-massacre-by-the-texas-rangers/; Carlos Kevin Blanton, "The Secret History of Anti-Mexican Violence in Texas," *Texas Monthly*, September 21, 2018, www.texasmonthly.com/the-culture/anti-mexican-violence-in-texas/; Refusing to Forget, "The History of Racial Violence on the Mexico-Texas Border," https://refusingtoforget.org/the-history/.
7 *Transactions of the Texas State Medical Association*, vol. 30 (Austin, TX: The Eugene Von Boeckmann Publishing Co., 1898), 49.
8 *Journal of the American Medical Association*, vol. 31 (Chicago: American Medical Association Press, 1898), 1.

9 *Transactions of the Texas State Medical Association*, vol. 30, 47.
10 Ibid., 54.
11 Ibid.
12 *Transactions of the American Medical Association*, vol. 31 (Philadelphia: Collins Printer, 1880), 1123–24.
13 Ibid., 638.
14 See "Officers and Membership Rosters of Texas State Medical Association," *Transactions of the Texas State Medical Association*, vol. 31 (Austin, TX: The Eugene Von Boeckmann Publishing Co., 1899), vii–x, 331–51.
15 William D. Carrigan and Clive Webb, *Forgotten Dead: Mob Violence Against Mexicans in the United States, 1848–1928* (Oxford: Oxford University Press, 2013), 64–96; Ken Gonzales-Day, *Lynching in the West, 1850–1935* (Durham, NC: Duke University Press, 2006), 133–72; Monica Muñoz Martinez, *The Injustice Never Leaves You: Anti-Mexican Violence in Texas* (Cambridge, MA: Harvard University Press, 2018), 232–41.
16 David Montejano, *Anglos and Mexicans in the Making of Texas, 1836–1986* (Austin, TX: University of Texas Press, 1987), 18–19.
17 Manuel Ceballos-Ramírez and Oscar J. Martinez, "Conflict and Accommodation on the U.S.-Mexican Border, 1848–1911," in *Myths, Misdeeds, and Misunderstandings: The Roots of Conflict in U.S.-Mexican Relations*, eds. Jaime E. Rodríguez O. and Kathryn Vincent (Wilmington, DE: SR Books, 1997), 136–37; David J. Weber, *Foreigners in Their Native Land: Historical Roots of the Mexican Americans* (Albuquerque: University of New Mexico Press, 2003), 140. According to Weber, southern Arizona remained Mexican territory until 1853.
18 Alexander C. Diener and Joshua Hagen, *Borders: A Very Short Introduction* (Oxford: Oxford University Press, 2012), 41–42; Laura Lyons McLemore, *Inventing Texas: Early Historians of the Lone Star State* (College Station, TX: Texas A&M University Press, 2004), 11–16.
19 Brantz Mayer, *History of the War Between Mexico and the United States: With a Preliminary View of Its Origin* (New York: Wiley & Putnam, 1848), 49.
20 Saidiya V. Hartman, *Scenes of Subjection: Terror, Slavery, and Self-making in Nineteenth-Century America* (Oxford: Oxford University Press, 1997), 153.
21 Ibid.
22 Gregory L. Cuéllar, "Introduction," In *Passages of the New World*, ed. Christopher L. Morrow (College Station, TX: Texas A&M University Press, 2006).
23 McLemore, *Inventing Texas*, 5.
24 Ibid.
25 Mary Austin Holley, *Texas* (Lexington: J. Clarke and Co., 1883; Austin, TX: The Steck Co., 1935), 128. Citations refer to the Steck Company edition.
26 Henry Stuart Foote, *Texas and the Texans; Or, Advance of the Anglo-Americans to the South-West; Including a History of Leading Events in Mexico, from the Conquest by Fernando Cortes to the Termination of the Texan Revolution* (Philadelphia: Thomas, Cowperthwait & Co., 1841), 91.
27 McLemore, *Inventing Texas*, 49.
28 A. B. Lawrence, *Texas in 1840, or the Emigrant's Guide to the New Republic; Being the Result of Observation, Enquiry and Travel in that Beautiful Nation* (New York: William W. Allen, 1840), 227.
29 Hartman, *Scenes of Subjection*, 32.
30 Melinda Rankin, *Texas in 1850* (Boston: Damrell & Moore, 1852), 3.
31 Ibid., 55–56.
32 John McCarty, *A Thanksgiving Sermon* (Mexico: American Star, 1847), 14.
33 Rankin, *Texas in 1850*, 55–56.
34 "Laredo Smallpox," *Austin Daily Statesman*, January 12, 1899.

35 Allen D. Candler et al., "Smallpox in the United States," *Public Health Reports (1896–1970)* 14, no. 9 (March 3, 1899): 280.
36 Ibid.
37 J. H. Oakley et al., "Smallpox in the United States," *Public Health Reports (1896–1970)* 14, no. 11 (March 17, 1899): 345.
38 Candler et al., "Smallpox in the United States," (March 3, 1899): 280.
39 L. M. Powers et al., "Smallpox in the United States," *Public Health Reports (1896–1970)* 14, no. 10 (March 10, 1899): 311.
40 Oakley et al., "Smallpox in the United States" (March 17, 1899): 343–44.
41 Powers et al., "Smallpox in the United States" (March 10, 1899): 311.
42 John Mckiernan-González, *Fevered Measures: Public Health and Race at the Texas-Mexico Border, 1848–1942* (Durham, NC: Duke University Press, 2012), 128.
43 Ibid., 124.
44 Candler et al., "Smallpox in the United States," (March 3, 1899): 280.
45 Mckiernan-González, *Fevered Measures*, 129.
46 Ibid.
47 "Historical and Biographical Sketch / Rev. Henry Barrington Pratt (1832–1912)," Box C035, 11–12, H. B. Pratt collection, 1848–1884, 1911–1913, 1938–1939, Austin Seminary Archives, Stitt Library, Austin Presbyterian Theological Seminary.
48 Lea Hume, "Smallpox in the United States," *Public Health Reports (1896–1970)* 14, no. 12 (March 24, 1899): 240.
49 "Laredo Smallpox Situation," *Austin Daily Statesman*, March 10, 1899.
50 W. F. Blunt to Gov. Joseph D. Sayers, letter, March 9, 1899, box 301-175 records, Texas Governor Joseph D. Sayers, Archives and Information Services Division, Texas State Library and Archives Commission.
51 Ibid.
52 Ibid.
53 Dr. W. F. Blunt, telegram to Dr. J. M. McKnight, March 9, 1899.
54 "Smallpox at Laredo Serious," *Austin Daily Statesman*, March 14, 1899.
55 Ibid.
56 "Laredo Smallpox," *Austin Daily Statesman*, March 17, 1899.
57 *A Twentieth Century History of Southwest Texas*, vol. 2 (Chicago: The Lewis Publishing Co., 1907), 83, https://archive.org/stream/twentiethcentury02unse/twentiethcentury02unse_djvu.txt.
58 Quintin Villegas and J. O. Nicholson to Governor Joseph D. Sayers, telegram, March 14, 1899, box 301-175 records, Texas Governor Joseph D. Sayers, Archives and Information Services Division, Texas State Library and Archives Commission.
59 Governor Joseph D. Sayers, telegram to US Surgeon General, March 14, 1899.
60 Dr. W. F. Blunt, letter to Governor Joseph D. Sayers, March 15, 1899.
61 Ibid.
62 Texas Congress, House, *Journal of the House of Representatives of Texas*, 26th Legislature, regular sess., March 15, 1899, 751–52.
63 Joseph D. Sayers to Surgeon General Marine Hospital Service, telegram, March 14, 1899, box 301-175 records, Texas Governor Joseph D. Sayers, Archives and Information Services Division, Texas State Library and Archives Commission; "Laredo Smallpox Situation," *Austin Daily Statesman*, March 18, 1899.
64 Dr. W. F. Blunt, telegram to Governor Joseph D. Sayers, March 17, 1899; "Laredo Smallpox Situation," *Austin Daily Statesman*, March 18, 1899.
65 "Aid Asked For," *Austin Daily Statesman*, March 19, 1899.
66 Mckiernan-González, *Fevered Measures*, 123.
67 Ibid., 138.

68 Ibid.
69 Ibid., 139.
70 *Transactions of the Texas State Medical Association*, vol. 31, 74. For smallpox, people were vaccinated with a prophylactic discovered by Edward Jenner in the late eighteenth century. His vaccination used cowpox virus, a milder infectious disease, as the therapeutic agent in the treatment of smallpox.
71 Mckiernan-González, *Fevered Measures*, 139.
72 Ibid.
73 J. M. Rodriguez to Governor Joseph D. Sayers, letter, March 18, 1899, box 301–175 records, Texas Governor Joseph D. Sayers, Archives and Information Services Division, Texas State Library and Archives Commission.
74 Dr. W. F. Blunt, telegram to Governor Joseph D. Sayers, March 19, 1899, box 301–175 records, Texas Governor Joseph D. Sayers, Archives and Information Services Division, Texas State Library and Archives Commission.
75 H. C. Corbin, telegram to Governor Joseph D. Sayers, March 19, 1899, box 301–175 records, Texas Governor Joseph D. Sayers, Archives and Information Services Division, Texas State Library and Archives Commission.
76 Dr. W. F. Blunt, telegram to Governor Joseph D. Sayers, March 19, 1899.
77 Montejano, *Anglos and Mexicans*, 33–34.
78 Ibid., 116–26.
79 Gregory Lee Cuéllar, "Contesting State Violence: The Bible, the Public Good, and Divinely Sanctioned Violence in the Texas Borderlands," in *La Violencia and the Hebrew Bible: The Politics and Histories of Biblical Hermeneutics on the American Continent*, eds. Susanne Scholz and Pablo R. Andiñach (Atlanta: Society of Biblical Literature, 2016), 51.
80 Michael L. Collin, *Texas Devils: Rangers and Regulars on the Lower Rio Grande, 1846–1861* (Norman, OK: University of Oklahoma Press, 2008), 5.
81 Laurence Armand French, *Running the Border Gauntlet: The Mexican Migrant Controversy* (Santa Barbara, CA: Praeger, 2010), 53; Miguel Antonio Levario, *Militarizing the Border: When Mexicans Became the Enemy* (College Station, TX: Texas A&M University Press, 2012), 20; Collin, *Texas Devils*, 11–12.
82 Sergeant C. Dubose, "Report of Rangers Work at Laredo Texas from March 19th to March 25th 1899," box 301–176 Records, Texas Governor Joseph D. Sayers, Archives and Information Services Division, Texas State Library and Archives Commission.
83 "A Clash with Mexicans," *The New York Times*, March 20, 1899.
84 Dubose, "Report."
85 Ibid.
86 "Rioting at Laredo," *Morning Oregonian*, March 21, 1899; Dubose, "Report."
87 Dubose, "Report."
88 Ibid.
89 Ibid.
90 "Rioting at Laredo."
91 Ibid.; "Casualties of the Bloody Riot," *Austin Daily Statesman*, March 22, 1899.
92 "Rioting at Laredo."
93 Dr. H. J. Hamilton, "Smallpox in the United States," *Public Health Reports (1896–1970)* 14, no. 13 (March 31, 1899): 424.
94 Levario, *Militarizing the Border*, 114; Martinez, *The Injustice Never Leaves You*, 14–15.
95 Frantz Fanon, *The Wretched of the Earth* (New York: Grove Press, 2004), 23.
96 Hartman, *Scenes of Subjection*, 126.
97 Howard Markel and Alexandra Minna Stern, "The Foreignness of Germs: The Persistent Association of Immigrants and Disease in American Society," *The Milbank Quarterly* 80, no. 4 (2002): 774–77; Chantal Da Silva, "Donald

Trump Says Migrants Bring 'Large Scale Crime and Disease' to America," *Newsweek*, December 11, 2018, www.newsweek.com/donald-trump-says-migrants-bring-large-scale-crime-and-disease-america-1253268; Talia Lavin, "How Trump's Immigrant Bashing Feeds White Supremacists' Obsession with Jews," *The Washington Post*, November 1, 2018, www.washingtonpost.com/outlook/2018/11/01/how-trumps-immigrant-bashing-feeds-white-supremacists-obsession-with-jews/?noredirect=on; Jason Le Miere, "Fox News Guest Claims Migrant Caravan Carries 'Leprosy,' Will 'Infect Our People,' Offers No Evidence," *Newsweek*, October 29, 2018, www.newsweek.com/fox-news-migrant-caravan-leprosy-1192605.

Bibliography

"Aid Asked For." *Austin Daily Statesman*, March 19, 1899.

Atkinson, William B. "Code of Ethics." Vol. 33 of *Transactions of the American Medical Association, 1882*. Philadelphia: Times Printing House, 1882.

———. "Minutes of the Thirty-First Annual Meetings of the American Medical Association." Vol. 31 of *Transactions of the American Medical Association*. Philadelphia: Collins Printer, 1880.

Blanton, Carlos Kevin. "The Secret History of Anti-Mexican Violence in Texas." *Texas Monthly*, September 21, 2018. www.texasmonthly.com/the-culture/anti-mexican-violence-in-texas/.

Candler, Allen D., C. P. Wertenbaker, R. D. Murray, J. A. Albright, Lea Hume and H. J. Hamilton, "Smallpox in the United States." *Public Health Reports (1896–1970)* 14, no. 9 (March 3, 1899): 273–81.

Carrigan, William D., and Clive Webb. *Forgotten Dead: Mob Violence Against Mexicans in the United States, 1848–1928*. Oxford: Oxford University Press, 2013.

"Casualties of the Bloody Riot." *Austin Daily Statesman*, March 22, 1899.

Ceballos-Ramírez, Manuel, and Oscar J. Martinez. "Conflict and Accommodation on the U.S.-Mexican Border, 1848–1911." In *Myths, Misdeeds, and Misunderstandings: The Roots of Conflict in U.S.-Mexican Relations*, edited by Jaime E. Rodríguez O. and Kathryn Vincent, 135–67. Wilmington, DE: SR Books, 1997.

"A Clash With Mexicans." *The New York Times*, March 20, 1899.

Colás, Alejandro. *Empire*. Cambridge: Polity Press, 2007.

Collin, Michael L. *Texas Devils: Rangers and Regulars on the Lower Rio Grande, 1846–1861*. Norman, OK: University of Oklahoma Press, 2008.

Cuéllar, Gregory Lee. "Contesting State Violence: The Bible, the Public Good, and Divinely Sanctioned Violence in the Texas Borderlands." In *La Violencia and the Hebrew Bible: The Politics and Histories of Biblical Hermeneutics on the American Continent*, edited by Susanne Scholz and Pablo R. Andiñach, 39–58. Atlanta: Society of Biblical Literature, 2016.

———. "Introduction." In *Passages of the New World*, edited by Christopher L. Morrow, xi–xv. College Station, TX: Texas A&M University, 2006.

Da Silva, Chantal. "Donald Trump Says Migrants Bring 'Large Scale Crime and Disease' to America." *Newsweek*, December 11, 2018. www.newsweek.com/donald-trump-says-migrants-bring-large-scale-crime-and-disease-america-1253268.

Diener, Alexander C., and Joshua Hagen. *Borders: A Very Short Introduction.* Oxford: Oxford University Press, 2012.

Fanon, Frantz. *The Wretched of the Earth.* New York: Grove Press, 2004.

Foote, Henry Stuart. *Texas and the Texans: Or, Advance of the Anglo-Americans to the South-West: Including a History of Leading Events in Mexico, from the Conquest by Fernando Cortes to the Termination of the Texan Revolution.* Philadelphia: Thomas, Cowperthwait & Co., 1841.

Foucault, Michel. *Discipline and Punish: The Birth of the Prison.* Translated by Alan Sheridan. New York: Random House, 1995.

———. *The Order of Things: An Archaeology of the Human Sciences.* London: Routledge, 1994.

French, Laurence Armand. *Running the Border Gauntlet: The Mexican Migrant Controversy.* Santa Barbara, CA: Praeger, 2010.

Goldstone, Jack A., and John F. Haldon. "Ancient States, Empires, and Exploitation: Problems and Perspectives." In *Dynamics of Ancient Empire*, edited by Ian Morris and Walter Scheidel. Oxford: Oxford University Press, 2009.

Gonzales-Day, Ken. *Lynching in the West, 1850–1935.* Durham, NC: Duke University Press, 2006.

Hamilton, H. J. "Smallpox in the United States." *Public Health Reports (1896–1970)* 14, no. 13 (March 31, 1899): 422–24.

Hardt, Michael, and Antonio Negri. *Empire.* Cambridge, MA: Harvard University Press, 2001.

Hartman, Saidiya V. *Scenes of Subjection: Terror, Slavery, and Self-making in Nineteenth-Century America.* Oxford: Oxford University Press, 1997.

"Historical and Biographical Sketch/Rev. Henry Barrington Pratt (1832–1912)." Box C035, 11–12. H. B. Pratt collection, 1848–1884, 1911–1913, 1938–1939. Austin Seminary Archives, Stitt Library, Austin Presbyterian Theological Seminary.

Holley, Mary Austin. *Texas.* Austin, TX: The Steck Co., 1935. First published 1883 by J. Clarke and Co, Lexington.

Hume, Lea. "Smallpox in the United States." *Public Health Reports (1896–1970)* 14, no. 12 (March 24, 1899): 240.

"Laredo Smallpox." *Austin Daily Statesman*, January 12, 1899.

"Laredo Smallpox." *Austin Daily Statesman*, March 17, 1899.

"Laredo Smallpox Situation," *Austin Daily Statesman*, March 10, 1899.

Lavin, Talia. "How Trump's Immigrant Bashing Feeds White Supremacists' Obsession with Jews." *The Washington Post*, November 1, 2018. www.washingtonpost.com/outlook/2018/11/01/how-trumps-immigrant-bashing-feeds-white-suprema cists-obsession-with-jews/?noredirect=on.

Lawrence, A. B. *Texas in 1840, or the Emigrant's Guide to the New Republic: Being the Result of Observation, Enquiry and Travel in that Beautiful Nation.* New York: William W. Allen, 1840.

Le Miere, Jason. "Fox News Guest Claims Migrant Caravan Carries 'Leprosy,' Will 'Infect Our People,' Offers No Evidence." *Newsweek*, October 29, 2018. www.newsweek.com/fox-news-migrant-caravan-leprosy-1192605.

Levario, Miguel Antonio. *Militarizing the Border: When Mexicans Became the Enemy.* College Station, TX: Texas A&M University Press, 2012.

Markel, Howard, and Alexandra Minna Stern. "The Foreignness of Germs: The Persistent Association of Immigrants and Disease in American Society." *The Milbank Quarterly* 80, no. 4 (2002): 757–88.

Martin, Jay. "Scopic Regimes of Modernity." In *Vision and Visuality*, edited by Hal Foster. Seattle: Bay Press, 1999.
Martinez, Monica Muñoz. *The Injustice Never Leaves You: Anti-Mexican Violence in Texas*. Cambridge, MA: Harvard University Press, 2018.
Mayer, Brantz. *History of the War Between Mexico and the United States: With a Preliminary View of Its Origin*. New York: Wiley & Putnam, 1848.
McCarty, John. *A Thanksgiving Sermon*. Mexico: American Star, 1847.
Mckiernan-González, John. *Fevered Measures: Public Health and Race at the Texas-Mexico Border, 1848–1942*. Durham, NC: Duke University Press, 2012.
McLemore, Laura Lyons. *Inventing Texas: Early Historians of the Lone Star State*. College Station, TX: Texas A&M University Press, 2004.
Montejano, David. *Anglos and Mexicans in the Making of Texas, 1836–1986*. Austin, TX: University of Texas Press, 1987.
Oakley, J. H., L. Hume, E. Alexander and A. C. Smith. "Smallpox in the United States." *Public Health Reports (1896–1970)* 14, no. 11 (March 17, 1899): 341–46.
Powers, L. M., W. J. Pettus, L. Haynes Buxton, L. Hume, and H. J. Hamilton. "Smallpox in the United States." *Public Health Reports (1896–1970)* 14, no. 10 (March 10, 1899): 308–12.
Rankin, Melinda. *Texas in 1850*. Boston: Damrell & Moore, 1852.
Refusing to Forget. "The History of Racial Violence on the Mexico-Texas Border." https://refusingtoforget.org/the-history/.
"Rioting at Laredo." *Morning Oregonian*, March 21, 1899.
Saldívar, Ramón. *The Borderlands of Culture: Américo Paredes and the Transnational Imaginary*. New Americanists, edited by Donald E. Pease. Durham, NC: Duke University Press, 2006.
"Smallpox at Laredo Serious." *Austin Daily Statesman*, March 14, 1899.
"Smallpox Situation." *Austin Daily Statesman*, March 18, 1899.
Stoler, Ann Laura. *Haunted by Empire: Geographies of Intimacy in North American History*. Durham, NC: Duke University Press, 2006.
Texas Congress, House. *Journal of the House of Representatives of Texas*. 26th Legislature, regular sess., March 15, 1899.
Texas Governor Joseph D. Sayers. Archives and Information Services Division. Texas State Library and Archives Commission.
Tyx, Daniel Blue. "Who Writes History? The Fight to Commemorate a Massacre by the Texas Rangers." *The Texas Observer*, November 26, 2018. www.texasobserver.org/who-writes-history-the-fight-to-commemorate-a-massacre-by-the-texas-rangers/.
Vol. 2 of *A Twentieth Century History of Southwest Texas*. Chicago: The Lewis Publishing Co., 1907. https://archive.org/stream/twentiethcentury02unse/twentiethcentury02unse_djvu.txt.
Vol. 30 of *Journal of the American Medical Association*. Chicago: American Medical Association Press, 1898.
Vol. 30 of *Transactions of the Texas State Medical Association*. Austin, TX: The Eugene Von Boeckmann Publishing Co., 1898.
Vol. 31 of *Transactions of the American Medical Association*. Philadelphia: Collins, 1880.
Vol. 31 of *Transactions of the Texas State Medical Association*. Austin, TX: The Eugene Von Boeckmann Publishing Co., 1899.
Weber, David J. *Foreigners in Their Native Land: Historical Roots of the Mexican Americans*. Albuquerque: University of New Mexico Press, 2003.

West, H. A. "Membership Rosters and Presidential Leadership of Texas State Medical Association." In *Transactions of the Texas State Medical Association*. Austin, TX: The Eugene Von Boeckmann Publishing Co., 1898.

———. "Minutes of Thirtieth Annual Meeting." Vol. 30 of *Transactions of the Texas State Medical Association*. Austin, TX: The Eugene Von Boeckmann Publishing Co., 1898.

3 The sacralizing performance of a counter archive

The Mexican tradition of storytelling in the US-Mexico borderlands has as its antecedents the *pastorela* (religious folk drama), *corrido* (ballad), *dicho* (vernacular proverbs), *décima* (ten-line stanza), *versos* (verses), *adivinanzas* (riddles), *cuentos* (folk tales), *rezos* (prayers), and *chistes* (jokes).[1] Although this oral tradition is viewed in what Hazel Carby calls "weapons for social change," these cultural productions have also structured and shaped Mexicans' religious, social, and cultural identities in the border region.[2] These speech genres point to a communal oral archive of sacralizing stories about kinships, romance, miracles, triumphs, and acts of resistance. In his book, *The Legacy of Américo Paredes*, José López Morín describes Paredes's exposure to the spoken word on the Texas-Mexico border:

> For centuries Paredes's ancestors had celebrated life through music and related events through the spoken word. Oral tradition represented the collective memory of his people, and ballads of heroic events, legends of fabulous treasures, and tales of supernatural apparitions were all an integral part of the cultural forces that shaped Mexican life.[3]

Part of the impetus to creating an oral archive stems from a collective will to reject the State's sacred apparatus of US Manifest Destiny, Anglo-American Protestant superiority, state archives, Western scientific objectivity, and the border-sovereignty-citizenship triplex. From such an apparatus, which admittedly is not limited to these components, elite power has generated an effective desacralizing force that aims to eradicate ethnic Mexican border culture. At issue in this chapter is the State's desacralization of ethnic Mexicans through its archived stories about the Texas-Mexico border. This emphasis is less about archive as process than a state-approved meta-narrative that official archives preserve and disseminate. In Texas, the approved meta-narrative coincides with events, figures, achievements, and ideas that legitimate elite Anglo-American superiority. Sacralizing the meta-narrative is the State's archival complex, which includes repositories of state papers, museums, monuments, historical markers, architecture, ceremonies, and traditions. There are the formal institutions whose name and function clearly point to archive, as in the Texas State Library and Archives Commission, and then the spectacle and performance of archive in the public square. At both the macro- and micro-levels of the State's archival complex, the aim is to sacralize the State's meta-narrative in ways that ensure the reproduction of elite power. For the archives of the State, elite power represents the standard for culture, personhood, and meaning in dominant white US society. Yet the nonstandard in the State's archives consist of those that elite power has deemed their nonsacred other. In the case of the Texas-Mexico border region, ethnic Mexicans are the State's designated nonsacred other and hence written out of its archives. In preserving and retelling the State's meta-narrative, archival agents have been used wittingly or unwittingly to silence, conceal, suppress, and ultimately erase ethnic Mexican cultural and social contributions. In the words of Antoinette Burton, "national identities are founded on archival elisions, distortions, and secrets."[4] Being written out of the State's archives also occurs through the desacralization of ethnic Mexicans, such that their genuine personhood has been skewed, contorted, and fragmented beyond recognition. As Monica Muñoz Martinez writes, ethnic Mexican subjects "appear in institutional archives as anonymous criminals."[5]

Arguably, the archive par excellence of the State, both in stewarding the meta-narrative of elite power and excluding the ethnic Mexican Other, is the territorial border imposed on the landscape after the Mexican-American War. As archive, the US-Mexico border retells the story about Anglo-American imperialism. For ethnic Mexicans this is the source of a perpetual social wound, which as Gloria Anzaldúa describes, "*es una herída abierta* [is an open wound] where the Third World grates against the first and bleeds. And before a scab forms, it hemorrhages again, the lifeblood of two worlds merging to form a third country—a border culture."[6] Yet for elite Anglo-American power, the story of the US-Mexico border transmits a heritage of divinely sanctioned domination (Manifest Destiny), which is exclusive to Anglo-Americans and their posterity. For past, present, and future ethnic Mexicans, the story of the border bequeaths a social wound and makes exclusive their perpetual subjugation. For this chapter, emphasis is placed not on what the border keeps in but rather what it keeps out. It is this latter part of the border's story that the archive of the wounded emerges. Those kept out from the story circulating within the US (i.e. meta-narrative) are black- and brown-bodied migrants, asylum seekers, and refugees. They are the undocumented, the detained, and the deported. Hearing from their archive tells an alternative story of the US-Mexico border. Although their stories define the contours of evil in the US, they more importantly want to be brought into the border's meta-narrative and change its truth claims about those the border keeps in. As those kept out, their archive debunks Anglo-American Protestant superiority simply by crossing the border. Such an act renders the border an archive of migrant intervention. By border crossing, they defy the border's claims about their inferiority by evidencing their resilience, courage, ingenuity, stamina, and creativity.

The perpetual social wound caused by the border not only wears on the well-being of ethnic Mexicans, but it also provokes a counter-will that creatively undercuts the wound's intended goal of Mexican exclusion. In defiance of this social wound, ethnic Mexicans—on both sides of the border—offer a counter archive that resacralizes their personhood, values, beliefs, achievements, and capacities.[7] It intervenes into the domain of identity politics by saturating the ethnic Mexican imaginary with ideas of self-worth and self-determination in a "*gringo*" society.[8] In the words of Ramón Saldívar:

> The narrative of their identities, troubled and painful as it might be, is nonetheless ascertainable, reinforced by the icons of Mexican material culture, and especially by the expressions of the popular imagination: the jokes, riddles, popular sayings, legends, and songs—in sum, the entire repertoire of speech genres of their collective vernacular life experiences—that name a way of life. These forms of typical utterances express the specific themes associated with communal identity in highly standardized ways.[9]

The orality of this counter archive not only points to its discursive nature, as jokes, riddles, popular sayings, legends, and *corridos* (ballads), but also its performance by border musicians, poets, storytellers, and jokesters. As Anzaldúa states, "These folk musicians and folk songs are our chief cultural myth-makers, and they made our hard lives seem bearable."[10]

Border *corridos* as counter archive

In greater Mexico, the *corrido* (ballad) has been a male-centric musical genre that often narrates the deeds, activities, aspirations, romantic relationships, and adventures of male-related events such as war, battles, horse racing, and bullfighting. In spite of this, female *corridistas* (balladeers) like Lydia Mendoza—*La Alondra de la Frontera* (The Lark of the Border)—have played an important role in challenging what Manuel Peña calls "the folklore of *machismo*" within the Mexican musical tradition.[11] In the Texas-Mexico border region, the *corrido* repertoire shares some elements with the broader Mexican *corrido* genre, such as lyrical style and narrative layout. Yet its most distinctive feature since the early twentieth century is the theme of intercultural conflict between Anglo-American and ethnic Mexican male prowess.[12] As Monica Muñoz Martinez describes, "these songs celebrated men who fought for their rights armed with pistols in their hands and rarely depicted women as active contributors to the borderlands."[13] In the violent face-off between two opposing cultures, Anglo-Protestant America and *Mestizo*-Catholic Mexico, the early border *corridos* privileged a Mexican male warrior position as a way to invalidate the ruling paradigm of Anglo-American male superiority in US society. Subtending the heightened attention to Mexican male warriorhood in border *corridos* was not only the male's patriarchal privilege to express social wound but also the scope of postcolonial trauma Anglo-American vigilantism had caused to ethnic Mexican males in the border region.[14] Hence they constitute a counter archive in which the emasculated ethnic Mexican male found self-worth within a warrior-hero imaginary.[15] As Peña indicates, "lacking the means to raise their material or political status, the Texas-Mexicans turned to symbolic expression as a compensatory outlet for their sense of oppression."[16] As a counter archive, the border *corridos* admit to the therapeutic value of verbal art in coping with postcolonial male trauma. By turning to the art of border balladry, emasculated Mexican males are able to imagine themselves not according to the criminalizing inscriptions of the State but rather as men with honor, courage, wit, and dignity. Though social critique, therapeutic artistry, and warrior-hero imaginary mark the border *corridos* as a powerful counter archive, they are also grossly incomplete in that they leave unimagined the postcolonial and patriarchal traumas of ethnic Mexican females in the border region. In other words, they only intervene in the repair of the wounded Mexican male body, often under the notion that their healing is by extension healing for ethnic Mexican women. As Anzaldúa reminds us in her poem *sus plumas el viento*, the ethnic Mexican female body was also a target of Anglo-American colonialism. Often the victims of wanton sexual violence, they were forced to bear a different version of postcolonial trauma. In the second stanza, Anzaldúa describes the horrors of this violence:

> *Ayer entre las matas de maíz* (Yesterday between the corn stalks)
> she had stumbled upon them
> Pepita on her back
> grimacing to the sky,
> the anglo buzzing around her like a mosquito,
> landing on her, digging in, sucking.
> When Pepita came out of the irrigation ditch
> some of the men spit on the ground.[17]

Anzaldúa indicates below the title of this poem that it is "for my mother, Amalia."[18] In the first stanza, she introduces the poem's protagonist named Pepita, who we later discover is a Mexican female field worker and "maid" to "white folks."[19] It is in between the high corn stalks, hidden from sight, that her body is flattened, ravaged, and raped by her field boss, who is "the anglo buzzing around her like a mosquito." From the ditch she emerges to some men who spit on the ground in disgust and shame. Already wounded from the fall ("grimacing"), she is wounded again by sexual violence. Here Anzaldúa captures the doubly pained female body, both the target of Anglo male lust (ninth stanza: "the men staring at her ass") and yet the field hands for his wealth and dominance (eighth stanza: "she stares at her hands, *Manos hinchadas, quebradas*, thick and calloused like a man's"). Following the rape scene,[20] Anzaldúa pivots to the singing of *corridos*. The singer and composer is a fellow female Mexican fieldworker named Chula:

> She listens to Chula singing *corridos*
> Making up *los versos* as she
> plants down the rows
> hoes down the rows
> picks down the rows
> the chorus resounding for acres and acres
> Everyone adding a line
> The day crawls a little faster.[21]

The singing of the *corridos* in this scene advances the poem's biographical story of Pepita's life as a field worker in the borderlands. This stanza begins with her as the subject: "She listens to Chula singing *corridos*." Her rape in the prior stanza still lingers, such that it frames the *corridos* not as a celebratory response but rather as performance that attends to Pepita's ravaged body. In contrast to the traditional male-centric function of the border *corrido* genre, Anzaldúa has us image it as an ethnic Mexican female art form used for channeling away the traumas of Anglo-American sexual violence and domination. Chula is described as "making up" the lyrics as she "plants," "hoes," and "picks," thereby archiving the lived moment in the form of song. Perhaps what attracted Pepita's listening ear were improvised lyrics that sacralized her ethnic Mexican female body.[22] Also imagined in this stanza is the *corrido*'s therapeutic value for the field workers. Here, Chula's *corridos* resound "for acres and acres" to the extent that the surrounding field workers affix their lyrics of the lived moment to them. In the world of this poem, Anzaldúa not only feminizes the wounds of Anglo-male violence and domination but also the border *corrido* genre in ways that affirm its storytelling power while inverting this genre's male-centric associations.

In Paredes's view, the Anglo romantics were more likely to "sentimentalize" the people they had colonized than to confront the reality of violent conflict and the racial inequality that they imposed on the border region.[23] In contrast, border *corridos* undermine this archival strategy by annulling Anglo-American emasculating and criminalizing stereotypes of ethnic Mexican males through the theme of intercultural conflict. In the late-nineteenth-century border ballad "*El Corrido de Kiansis*,"[24] the theme of Anglo/Mexican conflict unfolds within the quintessential Anglo-American cowboy activities of a cattle drive from Texas to Kansas stockyards:

> *Quinientos novillos eran,*   Five hundred steers there were,
> *todos grandes y livianos,*   all big and quick;
> *y entre treinta americanos*   Thirty American boys
> *no los podían embalar.*   could not keep them bunched together.
>
> *Llegan cinco mexicanos,*   Then five Mexicans arrive,
> *todos bien enchivarrados,*   all of them wearing good chaps;
> *y en menos de un cuarto de hora* And in less than a quarter-hour,
> *los tenían encerrados.*   they had the steers penned up.

By design, this border *corrido* seeks to sacralize the Mexican cowboy (*vaquero*) as the superior cattle driver. Through a series of contrasting amounts: "*cinco mexicanos*" (five Mexicans) and "*menos de un cuarto de hora*" (less than a quarter-hour) versus "*treinta americanos*" (thirty American boys), the *corrido* targets those attributes of the Anglo-American cowboy that are associated with his superior masculine status—such as tamer of the Wild West, rugged pioneer, and natural marksman. Instead, the ideal male is the Mexican *vaquero* such that one Mexican cowboy is equal to six American cowboys in terms of strength, and yet far more superior than the six in terms of ingenuity and skill. In the words of the border *corrido*:

Esos cinco mexicanos	Those five Mexicans
al momento los echaron,	penned up the steers in a moment,
y los treinta americanos	And the thirty Americans
se quedaron azorados.	were left staring in amazement.

The border *corrido* brings the Mexican male imaginary into a critical moment in the cattle drive event when male strength, skill, and leadership are confirmed. The scene of five Mexicans corralling five hundred steers leads the audience to imagine an extraordinary display of *vaquero* power that leaves the thirty American cowboys "staring in amazement (*se quedaron azorados*)." As a counter archive, this border *corrido* undermines many of the core tenets of ethnic Mexican desacralization in Anglo-American Protestant society, particularly those that claim they are morally bankrupt, mentally deficient, and incapable of leading. Instead, they are casted here as the ideal frontiersmen of the Wild West—strong, decisive, efficient, and adroit.

The lyrical style, narrative framework, vocal performance, and musical composition of border *corridos* worked jointly to invalidate the sacralized ideology of Anglo-American male superiority. In the same way racially criminalizing stereotypes of ethnic Mexicans legitimated Anglo-American male superiority in elite US society, border *corridos* reversed this strategy, leaving the Mexican *vaquero* as the true North American frontier hero. In targeting the standard bearer of US society, border *corridos* not only reinforced patriarchy as the preferred mode for attending to communal postcolonial trauma, but also they conversely show how their idealized depictions of Mexican masculinity were commensurate to the emasculating impact of Anglo-American male colonization in the border region. Though shaming icons of Anglo-American masculinity was an important first step in decolonizing the shamed Mexican male imaginary, the critical gaze must also attend to what Muñoz Martinez identifies as "the aftermath of violence to document what happened next—the parts of life rarely recorded in mainstream histories or border *corridos*."[25]

Rising to the iconic status of the Anglo-American cowboy in US frontier lore were the Texas Rangers. In the early twentieth century, their claim to Anglo-American male superiority was based not on corralling cattle but rather on exterminating Mexican "border bandits." (See Fig 3.1) In his 1909

The sacralizing performance of a counter archive 61

Figure 3.1 A 1915 picture postcard of Captain James Fox, Texas Ranger (left); a member of Fox's Ranger force (middle); Tom Tate, Cowboy/Special Ranger (right); and the bodies of four roped Mexican men: Jesús García, Mauricio García, Amado Muñoz, and Muñoz's brother. It was sold at public postcard stands in Brownsville, Texas to intimidate ethnic Mexicans in the border region.[26]

Source: Photograph by Robert Runyon; Dolph Briscoe Center for American History.[27]

book *Captain Bill McDonald, Texas Ranger: A Story of Frontier Reform*, Albert Bigelow Paine provides a prototypical portrayal of the Texas Rangers:

> Early in 1836 Texas fought for and gained her independence, the only State in the Union to achieve such a triumph. On the following year the Texas congress recognized the Ranger Movement and authorized several persons to raise Ranger companies to scour the country and annihilate marauding bands. Indians and low class Mexicans ("greasers") often consorted, and the work, desperate and bloody, continued along the ever widening and westering frontier up to within a period easily remembered today by men not beyond middle age.[28]

Hence, targeting the Texas Rangers in border *corridos* like "Ignacio Treviño," "Jacinto Treviño," and "Los Sediciosos" admit to their centrality within the sacralized ideology of Anglo-American male superiority. This critical awareness was generated from firsthand encounters with Texas

Ranger violence and terror in the border region.[29] Functioning under a Mexican male-centric optic, the border *corridos* did fall short of empowering traumatized ethnic Mexican women. For as Anzaldúa reminds us, their wounds were not always bound up in the emasculated Mexican male body but rather in exclusive acts of Anglo-male sexual violence and labor exploitation. Yet despite this constraint, they register a hermeneutical process of the borderlands for the context of state-sanctioned violence that on a therapeutic level is still useful as a source of healing. They show how turning to musical art and storytelling can resacralize shamed and wounded ethnic Mexican personhood. Their creation and design are inextricably linked to ethic Mexican border culture and appeal to both male and female listeners. The ethical aim, however, is not to monopolize the story the *corridos* tell but rather allow for what Anzaldúa describes in her poem *sus plumas el viento*, "Everyone adding a line."[30]

The social critique of border *corridos*

In the 1919 investigations of the Texas Rangers, Representative J.T. Canales submitted as evidence a 1918 report by Mexican Ambassador Y. Bonnilla of Jose Hernandez's emasculating experience with the Texas Rangers:

> Rangers, whose names he doesn't know, came to his house and took him and his young son of about ten years of age, both tied, to a grove and there told Hernández that if he did not confess that he had stolen a *burro* they would hang him together with the boy. Hernández firmly protested his innocence and they immediately put a lariat around his neck and threw the end over the limb of the tree, pulling on it so that Hernández barely touched the ground with his feet, and with another lariat flogged him until he became unconscious. The boy witnessed the whole proceedings but was not hurt. When I saw Hernández six days had already gone by, but black and yellow stripes could still be seen from his belt down to the knees. The lashes could still be seen well marked. The condition in which the man was about such that he could neither sit nor lie down for several days.[31]

This witness account chronicles a pathology of violence against ethnic Mexicans within the Texas Ranger force in the twentieth century. As revealed here, they administered the State's justice through torture, humiliation, and trauma. In many ways their grotesque mutilation of the ethnic Mexican male body served to bolster their own sense of superior masculinity. What is haunting in this account was the spectacle of this terror for Hernández's ten-year-old son. The sight of his father's body hanging at the end of a lynching rope and then flogged unconscious would indeed have been wounds that scarred his childhood and even transferred over to his offspring in his adult years.[32] The border *corridos* channeled these social wounds in the form of a social critique against those deemed central to the State's sacred apparatus. This fostered more than a "compensatory outlet."[33] Their social critique facilitated a critical awareness among the audience of the State's key enforcers of its threshold of eradicating violence in the Texas-Mexico border region. Hence, by targeting the Texas Rangers, the border *corridos* affirmed for their audience their victimization while also offering their wounded imaginations scenes of ethnic Mexican superiority. For instance, in "Jacinto Treviño,"[34] Mexican male courage and strength are proven true in a saloon conflict with the Texas Rangers:

> *Entrenle, rinches cobardes,*   Come on, you cowardly *rinches*,
> *que el pleito no es con un niño*   you're not playing games with a child
> *querían conocer su padre,*   You wanted to meet your father?
> *¡yo soy Jacinto Treviño!*   I am Jacinto Treviño!
>
> *Entrenle, rinches cobardes,*   Come on, you cowardly *rinches*,
> *validos de la ocasión,*   you always like to take the advantage;
> *no van a comer pan blanco*   this is not like eating white bread
> *con tajadas de jamón.—*   with slices of ham.

The term "*rinches*" was a name created by ethnic Mexicans in the border area for the Texas Rangers and, as Richard R. Flores indicates, makes use of the negative Spanish language suffix "*-inche*."[35] Essential to its vernacular appeal was how its meaning carried an indictment of the Texas Rangers as a tyrannical Anglo-American law enforcement organization. In the border *corrido*, the plural *rinches* confront the single Mexican, Jacinto Treviño, in the saloon of Bekar.[36] Rather than avoid them, Jacinto speaks directly to the *rinches* with the repeated command, "*Entrenle*." This signals Jacinto's boldness in the face of the State's revered enforcer of the law. Both stanzas begin with his command followed by his words "you cowardly *rinches*." Rhetorically, this undergirds the notion that the conflict is not only central to the *corrido*'s message, but also that the conflict is initiated by a fearless ethnic Mexican male. In the same way the Texas Rangers used the tortured body of Hernández to affirm their superior masculinity, the border *corrido* casts the Texas Rangers as cowards in order to show Jacinto Treviño as the superior male in the border region.

Where in the Anglo-American world, ethnic Mexicans were rendered inferior,[37] the world of the border *corrido* disparages the very attribute that gave iconic status to the Texas Rangers: their bravery. Throughout Texas Rangers lore, great emphasis is placed on their bravery in order to build up their superior manhood persona. In her late-nineteenth-century ballad "Song of the Texas Rangers," Mrs. J.D. Young writes these words:

> Our men come from the prairies rolling broad, proud and free,
> From the high and craggy mountains to the murmuring Mexic' sea;
> And their hearts are open as their plains; their tho'ts as proudly brave
> As the bold cliffs of the San Bernard, or the Gulf's resistless wave.[38]

Elevating the value of ethnic Mexican men via the discrediting of Texas Ranger bravery was a staple strategy in the border *corridos*. In contrast to Texas Rangers lore, the border *corridos* offered the ethnic Mexican male imaginary an emboldening set of truth claims about their manhood.[39] In redressing their wounded masculinity, these border *corridos* cast their ethnic Mexican protagonists as men who are fearless in the face of the State's sacralized police force of Mexican terror.[40] Subtending their bravery is not criminality but rather an ethics of resistance to state-sanctioned violence, as embodied in the Texas Rangers. Within the official archives of the State, the Texas Rangers were given superior warriorhood status, possessing model characteristics like God-fearing, brave, honorable, law enforcer, and protector of the public good. Indeed, these male attributes were not assigned outright to the Texas Rangers but rather affirmed through the capture and extermination of ethnic Mexicans. Rather than submit to this latter dynamic, the border *corridos* intervene by providing a counter image of Mexican masculinity at the expense of emasculated *rinches*. Consider these words in "Ignacio Treviño": "*Decía Ignacio Treviño con su pistola en la mano:—No corran, rinches cobardes, con un solo Mexicano*" (Then said Ignacio Treviño, with his pistol in his hand, "Don't run, you cowardly *rinches*, from a single Mexican"). Also in "*Los Sediciosos*," which commemorates the Texas-Mexican uprising of 1915 (*Plan de San Diego*), Aniceto Pizaña declares: "*Esos rinches de la Kiñena, dicen que son muy valientes, hacen llorar las mujeres, hacen correr alas gentes*" (Those rangers from the King Ranch, say that they are very brave; they make the women cry, and they make the people run).[41] With the combination of embodied performance, musical technique, and vocal emphasis, these images of single Mexican male strength and bravery took command of the public sphere and unleashed into the Mexican imagination a different archive.

This audacious portrayal of Mexican masculinity was commensurate with lived postcolonial trauma in which the lynching and massacring of brown bodies was a common public spectacle in the border region.[42] In this way, they name the social wound through audacious scenes of Mexican male prowess and bravery that leave the Texas Rangers awestruck. As in the border *corrido* "Jacinto Treviño," Jacinto boldly declares himself the father of the Texas Rangers, "*querían conocer su padre, ¡yo soy Jacinto Treviño!*" (You wanted to meet your father? I am Jacinto Treviño!),[43] to which the chief Texas Ranger responds:

Decía el Rinche Mayor,	The chief to the *rinches* said,
Como era un americano:	even though he was an American
—¡Ah, qué Jacinto tan hombre,	Ah, what a brave man is Jacinto
No niega el ser mexicano!	—you can see he is a Mexican![44]

In the world of the border *corrido*, the Anglo-American chief Texas Ranger legitimates Mexican male bravery, hence reversing the State's desacralization mission. Instead of racially criminalized Mexican males affirming Anglo-American male superiority, the State's iconic figure is defamed, thereby inspiring the public's imagination about the value and worth of ethnic Mexican masculinity.

Border *corridos* and the Bible

After a momentary decline in the 1930s,[45] the border *corrido* experienced a "renaissance" in the 1960s. The Chicano Movement, Luis Valdez's *Teatro Campesino*, and Cesar Chávez's drive to unionize the farm workers energized ethnic Mexican balladeers to take up anew the border *corrido* musical form. Currently, the border *corrido* serves as an effective artistic template for telling the counter-stories of Mexican migration to the United States and border *narco*-traffic.[46] Even more provocative, however, is the use of the border *corrido* musical form to read the Bible. The result is border *corridos* that focus not on redressing shamed Mexican masculinity but on sacralizing the culture, context, and religious outlook of mainly evangelical Mexican audiences. Like their predecessors, these Bible border *corridos* draw their currency from a Mexican borderlands' vernacular and, as such, identify their target audience as people from this context. Rather than have the defamed iconic Anglo-American frontiersman serve as the portal for sacralizing ethnic Mexican manhood, the Bible border *corridos* turn to the Bible and its revered stories of God-fearing heroes. This performative storytelling dynamic distills the Bible through a musical Mexican form of the borderlands, producing a sacralizing effect on its designated audience. Here, the Bible becomes a sacred borderlands Mexican Bible with Mexicanized biblical heroes, God, and Jesus.

Known throughout the borderlands for their Bible border *corridos* is *Grupo Juda*. In 1998, this evangelical *norteño* musical band from Monterrey, Nuevo León, Mexico, signed on with record label Lion of Judah Music *Producciones* and recorded five albums, two of which had an extensive Bible border *corrido* repertoire.[47] In 2005, the band created the independent record label Judah Music *Producciones*, recording only two albums with Bible border *corridos*. Each year, *Grupo Juda* undertakes an extensive touring schedule throughout the US-Mexico borderlands region. Often the featured band, their concerts draw large sing-along audiences and are given generous airtime on numerous evangelical/Pentecostal AM/FM radio stations in the US Southwest. Several of their live performances, music videos, interviews, and video blogs register high viewing counts on their YouTube channel GRUPOJUDAOFICIAL, and a growing number of fans have joined their community Facebook page (Grupo Juda Monterrey). In a recent interview with the band, bass player Alfredo Martínez Mata was asked about the band's use of the popular border *corrido* genre in telling the stories about biblical figures. He stated, "we have seen that *corridos* are liked very much here in the north, powerful stories that give us examples for our daily lives and I think that the people like them and the people are being ministered by them, therefore we try very hard to create them."[48] For their 1998 album, *Corridos II*, they recorded two original Bible border *corridos*, "*Corrido de José*" and "*Corrido de Pablo.*" In 1999, the band released their album *Edición Especial Corridos*, which featured four original Bible border *corridos*, "*Corrido de Lázaro,*" "*Corrido de Noé,*" "*Corrido de Ester,*" and "*Corrido de Moisés.*" Also appearing in this album is their rendition of a classic Bible border ballad "*Corrido de Daniel,*" which according to lead singer Sergio Mata, its author is unknown. In 2006, they released their album *Corridos III: El Mejor de los Corridos*, which contained three original Bible border *corridos*, "*El Corrido del Samaritano,*" "*Corrido de Jonás,*" and "*Corrido de Abram y Sara.*" The "*Corrido de Daniel*" has been one of the band's most popular Bible border *corridos*, which earned it a spot on the religious compilation album titled *Las Mejores 20 Norteñas de Todos los Tiempos* (The best 20 Border-Region songs of all time).

Sacralizing Bible-believing Mexicans

As is typical of early-nineteenth-century border *corridos*, the "*Corrido de Daniel*" contains thematic elements of challenge, confrontation, and defeat.[49] In terms of its narrative structure, it also follows the border *corrido* tripartite narrative sequence of place and name of the main character, message of heroics/conflict, and farewell.[50] Focusing primarily on the book of Daniel Chapter 6, the "*Corrido de Daniel*" features six stanzas of six octosyllabic lines with a rhyme scheme that coincides in the even lines. With the basic instrumentation indicative of the *norteña*-ensemble tradition (i.e. borderlands), the "*Corrido de Daniel*" is played in major keys and remains within the vocal range of an octave, both of which are distinctive features of the border *corrido* storytelling performance.[51] This fusion of the Bible and the border *corrido* musical form yields a sacralizing dynamic of the US-Mexico borderlands that enlivens the cultural senses and sanctifies the religious imaginations of mainly evangelical Mexican audiences. Similar to the ways in which early border *corridos* undermined the iconic currency of the Texas Rangers by emboldening the ethnic Mexican male imagination, the Bible border *corrido* harnesses the sacredness of the Spanish Bible to elevate and affirm the sacred worth of Bible-believing Mexicans. Indeed, this is a twofold sacralization process of *corrido* performance and the Bible. The former represents the sacred domain of Mexican border culture and its set ways of truth-making (counter archive); whereas the latter is ascribed sacred authority as part of the audience's religious faith. The Bible border *corrido* performance has in view communal sacralization such that the cultural heritage and religious faith of entire Mexican communities are simultaneously given divine worth.

In typical border ballad form, the first stanza gives the place and name of the main character:

En la babilonia antigua　　In ancient Babylon
ciudad de grandes misterios　the city of great mysteries
hay vivía un gran profeta　　There lived a great prophet
y siervo del Dios eterno　　and servant of the eternal God
Daniel así se llamaba　　　Daniel was his name
consejero de los reinos[52]　Councilor of the king's dominions

Here, both the narrator and author remain anonymous. As Ramon Saldívar notes, "the distinction between reliable and unreliable narrators is totally inapplicable in the *corrido* context."[53] On the other hand, the ancient biblical city of Babylon carries a familiar proximity, immediately integrating the audience into the biblical story. Through the artistic medium of the *corrido*, the audience is expected to imagine themselves in the ancient city of Babylon and more importantly identify personally with the exiled prophet-hero Daniel. In vernacularizing the Bible through the border *corrido* performance, an enculturation process takes place in which biblical history, geography, and figures are imbued with Mexican familiarity. In other words, the Bible border *corrido* invites evangelical Mexican audiences to enter the biblical story not as an outsider but rather as the story's natural heirs. This form of narrative presence is multifarious and includes cultural preferences, religious beliefs, and ways of truth-making specific to the US-Mexico borderlands. Through the Mexicanizing performance of the border *corrido*, the otherness of the Bible recedes, leaving its sacredness to be inherited by Bible-believing Mexicans. By distilling the sacred from the Bible in this way, a desacralized people are sacralized as a biblical people and hence the people of God. The Bible border *corrido* gives cultural specificity to the Bible's sacredness, connecting it to distinctive Mexican values, beliefs, convictions, and ways of being. Bible-believing Mexican audiences are under no suspicion of the border *corrido*'s intentions, for they are confident that it exists solely for their benefit. The Bible border *corrido* fuses their story with the biblical story and as such renders their lives sacred.

The core message of the Bible border *corrido* begins in the second stanza, introducing the biblical hero's challenge:

Príncipes y magistrados　　Princes and magistrates
lo miraban con recelo　　　Looked at him with jealousy
buscando ponerle en el mar　Looking to put him in evil
conspiraron un acuerdo　　They conspired an agreement
que se prostrara ante el rey　That he should bow before the king
porque así querían verlo[54]　Because that's how they wanted to see him

The Bible border *corrido* is calibrated to a Mexican borderlands social imagination and, as such, receives its currency from audiences imbued with this context. Within this cultural and religious collective, the biblical figures of "*Príncipes y magistrados*" (princes and magistrates) correspond to real-life antagonistic figures in the socio-political milieu of the US-Mexico borderlands—from local civic leaders to US border patrol officers. In a region overwhelmed by acts of racial and economic injustices at the state level, the border *corrido* genre grants Bible-believing Mexican audiences a sacralizing vision in which Daniel's oppression is equivalent to their own. This mode of sacralization attends to both the social and spiritual needs of the audience. Accompanying the vernacularizing and enculturating strategies of the Bible border *corrido* is a concern for the audience's social location. In many ways, the links it makes to the social constitute a significant portion of its truth-making authority for Bible-believing Mexican audiences. Yet, by incorporating the Bible, the *corrido* is also able to attend in profound ways to their spiritual realities.

In tying Daniel's oppression to a particular social need, mass detention and deportation in the US would not be out of reach for the *corrido*'s social vision.[55] Within the evangelical Latina church, several undocumented immigrant pastors in the US have been targets of President Donald Trump's mass deportation operations. Among the undocumented evangelical Latino pastors the US Immigration and Customs Enforcement (ICE) arrested in 2017 were Rev. Antonio Velasquez of Guatemala, Pastor of *Iglesia Internacional el Cordero de Dios* in Phoenix Arizona;[56] Rev. Jorge Ramirez of Mexico, Worship Pastor at Fountain of Praise Apostolic Church, Oceanside, CA;[57] Rev. Noe Carias of Guatemala, Pastor of Evangelical Assemblies of God Church, Los Angeles, CA;[58] and Rev. José Chicas of El Salvador, Pastor of *Iglesia Evangélica Jesús el Pan de Vida*, Raleigh, North Carolina.[59]

In casting an applicable social vision, the *corrido* is not limited to male biblical heroes, as shown with *Grupo Juda*'s Bible border *corrido* "*Corrido de Ester*." Here, the audience is led to imagine themselves as the brave exilic-queen Esther:

Amán era un desalmado	Haman was a fiend
Ester la joven valiente	Esther the brave young lady
el intentaba matarla	he attempted to kill her
en companía de su gente	in the company of his people
mas ella expuso su vida	but she laid out her life
por conservar su simiente[60]	to conserve her seed

In this stanza, Esther overcomes the murderous plot of Haman, who in the biblical story (Esther 3:1) is a high royal official of the Persian King Ahasuerus. For evangelical Mexican audiences of the borderlands, their repertoire of corresponding figures perpetrating life-threatening violence against them range from cartel leaders to ICE to white nationalist terrorists. The social vision casted in both *corridos* not only sets up links between the violence of the princes, magistrates, and officials in the biblical story and contemporary violence by figures of elite power, but also between exiled Daniel and Esther and US immigrant audiences. Here their lived victimization coalesces with

The sacralizing performance of a counter archive 69

the victimization of Daniel or Esther, thereby sacralizing their contemporary social struggles. At the same time, these contemporary social links also facilitate the desacralization of the current figures of elite power who are manufacturing the violence that the audience is facing.

The socio-cultural currency of *corrido* conflict

The third stanza introduces the biblical hero's conflict, which is also a key feature of the early-nineteenth-century border *corrido* tradition:

A tan terrible ordenanza	To a very terrible ordinance
Daniel nunca le temió	Daniel never feared it
solo al Señor de los cielos	Only to the Lord of heaven
su vida toda entregó	Did he give his whole life
solamente en el confiaba	Only in him did he confide
y la fé no le faltó[61]	And faith he didn't lack

Although present in the biblical text, the emphasis on Daniel's conflict with the princes and magistrates fulfills a socio-cultural requirement of the border *corrido* form. As reflected in the border *corrido* "Jacinto Treviño," its socio-cultural currency hinges on the hero's conflict with nefarious figures of elite power.[62] Drawing on Manuel Peña's notions of status reversal,[63] this may be schematized as follows:

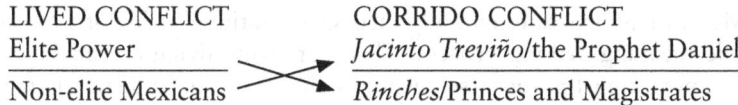

LIVED CONFLICT   CORRIDO CONFLICT
Elite Power   *Jacinto Treviño*/the Prophet Daniel
Non-elite Mexicans   *Rinches*/Princes and Magistrates

From this vicarious dynamic, audience members translate their personhood through the lives of the biblical heroes. Seeing themselves in this way boosts their confidence enough so as not to be afraid of evil elite power. As a northern Mexican musical form, this building up of personhood is especially potent for evangelical Mexican audiences in the borderlands. Here, culture and sacred scripture intermingle in ways that affirm their Mexican-ness and yet elevates it to the realm of the divine. Here, they are sacralized as valiant and heroic people who possess high moral agency and spiritual fortitude to confront evil elite power.

Equally important to the socio-cultural currency of the Bible border *corrido* is to have its conflict reach an extraordinary and awe-inspiring level. Underlying this narrative strategy is the view that higher levels of conflict with representatives of evil elite power yield higher levels of superiority for the *corrido*'s hero-underdog. The heightened conflict sets up the hero-underdog to respond in extraordinary fashion, which in turn places them in a status superior to evil elite power. The ultimate beneficiary of the hero's elite status in the *corrido* is the non-elite Mexican audience. The intensity of the *corrido* conflict with elite power not only affirms their lived conflict but more importantly grafts it to the biblical story as to sacralize it. In the stanza above, it is Daniel's bravery and faith in God in the face of life-threatening elite power that serves as a sacred template for how non-elite Bible-believing Mexicans are to respond to their lived conflict with evil elite power.[64] The versatility of this correspondence between Daniel (*corrido*) and Bible-believing Mexicans (*lived*) has the capacity to align the sacred with a spectrum of lived conflict on both sides of the US-Mexico border. Whether the lived conflict relates to racist US immigration policies or a cartel kidnapping for ransom, the Bible border *corrido* allows these lived conflicts with evil elite power to be given sacred importance. This dynamic points to the *corrido's* archiving function in that through its sacralization of lived experiences, these experiences in turn are given Bible-like permanence. Through the *corrido*, their lived conflicts with evil elite power as well as their courageous responses to them are conjoined to the biblical story. Each time they hear the *corrido*, they recall anew the past conflicts they overcame as well as add their current conflicts to the biblical story. Hence, the sacralization that the Bible border *corrido* provides for Mexican audiences both offsets desacralizing regimes—like those in the US that cast Mexicans as morally bankrupt, criminal, and culturally inferior—and archives their victories over lived conflicts.

The sacralizing interchange between the biblical Daniel and lived experience occurs not through discourse alone, but rather at the nexus of embodied performance, a borderlands musicality, and an evangelical/Pentecostal Mexican belief system. In this way, the Bible border *corrido* enables non-elite Mexican audiences to embody their sacralization outside of a Western scientific meaning-making process. This sacralizing dynamic can be especially empowering for those segments of the Mexican audience living as immigrants in the United States. For in this context, elite power has deemed Mexican immigrant bodies criminal and therefore decreed their removal from the US body politic.[65]

In the fourth stanza, the theme of conflict intensifies for the biblical hero-underdog:

Y echaron al Daniel	And they threw Daniel
al foso de aquellos leones	Into the den of those lions
por no cumplir el decreto	For not completing the decree
que inventaron los traidores	That the traitors invented
pagaron un precio caro	They paid an expensive price
se los cenaron los leones	The lions had them for supper

Consistent with the biblical narrative, the insidious plot of the princes and magistrates culminates with the throwing of Daniel into "*al foso de aquellos leones*" (the den of those lions). For this climatic stanza, the Bible border *corrido* depends on the audience's biblical literacy to decipher terms like "*decreto*" (decree), "*traidores*" (traitors), and "*aquellos leones*" (those lions).⁶⁶ Rather than quote directly from the biblical text ("*echáronle en el foso del los leones*," Daniel 6:16, RVA), the *corrido* stays true to its octosyllabic meter and ABCBCB rhyme scheme. The elite men persecuting Daniel in the biblical text (Daniel 6) are cast in the Bible border *corrido* as "*los traidores*" (the traitors). This designation of elite power is not a loose paraphrase of the biblical text; instead it is tied to the lived experiences of non-elite Bible-believing Mexicans. Equal to meeting the requirements of the border *corrido* form is attending to a meaning-making process that is rooted in lived Mexican experience. In this latter context, elite power takes the form of actual traitors who pose a threat to the listening community. Here, the Bible border *corrido* submits to the authorities of a borderlands artistic form and lived Mexican experience in reading the sacred. The driving impulse is not to prove the Bible but rather to harness its sacred currency for a hurting and often victimized community. Under this cultural ethic, the Bible border *corrido* allows its audience to connect their actual traitors with the defeat of the traitors in the *corrido*, "*se los cenaron los leones*" (the lions had them for supper). This performed movement between biblical text and border *corrido* form reveals an economy of truth-making outside of Western science-based methods of biblical interpretation. As argued in the previous chapter, Western scientific objectivity has been susceptible to a white supremacist logic and as such is more prone to desacralizing ethnic Mexicans on both sides of the US-Mexico border. Similar to the early-nineteenth-century border *corrido*, this Bible border *corrido* attends to social wounds at both the socio-cultural and spiritual levels. Like the former, it captures the imagination of the listening audience in order to elevate their human worth and inspire acts of courage and justice. This mode of biblical reading casts a social vision that is human-centric and culturally specific. Where Western science-based readings approach the Bible as object, separate from any social wounds, the Bible border *corrido* represents a therapeutic art form that intervenes in the desacralized Mexican imagination by resacralizing body, mind, and soul.

Mexicanizing the biblical hero-underdog

Through the Bible border *corrido* performance, the sacralization of the lived conflict also extends to the audience's response to it, inasmuch as their response mirrors the heroic actions of a Mexicanized Daniel. In the fifth stanza, the biblical hero-underdog emerges victorious:

Al otro día Darío   On the next day Darius
fue a ver qué había sucedido   Went to see what had happened
llego gritando al Daniel   He arrived crying out to Daniel
¿estás a ya 'migo mío?   "Are you over there my friend?"
grande es tu dios viviente Great is your Living God
quien siempre ha sido contigo Who always has been with you.

In both the biblical narrative and the *corrido*, King Darius uses direct speech to address Daniel (Daniel 6:20). Yet in the *corrido*, Darius's use of Mexican colloquialisms like "*migo*" for "*amigo*" (friend) as well as their pronunciation and inflection by the performers serve as markers to community listeners that their way of knowing the world constitutes the ultimate hermeneutical authority.[67] Here, their authority of truth-making lies not in the *corrido*'s literal reading of the Bible but instead in its storytelling performance. Under this hermeneutical authority, the aim is precision and accuracy as it pertains to the established components of the border *corrido* genre. Thus, what appears as a deviation from the literal biblical text instead reflects a careful fulfillment of the border *corrido* meaning-making process. Consider, for instance, the Bible border *corrido*'s narrative scene sequence. In Daniel 6, the elite antagonists are eaten by the lions after King Darius speaks with uneaten Daniel in the lions' den. Yet in the *corrido*, these scenes are reversed in order to meet the storytelling requirements of the border *corrido* genre. Although this may be construed as a mishandling of the biblical material, the socio-cultural needs are what drives this change in scene sequence. In other words, the Bible border *corrido* is concerned more about empowering its audiences with sacralizing images that inspire self-confidence, stronger faith in God, and courage to confront evil elite power than historical accuracy as reflected in Western science-based readings of the Bible.

Integral to the Mexicanizing function of the Bible border *corrido* is the replacement of the Mexican *vaquero* with the biblical hero-underdog. This exchange utilizes the emboldening dynamic of the former while at the same time assigning it biblical sacredness. In the sixth stanza, the Mexicanization of the biblical hero Daniel is made explicit:

Así como este varón	Just like this man
Cristo quiere recordarte	Christ wants to remind you
que no quebrantes tu fé	Not to fail in your faith
en esta lucha constante	In this constant struggle
como Daniel confió en Dios	As Daniel confided in God
tu también saldrás triunfante	You also will come out triumphant

As required by the border *corrido* genre, the last stanza bids farewell to the listening audience. In the words of José López Morín, "the scenes swing back and forth and point of view moves from protagonist to adversaries, to common people alike."[68] Here in the farewell, the *corrido* affirms its evangelical Christian connection with a reference to Christ (*Cristo*) in the second line. In the end, Christ serves as the person who is calling the listening audience to envision themselves as Daniel, a strategy that renders the *corrido* more than a counter archive but rather sacred word. Ultimately, the words assigned to Christ pertain specifically to the vicarious dynamic that the audience has encountered through the *corrido* performance. It is Christ who desires the audience to see themselves as biblical heroes and to be confident enough in their faith to confront evil elite power, which in the words of the fourth line is a constant struggle, *"en esta lucha constante."*

Conclusion

Current conservative political discourse has resurrected early-twentieth-century anti-Mexican sentiments in order to desacralize ethnic Mexicans anew and thereby exclude them from the body politic.[69] Unlike the previous century, however, the current anti-Mexican rhetoric is supported by a much larger complex of border security and policing agents than the Texas Rangers. Today's criminalization of ethnic Mexicans is archived not only on paper but also on the physical landscape. The buildings, barriers, and agents charged by the State to exclude, imprison, and deport Mexican immigrants represent the current archival strategy of elite power. Security structures intended for ethnic Mexican capture and exclusion function as the State's new archive. Despite its expansive structural form, however, the State's archive still relies on white supremacist logic and abiding stereotypes of ethic Mexican criminality to legitimate its existence. In contrast to the State's archive of the early twentieth century, its current structural form allows for a broader scale of Mexican desacralization to occur in the US-Mexico borderlands region. The expansion of Mexican desacralization through the State's border security industrial complex has now spread to all brown-bodied people migrating on a south-to-north trajectory.

Similar to the early twentieth century, the Bible border *corrido* storytelling performance has come to the fore in the borderlands offering a counter archive that sacralizes those deemed the criminal other. Just as President Trump appeals to the Bible to sacralize white US society and desacralize the Mexican other, this artistic musical form Mexicanizes biblical heroes as a way to sacralize Bible-believing Mexicans. As a hermeneutic of the borderlands, the Bible border *corrido* genre inhabits a different sphere of meaning-making that ensures optimum sacralization of those deemed by elite power as the nonsacred other. Where it begins is not with Western scientific epistemologies, white supremacist logic, or ecclesiastical jurisdictions, but rather with the social vision of the desacralized Mexican other.

Notes

1 *Decimas* are Spanish stanzas consisting of verses of usually eight syllables. The form is distinguished by its dialogue with other poets. Américo Paredes, *Canto de adolescencia: Songs of Youth (1932–1937)* (Houston, TX: Arte Público Press, 2007), 186; See also María Herrera-Sobek, *Chicano Folklore: A Handbook* (Westport, CT: Greenwood Press, 2006), 182; For the Sephardic origins of the *corrido*, all of which have roots in Judeo-Spanish oral tradition, see Tomás Lozano and Rima Montoya, *Cantemos al alba: Origins of Songs, Sounds, and Liturgical Drama of Hispanic of New Mexico* (New Mexico: University of New

Mexico Press, 2007), 432–572; For additional readings on the emergence and development of the Texas-Mexico *corrido*, see Rafaela Castro, *Chicano Folklore: A Guide to the Folktales, Traditions, Rituals and Religious Practices of Mexican Americans* (Oxford: Oxford University Press, 2001), 67–69; Rafael Pérez-Torres, *Mestizaje: Critical Uses of Race in Chicano Culture* (Minneapolis: University of Minnesota Press, 2006), 85–116; José R. López Morín, *The Legacy of Américo Paredes* (College Station, TX: Texas A&M University Press, 2006), 70–97; Arnoldo De León and Richard Griswold del Castillo, *North to Aztlán: A History of Mexican Americans in the United States* (Wheeling, IL: Harlan Davidson, 2006), 63–85.

2 Elizabeth Netto Calil Zarur and Charles Muir Lovell, eds., *Art and Faith in Mexico: The Nineteenth-Century Retablo Tradition* (Albuquerque: University of New Mexico Press, 2001); Gloria Fraser Giffords, *Mexican Folk Retablos* (Albuquerque: University of New Mexico Press, 1974); Angelico Chavez Kunin, *From an Altar Screen: El Retablo: Tales from New Mexico* (New York: Farrer, Straus and Cudahy, 1957), 11, 139, 156; Hazel V. Carby, *Reconstructing Womanhood: The Emergence of the Afro-American Woman Novelist* (New York: Oxford University Press, 1987), 95; José David Saldívar, *Border Matters: Remapping American Cultural Studies* (Berkeley, CA: University of California Press, 1997), 36.

3 Morín, *The Legacy of Américo Paredes*, 2.

4 Antoinette Burton, "Introduction: Archive Fever, Archive Stories," in *Archive Stories: Facts, Fictions, and the Writing of History* (Durham, NC: Duke University Press, 2005), 2; For more details about the links between elite power and archives see Thomas Richards, *The Imperial Archive: Knowledge and the Fantasy of Empire* (London: Verso, 1993); See also Carolyn Steedman, *Dust: The Archive and Cultural History* (New Brunswick, NJ: Rutgers University Press, 2002); Nicholas B. Dirks, *Autobiography of an Archive: A Scholar's Passage to India* (New York: Columbia University Press, 2015); Achille Mbembe, "The Power of the Archive and Its Limits," in *Refiguring the Archive*, eds. Carolyn Hamilton et al. (Dordrecht, The Netherlands: Kluwer Academic Publishers, 2002), 19–26; Natalie Zemon Davis, foreword to *The Allure of the Archive*, by Arlette Farge, trans. Thomas Scott-Railton (New Haven, CT: Yale University Press, 2013); Ann Laura Stoler, *Along the Archival Grain: Epistemic Anxieties and Colonial Sense* (Princeton: Princeton University Press, 2008).

5 Monica Muñoz Martinez, "Recuperating Histories of Violence in the Americas: Vernacular History-Making on the US-Mexico Border," *American Quarterly* 66, no. 3 (September 2014): 663.

6 Gloria Anzaldúa, *Borderlands/La Frontera: The New Mestiza* (San Francisco: Spinsters/Aunt Lute, 1987), 3.

7 José E. Limón, *Mexican Ballads, Chicano Poems: History and Influence in Mexican-American Social Poetry* (Berkeley, CA: University of California Press, 1992), 42.

8 Elizabeth Jacobs, *Mexican American Literature: The Politics of Identity* (Abingdon, UK: Routledge, 2006), 67.

9 Ramón Saldívar, *The Borderlands of Culture: Américo Paredes and the Transnational Imaginary* (Durham, NC: Duke University Press, 2006), 163. For more on Texas-Mexican vernacular culture, see José E. Limón, *Américo Paredes: Culture and Critique* (Austin, TX: University of Texas Press, 2012); See also John Moran Gonzalez, *Border Renaissance: The Texas Centennial and the Emergence of Mexican America* (Austin, TX: University of Texas Press, 2009).

10 Anzaldúa, *Borderlands/La Frontera*, 61.

11 Manuel Peña, *Música Tejana: The Cultural Economy of Artistic Transformation* (College Station, TX: Texas A&M University Press, 1999), 52, 54; Herrera-Sobek, *Chicano Folklore*, 35; Yolanda Broyles-Gonzalez, *Life in Music/La Historia de Lydia Mendoza* (Oxford: Oxford University Press, 2001), xi.

12 Américo Paredes, *Folklore and Culture on the Texas-Mexican Border*, ed. Richard Bauman (Austin, TX: CMAS Books, 1995), 27; Peña, *Música Tejana*, 74; Monica Muñoz Martinez, *The Injustice Never Leaves You: Anti-Mexican Violence in Texas* (Cambridge, MA: Harvard University Press, 2018), 24.
13 Martinez, *The Injustice Never Leaves You*, 24.
14 Ibid., 9, 21–22, 77, 159–71.
15 Peña, *Música Tejana*, 36; Américo Paredes, *A Texas-Mexican Cancionero: Folksongs of the Lower Border* (Austin, TX: University of Texas Press, 1995), xxix, 140.
16 Peña, *Música Tejana*, 74.
17 Anzaldúa, *Borderlands/La Frontera*, 138.
18 Ibid.
19 Ibid., 140.
20 Ibid., 10–11.
21 Ibid., 138.
22 Ibid., 10–11.
23 Paredes, *A Texas-Mexican Cancionero*, xxx.
24 Ibid., 54–55.
25 Martinez, *The Injustice Never Leaves You*, 24.
26 Ibid., 237–38; R. B. Creager, testimony, "Proceedings of the Joint Committee of the Senate and the House in the Investigation of the Texas State Ranger Force," in *Adjutant General Records* (Austin, TX: Texas State Archives), 365–68; Captain W. T. Vann, testimony, "Proceedings," 576–77.
27 The Robert Runyon Photograph Collection, RUN00096, *The Dolph Briscoe Center for American History*, The University of Texas at Austin, http://runyon.lib.utexas.edu/n2c?urn:utlol:runyon.00096.
28 Albert Bigelow Paine, *Captain Bill McDonald, Texas Ranger: A Story of Frontier Reform* (New York: J. J. Little & Ives Co., 1909), 130.
29 Limón, *Mexican Ballads, Chicano Poems*, 16; Martinez, *The Injustice Never Leaves You*, 3–5; Nashwa Bawab, "A Century After the Porvenir Massacre, Remembering One of Texas' Darkest Days," *The Texas Observer*, January 31, 2018, www.texasobserver.org/century-porvenir-massacre-remembering-one-texas-darkest-days/; Madlin Mekelburg, "Porvenir Massacre on Texas Border Haunts Descendants 100 Years Later," *El Paso Times*, January 26, 2018, www.elpasotimes.com/story/news/2018/01/26/100-years-later-porvenir-massacre-haunts-descendants-texas-border/1058345001/?fbclid=IwAR1IPfsu-tVu4k2TQXWmCPiWW1xw6yVjzzRGPJ20j8Fv1fy8YaCO0aGmQlI.
30 Anzaldúa, *Borderlands/La Frontera*, 138.
31 Y. Bonnilla, Report, "Proceedings," 824.
32 For more on the notion of inherited trauma or "inherited loss," see Martinez, *The Injustice Never Leaves You*, 104–19.
33 Peña, *Música Tejana*, 74.
34 Paredes, *A Texas-Mexican Cancionero*, 70–72.
35 Julian Samora, Joe Bernal, and Albert Peña, *Gunpowder Justice: A Reassessment of the Texas Rangers* (Notre Dame, IN: University of Notre Dame Press, 1979), 7; Richard R. Flores, "The Corrido and the Emergence of Texas-Mexican Social Identity," *The Journal of American Folklore* 105, no. 416 (Spring 1992): 169.
36 Paredes, *A Texas-Mexican Cancionero*, 32.
37 Eugene C. Barker, Charles Shirley Potts, and Charles W. Ramsdell, *A School History of Texas* (Chicago: Row, Peterson & Co., 1913), 64; Felipe de Ortego y Gasca, "Brands, Bandits, and Ballads: Eiconic Images of Tejanos in the Literature of the Borderlands," *Journal of South Texas* 15, no. 2 (Fall 2002): 93–101; In 1852 Colonel Monroe, a regional military commander, reported to Washington that "the Mexicans are thoroughly debased, totally incapable of self-government, and there is no latent quality about them that can ever make them

respectable. They have more Indian blood than Spanish, and in some respects are below the Pueblo Indians, for they are not as honest or as industrious." In his book *Mexico, Aztec, Spanish and Republican*, vol. 2 (Hartford, CT: S. Drake and Co., 1852), 22; Brantz Mayer writes, "The Mexican native, in whose veins there is almost always a few drops of indigenous blood, is commonly indolent and often vicious. The bland climate and his natural temperament predispose him for an indulgent, easy, and voluptuous life."

38 William Long Fagan, *Southern War Songs: Camp-Fire, Patriotic and Sentimental* (New York: M. T. Richardson, 1890), 287. For more on the link between the Texas Rangers and their bravery continues in the historical literature, see B. Roberts Lackey, *Stories of the Texas Rangers* (San Antonio, TX: Naylor Co., 1955), 47–53; William Warren Sterling, *Trails and Trials of a Texas Ranger* (Norman, OK: University of Oklahoma Press, 1959), 21–52. Their bravery is also emphasized in Texas Ranger monuments and museum around the State of Texas, see https://trhc.org/index.html and www.texasranger.org/.

39 Fremont B. Deering, *The Border Boys with the Texas Rangers* (New York: Hurst & Co., 1912), 12; William J. Maltby, *Captain Jeff: Or Frontier Life in Texas with the Texas Rangers* (Colorado, TX: Whipkey Printing Co., 1906), 84–85; Daniel Webster Roberts, *Rangers and Sovereignty* (San Antonio, TX: Wood Printing & Engraving Co., 1914), 11–12; Paine, *Captain Bill McDonald, Texas Ranger*, 131–32; N. A. Jennings, *A Texas Ranger* (New York: C. Scribner's Sons, 1899), 141–58.

40 Jennings, *A Texas Ranger*, 141–58.

41 Paredes, *A Texas-Mexican Cancionero*, 32–33, 68, 73.

42 Jennings, *A Texas Ranger*, 138–58.

43 Paredes, *A Texas-Mexican Cancionero*, 70–72.

44 Ibid.

45 José David Saldívar, ed., *The Rolando Hinojosa Reader: Essays Historical and Critical* (Houston: Arte Público Press, 1985), 143.

46 Herrera-Sobek, *Chicano Folklore*, 35; Gregory Lee Cuéllar, *Voices of Marginality: Exile and Return in Second Isaiah 40–55 and the Mexican Immigrant Experience* (New York: Peter Lang Publishing, 2008), 82–95; Mark Cameron Edberg, *El Narcotraficante: Narcocorridos and the Construction of a Cultural Persona on the U.S.-Mexico Border* (Austin, TX: University of Texas Press, 2004), 25–46.

47 Juda—Topic, "Corrido de Jose (En Vivo)," filmed November 2015, *YouTube Video*, 2:56, www.youtube.com/watch?v=vfI9eembQmg.

48 Ernesto Sifuentes, "GRUPO JUDÁ en Monclova, Coah. Méx. 'La Entrevista'," filmed March 31, 2010, *YouTube Video*, 9:08, www.youtube.com/watch?v=O5gw4CZfzlk; Paredes, *Folklore and Culture*, 230.

49 Guillermo E. Hernández, "What Is a Corrido? Thematic Representation and Narrative Discourse," *Studies in Latin American Popular Culture* 18 (January 1999): 69.

50 Cathy Ragland, *Música Norteña: Mexican Migrants Creating a Nation Between Nations* (Philadelphia: Temple University Press, 2009), 38.

51 Ibid; Paredes, *A Texas-Mexican Cancionero*, xxi.

52 "*Corrido de Daniel*," audio, track on Grupo Juda, *Edición Especial Corridos*, Lion of Judah Music Productions, 1999. (My English translation.)

53 Ramón Saldívar, *Chicano Narrative: The Dialectics of Difference* (Madison, WI: The University of Wisconsin Press, 1990), 36.

54 "*Corrido de Ester*," audio, track number on Grupo Juda, *Edición Especial Corridos*, Lion of Judah Music Productions, 1999. (My English translation.)

55 Miriam Jordan, "ICE Arrests Hundreds in Mississippi Raids Targeting Immigrant Workers," *The New York Times*, August 7, 2019, www.nytimes.com/2019/08/07/us/ice-raids-mississippi.html; Jenny Jarvie, "A Mississippi Church Counts Its

Missing After ICE Raids: 'This Is a Very Dark Moment'," *Los Angeles Times*, August 19, 2019, www.latimes.com/world-nation/story/2019-08-19/mississippi-catholic-church-after-ice-raids.

56 Daniel Gonzalez, "Phoenix Pastor, Guatemalan Migrant Granted Reprieve from ICE Deportation," *AZ Central*, July 19, 2017, www.azcentral.com/story/news/politics/immigration/2017/07/19/local-pastor-guatemalan-migrant-granted-reprieve-ice-deportation/489901001/.

57 Kate Morrissey, "Oceanside Minister Faces Bond Hearing on Deportation Case," *The San Diego Union-Tribune*, June 28, 2017, www.sandiegouniontribune.com/news/immigration/sd-me-oceanside-deport-20170628-story.html.

58 Kyung Lah, "California Pastor Caught in Immigration Enforcement Net," *CNN*, August 7, 2017, www.cnn.com/2017/08/07/us/california-pastor-ice-detainee-noe-carias/index.html.

59 Edgar Zúñiga Jr., "Church Community Rallies Around North Carolina Pastor Seeking Sanctuary from Deportation," *NBS News*, July 13, 2017, www.nbcnews.com/news/latino/church-community-rallies-around-north-carolina-pastor-seeking-sanctuary-deportation-n782511.

60 "Corrido de Ester."

61 "Corrido de Daniel."

62 Saldívar, *Chicano Narrative*, 35.

63 Peña, *Música Tejana*, 75.

64 Ragland, *Música Norteña*, 38; Saldívar, *Chicano Narrative*, 36.

65 For Fiscal Years 2016 and 2017, ICE deported a total of 278,586 Mexican nationals, which was more than any other nationality. See US Immigration and Customs Enforcement, "Fiscal Year 2017 ICE Enforcement and Removal Operations Report," 15, www.ice.gov/sites/default/files/documents/Report/2017/iceEndOfYearFY2017.pdf; See also Julia Love, "Scores from Mexico, Guatemala Detained in Mississippi Raids," *Reuters*, August 8, 2019, www.reuters.com/article/us-usa-immigration-mexico/scores-from-mexico-guatemala-detained-in-mississippi-raids-idUSKCN1UY29D and Ashton Pittman, "No One Is Coming Out': Ice Raids Leave Latino Community Paralyzed with Fear," *The Guardian*, August 11, 2019, www.theguardian.com/us-news/2019/aug/11/ice-raids-latino-community-mississippi-fear.

66 María Herrera-Sobek, *Recovering the U.S. Hispanic Literary Heritage*, vol. 4 (Houston: Arte Público Press, 2006), 243.

67 Guillermo Hernandez, *Chicano Satire: A Study in Literary Culture* (Austin, TX: University of Texas Press, 1991), 13.

68 Morín, *The Legacy of Américo Paredes*, 81.

69 Michelle Goldberg, "Trump Is a White Nationalist Who Inspires Terrorism," *The New York Times*, August 5, 2019, www.nytimes.com/2019/08/05/opinion/trump-white-supremacy.html; Adam Serwer, "Conservatives Have a White-Nationalism Problem," *The Atlantic*, August 6, 2019, www.theatlantic.com/ideas/archive/2019/08/trump-white-nationalism/595555/; Anthony Rivas, "Trump's Language About Mexican Immigrants Under Scrutiny in Wake of El Paso Shooting," *ABC News*, August 4, 2019, https://abcnews.go.com/US/trumps-language-mexican-immigrants-scrutiny-wake-el-paso/story?id=64768566.

Bibliography

Anzaldúa, Gloria. *Borderlands/La Frontera: The New Mestiza*. San Francisco: Spinsters/Aunt Lute, 1987.

Barker, Eugene C., Charles Shirley Potts, and Charles W. Ramsdell. *A School History of Texas*. Chicago: Row, Peterson & Co., 1913.

Bawab, Nashwa. "A Century After the Porvenir Massacre, Remembering One of Texas' Darkest Days." *The Texas Observer*, January 31, 2018. www.texasobserver.org/century-porvenir-massacre-remembering-one-texas-darkest-days/.

Broyles-Gonzalez, Yolanda. *Life in Music/La Historia de Lydia Mendoza*. Oxford: Oxford University Press, 2001.

Burton, Antoinette, ed. *Archive Stories: Facts, Fictions, and the Writing of History*. Durham, NC: Duke University Press, 2005.

Carby, Hazel V. *Reconstructing Womanhood: The Emergence of the Afro-American Woman Novelist*. New York: Oxford University Press, 1987.

Creager, R. B. "Proceedings of the Joint Committee of the Senate and the House in the Investigation of the Texas State Ranger Force." In *Adjutant General Records*. Austin, TX: Texas State Archives, 1919.

Cuéllar, Gregory Lee. *Voices of Marginality: Exile and Return in Second Isaiah 40–55 and the Mexican Immigrant Experience*. New York: Peter Lang Publishing, 2008.

Deering, Fremont B. *The Border Boys with the Texas Rangers*. New York: Hurst & Co., 1912.

De León, Arnoldo, and Richard Griswold del Castillo. *North to Aztlán: A History of Mexican Americans in the United States*. Wheeling, IL: Harlan Davidson, 2006.

de Ortego y Gasca, Felipe. "Brands, Bandits, and Ballads: Iconic Images of Tejanos in the Literature of the Borderlands." *Journal of South Texas* 15, no. 2 (Fall 2002): 93–101.

Dirks, Nicholas B. *Autobiography of an Archive: A Scholar's Passage to India*. New York: Columbia University Press, 2015.

Edberg, Mark Cameron. *El Narcotraficante: Narcocorridos and the Construction of a Cultural Persona on the U.S.-Mexico Border*. Austin, TX: University of Texas Press, 2004.

Fagan, William Long. *Southern War Songs: Camp-Fire, Patriotic and Sentimental*. New York: M. T. Richardson, 1890.

Farge, Arlette. Foreword to the *Allure of the Archive*, by Natalie Zemon Davis. Translated by Thomas Scott-Railton. New Haven, CT: Yale University Press, 2013.

Flores, Richard R. "The Corrido and the Emergence of Texas-Mexican Social Identity." *The Journal of American Folklore* 105, no. 416 (Spring 1992): 166–82.

Giffords, Gloria Fraser. *Mexican Folk Retablos*. Albuquerque: University of New Mexico Press, 1974.

Goldberg, Michelle. "Trump Is a White Nationalist Who Inspires Terrorism." *The New York Times*, August 5, 2019. www.nytimes.com/2019/08/05/opinion/trump-white-supremacy.html.

Gonzalez, Daniel. "Phoenix Pastor, Guatemalan Migrant Granted Reprieve from ICE Deportation." *AZ Central*, July 19, 2017. www.azcentral.com/story/news/politics/immigration/2017/07/19/local-pastor-guatemalan-migrant-granted-reprieve-ice-deportation/489901001/.

Grupo Juda. *Edición Especial Corridos*. Lion of Judah Music Productions, 1999. Spotify.

Hernández, Guillermo. *Chicano Satire: A Study in Literary Culture*. Austin, TX: University of Texas Press, 1991.

———. "What Is a Corrido? Thematic Representation and Narrative Discourse." *Studies in Latin American Popular Culture* 18 (January 1999): 69–93.

Herrera-Sobek, María. *Chicano Folklore: A Handbook*. Westport, CT: Greenwood Press, 2006.

———. Vol. 4 of *Recovering the U.S. Hispanic Literary Heritage*. Houston: Arte Público Press, 2006.

Jacobs, Elizabeth. *Mexican American Literature: The Politics of Identity*. Abingdon, UK: Routledge, 2006.

Jarvie, Jenny. "A Mississippi Church Counts Its Missing After ICE Raids: 'This Is a Very Dark Moment'." *Los Angeles Times*, August 19, 2019. www.latimes.com/world-nation/story/2019-08-19/mississippi-catholic-church-after-ice-raids.

Jennings, N. A. *A Texas Ranger*. New York: C. Scribner's Sons, 1899.

Jordan, Miriam. "ICE Arrests Hundreds in Mississippi Raids Targeting Immigrant Workers." *The New York Times*, August 7, 2019. www.nytimes.com/2019/08/07/us/ice-raids-mississippi.html.

Juda—Topic. "Corrido de Jose (En Vivo)." Filmed November 2015. *YouTube Video*, 2:56. www.youtube.com/watch?v=vfI9eembQmg.

Kunin, Angelico Chavez. *From an Altar Screen: El Retablo: Tales from New Mexico*. New York: Farrer, Straus and Cudahy, 1957.

Lah, Kyung. "California Pastor Caught in Immigration Enforcement Net." *CNN*, August 7, 2017. www.cnn.com/2017/08/07/us/california-pastor-ice-detainee-noe-carias/index.html.

Limón, José E. *Mexican Ballads, Chicano Poems: History and Influence in Mexican-American Social Poetry*. Berkeley, CA: University of California Press, 1992.

Maltby, William J. *Captain Jeff: Or Frontier Life in Texas with the Texas Rangers*. Colorado, TX: Whipkey Printing Co., 1906.

Martinez, Monica Muñoz. *The Injustice Never Leaves You: Anti-Mexican Violence in Texas*. Cambridge, MA: Harvard University Press, 2018.

———. "Recuperating Histories of Violence in the Americas: Vernacular History-Making on the US-Mexico Border." *American Quarterly* 66, no. 3 (September 2014): 661–89.

Mayer, Brantz. Vol. 2 of *Mexico, Aztec, Spanish and Republican*. Hartford, CT: S. Drake and Co., 1852.

Mekelburg, Madlin. "Porvenir Massacre on Texas Border Haunts Descendants 100 Years Later." *El Paso Times*, January 26, 2018. www.elpasotimes.com/story/news/2018/01/26/100-years-later-porvenir-massacre-haunts-descendants-texas-border/1058345001/?fbclid=IwAR1IPfsu-tVu4k2TQXWmCPiWW1xw6yVjzzRGPJ20j8Fv1fy8YaCO0aGmQlI.

Mbembe, Achille. "The Power of the Archive and its Limits." In *Refiguring the Archive*, edited by Carolyn Hamilton, Verne Harris, Jane Taylor, Michele Pickover, Graeme Reid, and Razia Saleh, 19–26. Dordrecht, The Netherlands: Kluwer Academic Publishers, 2002.

Morín, José R. López. *The Legacy of Américo Paredes*. College Station, TX: Texas A&M University Press, 2006.

Morrissey, Kate. "Oceanside Minister Faces Bond Hearing on Deportation Case." *The San Diego Union-Tribune*, June 28, 2017. www.sandiegouniontribune.com/news/immigration/sd-me-oceanside-deport-20170628-story.html.

Paine, Albert Bigelow. *Captain Bill McDonald, Texas Ranger: A Story of Frontier Reform*. New York: J. J. Little & Ives Co., 1909.

Paredes, Américo. *Canto de adolescencia: Songs of Youth (1932–1937)*. Houston, TX: Arte Público Press, 2007.

———. *Folklore and Culture on the Texas-Mexican Border*. Edited by Richard Bauman. Austin, TX: CMAS Books, 1995.

———. *A Texas-Mexican Cancionero: Folksongs of the Lower Border*. Austin, TX: University of Texas Press, 1995.

Peña, Manuel. *Música Tejana: The Cultural Economy of Artistic Transformation*. College Station, TX: Texas A&M University Press, 1999.

Pérez-Torres, Rafael. *Mestizaje: Critical Uses of Race in Chicano Culture*. Minneapolis: University of Minnesota Press, 2006.

Ragland, Cathy. *Música Norteña: Mexican Migrants Creating a Nation Between Nations*. Philadelphia: Temple University Press, 2009.

Rivas, Anthony. "Trump's Language About Mexican Immigrants Under Scrutiny in Wake of El Paso Shooting." *ABC News*, August 4, 2019. https://abcnews.go.com/US/trumps-language-mexican-immigrants-scrutiny-wake-el-paso/story?id=64768566.

Roberts, Daniel Webster. *Rangers and Sovereignty*. San Antonio, TX: Wood Printing & Engraving Co., 1914.

Saldívar, José David. *Border Matters: Remapping American Cultural Studies*. Berkeley, CA: University of California Press, 1997.

———, ed. *The Rolando Hinojosa Reader: Essays Historical and Critical*. Houston: Arte Público Press, 1985.

Saldívar, Ramón. *The Borderlands of Culture: Américo Paredes and the Transnational Imaginary*. New Americanists, edited by Donald E. Pease. Durham, NC: Duke University Press, 2006.

———. *Chicano Narrative: The Dialectics of Difference*. Madison, WI: The University of Wisconsin Press, 1990.

Samora, Julian, Joe Bernal, and Albert Peña. *Gunpowder Justice: A Reassessment of the Texas Rangers*. Notre Dame, IN: University of Notre Dame Press, 1979.

Serwer, Adam. "Conservatives Have a White-Nationalism Problem." *The Atlantic*, August 6, 2019. www.theatlantic.com/ideas/archive/2019/08/trump-white-nationalism/595555/.

Sifuentes, Ernesto. "GRUPO JUDÁ en Monclova, Coah. Méx. 'La Entrevista'." Filmed March 2010. *YouTube Video*, 9:08. www.youtube.com/watch?v=O5gw4CZfzlk.

Stoler, Ann Laura. *Along the Archival Grain: Epistemic Anxieties and Colonial Sense*. Princeton: Princeton University Press, 2008.

Zarur, Elizabeth Netto Calil, and Charles Muir Lovell, eds. *Art and Faith in Mexico: The Nineteenth-Century Retablo Tradition*. Albuquerque: University of New Mexico Press, 2001.

Zúñiga, Edgar, Jr. "Church Community Rallies Around North Carolina Pastor Seeking Sanctuary from Deportation." *NBS News*, July 13, 2017. www.nbcnews.com/news/latino/church-community-rallies-around-north-carolina-pastor-seeking-sanctuary-deportation-n782511.

4 The desacralizing power of immigrant detention

In President Trump's 2017 commencement address at Liberty University, a majority white evangelical Christian school,[1] he expressed the following:

> Now it falls on the shoulders of each of you here today to protect the freedom that patriots like George earned with their incredible sacrifice. Fortunately, you have been equipped with the tools from your time right here on this campus to make the right decisions and to serve God, family and country. As you build good lives, you will also be rebuilding our nation. You'll be leaders in your communities, stewards of great institutions and defenders of liberty.[2]

With 81 percent of white evangelicals having voted for Trump in the 2016 presidential election, it behooved him to cast this audience as the ideal protectors, rebuilders, and defenders of the public good.[3] Despite the contradictory nature of Trump's relationship with US evangelical voters, their alliance is not based on shared religious ethics but rather constitute what Andrew Arato and Jean Cohen describe as an entrepreneurship between a populist leader and the conservative religious right.[4] For Trump, US evangelicals afford him enough ethical currency to motivate the ultraconservative core of the Republican Party. Conversely, the conservative religious right has instrumentalized Trump to impose its evangelical Christian agenda over both public and private spheres. The result of their relationship is an Executive Office of the President that operates according to what Nicos Poulantzas calls a "personalized presidential system." As the man at the top of the Executive, State power is personalized in Trump by religion, capitalists, and white-nationalist entrepreneurs. In the words of Poulantzas, "the man at the top of the Executive is also the hostage of a political-administrative mechanism which, to a large degree, allocates him the preeminent position."[5] Defined in this way, we can see how Trump's presidency operates as the focal point of various administrative power centers and networks, the most prominent being monopoly capitalists, white nationalists, and the conservative religious right.[6] As Poulantzas rightly explains, "there is not *one* president, but *several in one*."[7]

Integral to my proposed borderland hermeneutic is registering opposing constructions of the sacred that vie for legitimacy throughout the border region. In the Trump era, defining the sacred in the US-Mexico borderlands has occurred through a white evangelical Christian-nationalist value system. This optic is layered with distinct nodal points (politicized evangelicalism; warrior masculinity; racial superiority; monopoly capitalism; heteronormativity; elite white male power) that frame how the body politic is to understand and hence engage the US-Mexico borderlands. Among its quintessential productions is a sacralized discourse of public safety that is instantiated by a bordering violence against racialized immigrant communities who are mainly black- and brown-bodied people.[8] Thus, for a borderland hermeneutic, knowledge of the sacred cannot avoid interrogating the political-ideological domain, in large part because the US-Mexico border was born out of violent state-sanctioned activity. Just as a political-ideological discourse of the sacred (e.g. Manifest Destiny) actualized a physical border on the landscape, it requires an intervening political hermeneutic to resacralize the borderlands as an inclusive terrain that brings together an array of otherness for the sake of mutual understanding and intercultural discovery. Suggested here are not surface encounters or celebratory theater, but rather knowing the social wounds that our respective otherness carries and converting them into ways of knowing that are Other to the very elite power structures that are producing and hence being reproduced by our otherness. For those desacralized in the borderlands by the current dispensation of elite power, the prospect of not intervening only has us yield to the fate that elite power's othering intends for us—utter eradication.

Marking Trump's iteration of a sacralizing discourse of public safety is how it hostilely desacralizes the people, places, and natural landscapes of the US-Mexico borderlands. The material effect of this insidious discourse is the militarization of a "war-zoned" borderlands and the criminalization of mainly black- and brown-bodied immigrants. In purifying the borderlands of the immigrant Other, Trump's sacralized public safety sanctions a bordering violence within the executive branches of US immigration enforcement and border security. Although the convergence of elite white male power, the sacred, public safety, and borderlands is personalized at the presidential level, there are specific sites on the ground level where this tailored convergence is made manifest in the everyday lives of racially criminalized immigrant communities. It is here on the ground level that the proposed borderland hermeneutic must concentrate its interrogating energies—for such a move constitutes the base meaning of borderland, a boundary/border marked on the ground/land. Thus, on the ground level, a worthwhile site of interrogation in which the above convergence materializes is at the nexus of privately run immigrant family detention centers in south Texas and their provision of religious care services. Herein lies an acute situation for the activist impulse of a borderland hermeneutic that involves carceral control—albeit in incremental doses—over the mind, body, soul, and spirit of immigrant parents and their children. In other words, religious care services, like chaplaincy, in privately run immigrant family detention centers interface between Trump's sacralized public safety (i.e. "Make America Safe Again!") and immigrant religious care needs. Because this juncture is framed by issues related to faith, the sacred, spiritual well-being, and emancipation, detained immigrant families are vulnerable to the full flexing of Trump's sacralized public safety.

Sacralized public safety and its bordering violence

In both his scripted and unscripted speeches, Trump often pivots from Americans as a righteous people to public safety as a sacred duty or vice versa. Beginning with his 2017 Inaugural Address, he declared that "Americans want great schools for their children, safe neighborhoods for their families, and good jobs for themselves. These are just and reasonable demands of righteous people and a righteous public."[9] For him, part of what renders Americans a righteous people is their patriotic love for the United States: "when you open your heart to patriotism, there is no room for prejudice. . . . The Bible tells us [Psalm 133: 11] 'How good and pleasant it is when God's people live together in unity.' "[10] With hearts filled with patriotism, the result is a united people, which based on Trump's reading of the Bible represents God's people. In tying patriotic Americans to divinely righteous people, Trump strategically weaves public safety into his religious nationalist narrative, thereby assigning it sacred status. At a rally in Melbourne, Florida, for instance, he expressed to his supporters that "the American nation remains the greatest symbol of liberty, of freedom, and justice on the face of God's Earth. . . . It's now that we have our sacred duty, and we have no choice, and we want this choice: to defend our country, to protect its values, and to serve its great, great citizens."[11] In aligning America's greatness with divine favor, Trump's tactic is what Arato and Cohen refer to as "the confiscation of religion by populists and attempts to use it to sanctify the nation, the people, or the leader."[12] Essentially, for Trump, an America under God renders its security a sacred duty. Similar to how Manifest Destiny served to sacralize Anglo-American imperialism in the mid-nineteenth century, Trump's investments in religious language aim to sacralize US security operations. At the forefront of Trump's sacralized security is the construction of a colossal wall at the US-Mexico border. Indeed, his entire border security operations—from wall to increased military personnel to tent courthouses—falls under his notion of sacred duty.[13]

In decoding Trump's sacralized public safety, it is important to define whose God he is invoking in his speeches. From a political standpoint, his "God" references have in view the 81 percent white evangelical Christian vote. On December 8, 2017, at the Faith and Freedom Coalition's Road to Majority Conference, Trump took the podium stating crassly, "thank you, Ralph. . . . He said we got 81 percent of the vote. I want to know, who are the 19 percent?"[14] In this setting, Trump deployed a repertoire of Christian references that resonated with his majority white evangelical audience. Using the Old Testament text of Isaiah 1:17, he aligned his "America First" cause with the righteous cause of the evangelical community. As he expressed, "we will not back down from doing what is right. Because, as the Bible tells us [applause]: We know that truth will prevail, that God's glorious wisdom will shine through, and that the good and decent people of this country will get the change they voted for and that they so richly deserve."[15] Here, the evangelical identity of Trump's "God" also represents the identity of what he views as authentic America. As he voiced to his supporters at a "Make America Great Again" rally in Pensacola, Florida, "we've stopped the Government's attacks on our Judeo-Christian values, because we know that families and churches, not Government officials, know best how to create a strong and loving community."[16] Ultimately, the links Trump makes between the public good, the religious right, and a "God" recognizable first and foremost to white evangelicals mark a form of religious nationalism that conflate public safety with divine will. As described in previous chapters, this strategy points to a sacred apparatus of burgeoning elite power that sets the threshold of violence to the realms of the divine. Here again, elite white male power has seized upon the sacred to enable its reproduction through sacralized acts of violence (i.e. public safety). While Trump's investments in the sacred are rhetorical, as President, he holds sufficient executive power to convert rhetoric into everyday activities that at one end reproduce his power base and on the other end legitimates eradicating forms of violence at all levels of government.[17]

Subtending Trump's mantra of "Make America Safe Again" is the formulation of an archenemy. Since the days of his presidential campaign, he has identified "Mexicans" and Muslims as the primary foes of Christian America and the US-Mexico border as the battlefront of national security and public safety. In typical apocalyptic fashion, Trump often describes the threat on the southern border as a national emergency where "illegal immigrants" assume the form of some large poisonous blob that is pouring into the country, preying on its citizens, and polluting the public good. With the sanctity of authentic American life at stake, public safety requires a bordering violence or, in Trump's favorite words, "throwing them the hell out of our country."[18] The "they" versus "we" dichotomy within Trump's sacralized public safety calls for physical acts of exclusion that are concentrated on the US-Mexico border.[19] As he declared in a 2017 rally speech in Cedar Rapids, Iowa, "No issue is more central to public safety than the issue of immigration and border security."[20] Such exclusionary acts involve the construction of a colossal border wall, mass deportation, family separation, and immigrant detention—all of which seek to inflict anew postcolonial-like traumas on mainly black- and brown-bodied border crossers. Rather than bridging communities together in the US-Mexico borderlands, Trump reinvests in the State's nineteenth-century sacred apparatus of white Protestant (now Evangelical) superiority, and the border-sovereignty-citizenship triplex in order to unleash the most devasting forms of bordering violence against the migrant Other. Indeed, this link between political discourse and border security reflects a historical pattern within the US-Mexico borderlands, starting with the Mexican-American War and the 1848 Treaty of Hidalgo. The recurrence of this bordering violence gives way to an intervening borderland hermeneutic that is vigilant of malicious political discourse, especially the kind directed at racialized minority communities in the borderlands. The yearly reports issued by US Immigration and Customs Enforcement (ICE) remind us of how Trump's sacralized public safety has a direct human correspondence, with Mexicans at the top of ICE's immigrant arrests and deportations in 2017.[21] In the words of Trump, "We are liberating. People are screaming from their windows, 'Thank you, thank you,' to the Border Patrol and to General Kelly's great people that come in and grab these thugs and throw them the hell out."[22] Trump's notion of liberation frames the State's border violence within the context of a war victory against an invading enemy, which here is the migrant Other. Moreover, liberation is also tied to Trump's sacralized public safety and as such sanctions the use of military war tactics as part of US border security. Though militarizing border security may appear as an exaggerated response to forced migration, it corresponds to the threshold of violence set by Trump's sacralized public safety. In the same way Manifest Destiny sacralized Anglo-American imperialism, Trump's sacralized public safety has legitimated the use of military-caliber violence to secure the US-Mexico border from the "invading" migrant other.

To legitimate the performance of bordering violence in the US-Mexico borderlands, Trump's sacralized public safety relies on abiding racist stereotypes (fostered by mass media, entertainment industry, school textbooks, etc.) of brown- and black-bodied immigrants as criminal, economically burdensome, low-skilled, physically diseased, and culturally inferior.[23] This pivot to brown- and black-bodied criminality marks the desacralizing strategies of Trump's sacred duty of public safety. Armed with a white supremacist logic, the ultimate aim is the desacralization of an entire people group via a series of dehumanizing and criminalizing categories, such as "animals," "not human," "criminal aliens," and "illegal immigrants."[24] By way of racial association, all brown- and black-bodied immigrants are implicated as criminals—rendering both child and adult as viable targets of the State's sacralized bordering violence.[25] Under Trump's sacred apparatus, the State's threshold of violence is on pace to reaching its intended level of human eradication. Here again, this admits to the potency of the sacred, not simply as an instrument for garnering political support but more importantly as the primary source for manufacturing eradicating forms of violence. From the sacred, the State is able to expand the depth of its othering operations to the realms of the divine, thereby rendering migrants, asylum seekers, and refugees as not just enemies of this age but cosmic enemies beyond time and space.

Global expansion of immigrant family detention market

The converging forces that gave rise to the US-Mexico borderlands reveal multiple agendas that range from the ideological-political to the socio-economic. Hence a borderland hermeneutic knows to turn its critical gaze toward the economic domain in rectifying the injustices of state-sanctioned bordering violence. Currently, monopoly capitalism, private prison companies, and corporatized government seek to profit from a desacralized migrant Other in the US-Mexico borderlands. Again, a borderland hermeneutic is attentive not only to the State's sacred apparatus that renders the migrant Other as a nonsacred being, but also the entrepreneurs investing in such a desacralization in order to make a lasting profit. In this way, the sacred materializes into economic gain, which in turn renews the public's confidence in the State's sacred apparatus as a facilitator of progress and wealth. With the eradication of the State's desacralized migrant other, elite power is credited hero status and therefore kept in power. Yet at the same time, the State's desacralization of the migrant other also relies on wealth production as crucial to the public currency of its sacred apparatus. At work here is not a new iteration of elite power, but rather the continuation of a US imperial impulse whereby the primary goal is total domination. Different from the mid-nineteenth century, the desacralization under Trump's sacred apparatus has in view domination through the exploitation of migrant bodies. It is not enough to simply remove migrant bodies from the body politic; Trump's desacralization of black- and brown-bodied migrants, asylum seekers, and refugees must also ensure the accumulation of massive sums of wealth for elite power. Hence the desacralization of the migrant other defines what is sacred for elite power (US white male evangelical superiority and the border-sovereignty-citizenship triplex) and as such defines what is exploitable. In the same way that the State's sacred apparatus sets the threshold of violence to the level of total eradication, it also sets the threshold of wealth production to the level of total domination. In the Trump era, it is the desacralized migrant other who is set to determine the fulfillment of these two thresholds. For as it stands, black- and brown-bodied migrants, asylum seekers, and refugees are the people destined for economic exploitation and then earthly eradication. In keeping with the US's early acts of conquest, the current form of elite power has reinvested in the sacred not so much to expand the US's territorial boundaries as with Manifest Destiny and the 1848 Treaty of Guadalupe Hidalgo, but instead to conquer migrant bodies. Here, their bodies represent the new frontier for US conquest. For on their bodies the war of conquest is waged, a new border is drawn, and a new resource is extracted for the production of wealth. In this new iteration of US imperialism, each desacralized body functions as disposable territory of elite power in which they are captured, consumed, ravaged, depleted, and discarded.

In the present era, Trump's sacralized public safety has reinvigorated the private prison sector in the US-Mexico borderlands by deeming nonsacred all border crossers (adults, youth, children, and infants). When viewed from the vantage point of the marketplace, the desacralization of mainly brown- and black-bodied migrants represents a conversion process in which racially criminalized border crossers serve as a revenue source for private prison companies. As the state's nonsacred, border crossers enter the profit-making machine of the private prison sector, where they are racially criminalized at the border and then separated, detained, and finally deported to their deaths.[26] As daunting as this machinery appears—in part because it morphs constantly—the immigrant family detention market represents a relatively stable domain for a borderland hermeneutic to unleash its critical energies.

Although immigrant family detention in the United States represents a fairly recent market niche for private prison companies, news of its profitability has gained the attention of international companies like the British security firm Serco.[27] In the summer prior to Donald Trump's presidency, Serco had successfully lobbied local government officials of Jim Wells County, Texas, near the Mexican border to enter into negotiations for a new 500-bed family detention facility at an abandoned nursing home.[28] Preceding such efforts was Serco's yearlong lobbying activity with federal lawmakers and key officials at the US Department of Homeland Security (DHS) and Immigration and Customs Enforcement (ICE) in Washington, DC.[29] It was reported that Serco had employed a number of US-based lobbyists, including a former senior ICE official, Kate Mills.[30] On June 9, 2016, elected government officials of Jim Wells County held a formal public hearing in which they and Serco representatives fielded questions from local residents and Texas-based immigrant rights advocates.[31] Prior to the meeting, Catholic Bishop Michael Mulvey of the Diocese of Corpus Christi issued a statement before the hearing urging county officials to reconsider allowing Serco to operate the detention facility, stating that "its existence goes against human decency."[32] There was also the pro bono legal group RAICES who launched an online petition drive urging people to send letters to President Barack Obama asking him to stop the negotiations between Serco, Jim Wells County, and the DHS.[33] At the public hearing, opponents gave examples of numerous scandals Serco had faced at its detention centers in the UK and Australia.[34] Among the most publicized examples was the Yarl's Wood immigration detention center in Bedfordshire, England, where since 2007 it had faced a series of abuse allegations, the most egregious being the repeated sexual assault of female detainees by male guards.[35] In response to the public's opposition, the elected officials voted unanimously against entering into contract agreements with Serco and the DHS.

Despite this setback, Serco was nevertheless determined to secure a spot within the lucrative family detention market in south Texas. Just a few days after the public hearing, its representatives moved on to Duval County, which is adjoined to Jim Wells County, and pitched the same contract proposal to its elected officials. On July 11, 2016, county officials voted to begin contract negotiations with Serco, and by July 15 they had submitted an application to ICE for federal approval of their contract agreement. Similar to its contract with Jim Wells County, Serco agreed to provide the physical structure, equipment, personnel, and services for a 500-bed family detention facility in the jurisdiction of Duval County.[36] A major concern for immigrant rights advocates was when Duval County Judge Ricardo O. Carrillo decided not to hold a public hearing on the county's contract agreement with Serco.[37] As Bishop Mulvey expressed in a formal statement issued on July 14, 2016:

> As a faith leader, I believe strongly that local communities and local people often hold the keys to local solutions and that we must let community voices lead us in discussions on what we want our communities to look like and what values we want them to reflect. Very few community voices were heard from on Monday.[38]

Moreover, the Texas-based immigrant advocacy group Grassroots Leadership sought signatures for a petition addressed to Duval County officials. In it, they emphasized Serco's history of human rights abuses in the UK and Australia as well as demanded a formal public hearing.[39] Undeterred by this opposition, Serco's contract agreement with Duval County continued through the process of federal approval without any community input.

As a last resort, Grassroots Leadership awaited a favorable final decision from Judge Karin Crump of the 250th District Court regarding its May 2016 lawsuit against the Texas Department of Family and Protective Services. For private prison companies like Serco, US-based CoreCivic (formerly the Corrections Corporation of America, or CCA) and GEO Group, this particular state department played a crucial role in the branding of family detention as a residential facility by issuing them temporary child care licenses.[40] Under the lawsuit, such a license was called into question by members of Grassroots Leadership and former detainees, arguing that the current family detention model constitutes a prison and not a child care facility. On December 2, 2016, Judge Crump issued a final judgment on the matter—ruling against the state of Texas from issuing child care licenses to the private prison companies operating family detention facilities in south Texas.[41] Although CoreCivic and GEO Group continued to cast their respective family detention facilities as residential centers,[42] Duval County officials decided to pull out of its contract agreement with Serco, hence thwarting—albeit temporarily—the global expansion of the family detention market in the US-Mexico borderlands.[43] Indeed, this victory was short-lived in that immediately after Donald Trump was declared winner of the 2016 presidential election, the stocks of CoreCivic and GEO Group began to rise significantly in value. Having campaigned on a religious nationalist/nativist platform in which immigrants from the global south were repeatedly demonized, his presidential win was described thusly by one press report: "Thanks to President Donald Trump, America's private prisons appear to be entering a gold age."[44]

Within a few weeks in office, Trump's sacralized public safety revealed its anti-immigrant agenda with the signing of two major executive orders (EOs). On January 25, 2017, at the DHS headquarters, he first signed Executive Order 13767 ("Border Security and Immigration Enforcement Improvements") followed by Executive Order 13768 ("Enhancing Public Safety in the Interior of the United States"). Central to these orders is the sanctioning of mass arresting raids, detention, and deportation of all "removable aliens."[45] Again, following these EOs, the stock values for CoreCivic and GEO Group continued their upsurge, marking a new era in the US immigrant detention market. Yet an even more resounding message of affirmation was sent to these companies when the Attorney General Jeff Sessions rescinded an Obama-era directive to either reduce or decline to renew private-prison contracts after they came due.[46] As he directed in his public memorandum, the Federal Bureau of Prisons are to return to using privately operated prisons. Within the first few months of Trump's administration, his public safety policies had firmly established his presidency as the grandmaster expander of the US immigration detention industrial complex.

On March 23, 2018, Trump signed a $1.3 trillion spending bill for Fiscal Year (FY) 2018, allotting $11 billion to ICE of which $4.1 billion was designated for mass arresting raids,[47] detention,[48] and removal operations.[49] From the latter sum, ICE budgeted over $3 billion[50] to expand its detention capacity to the average daily population (ADP) of 40,520 (38,020 daily adults and 2,500 daily families).[51] This was an increase of 2,414 from the cumulative ADP at the end of FY 2017 (36,628 daily adults and 1,476 daily families).[52] And compared to the cumulative ADP for FY 2016 during the Obama era, the increase was much higher, by a total of 6,144 (ADP of 32,770 daily adults and 1,606 daily families).[53] For Trump's FY 2019 annual budget, $2.8 billion was budgeted for ICE to expand detention capacity to an average daily adult population of 49,500 and an average daily family population of 2,500 for a total of 52,000 beds.[54] Under this regime, the aim has been to generate a sufficient supply of brown and black criminalized bodies to ensure the longevity and expansion of the US immigrant family detention market. Whether through family separation[55] on the US-Mexico border or ICE's interior enforcement efforts,[56] the average daily population in the US immigrant detention market is a booming industry.[57] As for the family immigrant detention market in particular, Trump ensured its permanent profitability with a new immigration rule in August 2019. Here, Trump replaced his inhumane family separation policy with a new family detention rule, allowing the Department of Homeland Security and ICE to detain families indefinitely.[58] This rule bypasses the terms of the 1997 Flores Settlement, which limited the time children can spend in detention and set minimum standards for the holding facilities for families and children.[59] These expansion measures are indicative of the thresholds of violence and wealth production that Trump's sacred apparatus has set for the migrant Other. The fact that the State's violence goes as far as targeting infants attests to the breadth and depth of Trump's othering strategies for border-crossing families. This human threshold marks less the consequences of criminally racializing narratives about border crossers than the lethal potency of Trump's investments in the sacred. Hence through the sacred, Trump produces a desacralizing force that expands the spectrum of othering. Its range encompasses the othering that criminally racializes border crossers in the physical as well as cosmically demonizes them in the metaphysical. Such a spectrum is commensurate with the radical nature of violence that the State has manufactured against border-crossing families. Though their eradication from the body politic is of utmost importance for the current iteration of elite US power, this result only occurs after they have been exhausted as a raw resource of revenue. With their desacralization immune to humanitarian reason, the extent of Trump's sacralized border violence against border-crossing families encounters minimal restraints. Trump's investments in the sacred (white American evangelicalism and the border-sovereignty-citizenship triplex) have delivered to him the sole command of the public good and its corresponding security. Hence, what from a humanitarian perspective may appear to be egregious inhuman treatment of border-crossing families—as in family separation, kids detained in cages,[60] "remain in Mexico" policy,[61] or indefinite detention—aligns perfectly within the governing logic of Trump's sacred apparatus. Although not limited to white supremacy, monopoly capitalism, and white American evangelicalism, these domains of Trump's sacred apparatus not only inform his version of the public good, but they are also prioritized under his public safety operations.

The current social wounds inflicted on border-crossing families are in many ways a continuation of the postcolonial traumas that ethnic Mexicans endured after the Mexican-American War (1846–1848). These interconnected wounds point to a reoccurring pathology of violence that is undergirded by sacralized notions of white supremacy and America's divine chosenness. For border-crossing families, however, their social wounds occur not at the outset of a burgeoning US empire but instead under the full weight of US monopoly capitalism. Hence, the social critique of their desacralization must have in view Trump's sacralization of monopoly capitalism in conjunction with white supremacy. Factoring in the concentration of wealth into Trump's sacred apparatus reveals a mode of desacralization that prefers to exploit and eradicate border-crossing families rather than colonize them. Here, the State has no intention of incorporating border-crossing families into the body politic, as suggested in colonization; instead their desacralization converts them into a disposable resource for the wealthy elite.

Privatized religious care in privately run immigrant family detention

Subtending Trump's desacralization of border-crossing families is the mass accumulation of wealth for the elite class in US society. Those directly in a position to profit are the private prison companies contracted to run the State's immigrant family detention operations. Though this industrial complex relies directly on the desacralization of border-crossing families, its ultimate legitimation comes from Trump's sacralized public safety. In other words, those charged with its implementation and supervision represent sacred actors, for they are securing what Trump has deemed sacred (white supremacy, monopoly capitalism, American evangelism, and the border-sovereignty-citizenship triplex). Here the private prison companies running immigrant family detention fulfill both the threshold of violence and the threshold of wealth production that Trump's sacred apparatus has set for border-crossing families. With ample ethical immunity under Trump's sacralized public safety, their security activities privilege long-term incarceration and maximum revenue production.

The effectiveness of the immigrant family detention industrial complex lies in its ability to exploit border-crossing families as a resource for wealth production and then eradicate them through deportation. This process can be plainly described as maximum wealth production through all-consuming micro-acts of violence. In terms of wealth production, the exploitable resource comes in bulk form of entire family units; whereas, the micro-acts of violence occur at the everyday level through regimented movements, surveillance, scare tactics, and daily containment.

Integral to Trump's sacralized public safety is how it legitimates for his constituents the immigrant family detention industrial complex. This ethical coverage, however, does not extend to the detained families themselves precisely because their aim as asylum seekers in not to affirm Trump's sacred apparatus but rather the freedom to settle in US society. In other words, they cross the border not in pursuit of their desacralization but with the hope of receiving asylum in the US. In many ways, their desire for peaceful and meaningful settlement underscores their self-understanding as asylum seekers.[62] Hence, to accept their criminalization in immigrant family detention would indeed run counter to how asylum-seeking families fundamentally understand themselves and their migratory journey.

The unwillingness of border-crossing families to accept their own desacralization is a mind-set that private prison companies seek to root out in immigrant family detention. Like the State, therefore, these companies also invest in the sacred as a way to sway detainees to embrace the State's desacralization of them and their ensuing fate of deportation. The key domain of the sacred that private prison companies have used to persuade detainees is religious care. Within the religious domain, detainees are less suspicious of religious care largely because they view it as a magnanimous force. Yet for private prison companies, the provision of religious care serves as the ideal instrument for ensuring the detainees' compliance to their profit-making agenda. In immigrant family detention, religious care consists of a complex assemblage of the sacred that seeks to induce a strong sense of culpability within asylum-seeking families, such that they view their border crossings and detainment as part of a series of sinful decisions. By conflating their detainment with sin, detainees are positioned to define their predicament as part of God's discipline. The aim here is not to fulfill their hopes for asylum but rather to subject them to the State's desacralization project.

Not only can religious care legitimate the State's desacralization of asylum-seeking families, but even more troubling it can ensure that private prison companies continue to profit from this form of migrant othering. Hence, essential to a borderland hermeneutic is to engage critically the nexus of privatized religious care, privately run immigrant detention, and corporatized government; for together they are brokering the sanctity of border-crossing families according to a white nationalist agenda and monopoly capitalism. Of vital concern in the present era is the clutching grip private prison companies, corporatized government, US evangelicalism, and white nationalism have on the levers that determine who is worthy of human sanctity in the US-Mexico borderlands. Yet even more acute is asylum-seeking families' forced acceptance of the State's desacralization within the domain of religious care in privately run immigrant family detention.

Maintaining cash flows through privatized religious care

Currently in the United States, CoreCivic and GEO Group are the only private prison companies federally contracted to manage two of ICE's three immigration family detention centers. Berks Family Residential Center in Pennsylvania is the only facility not under contract with a private prison company. At this facility, ICE officials in conjunction with Berks County manage all operations and services. Since 2014, GEO Group has managed Karnes County Residential Center in Karnes City, Texas (contract renewal date 2020), and CoreCivic has managed the South Texas Family Residential Center in Dilley, Texas (contract renewal date September 2021). As stipulated in their contracts with ICE, both companies are paid to supply and oversee all support services at their respective detention facilities. Among these services is included equal access to religious care, worship space, and religious literature. The provision of religious care for detainees is set forth in the ICE Family Residential Standards (FRS) as follows: "residents of different religious beliefs are provided reasonable and equitable opportunities to participate in the practices of their respective faiths, constrained only by concerns about safety, security, and the orderly operation of the facility."[63] As generic as these standards may appear, they mark the State's authority over religious faith and practice within facilities legally defined as residential.[64] According to federal detention standards, religious practices include "worship, observances, services, meetings, ceremonies, etc., associated with a particular faith; access to religious publications, religious symbolic items, religious counseling, and religious study classes; and adherence to dietary rules and restrictions."[65] Though the State has defined the standards for religious care in immigrant family detention, their interpretation and implementation are delegated to the private prison companies rather than separate local ecclesial bodies or faith communities. The State's encroachments into the religious domain are indeed unwarranted given the noncriminal status of the detainees themselves, in particular children and infants. As asylum seekers, the parents with children in family detention should be afforded their constitutional right of complete religious freedom without state constraints or involvement.[66] Yet in the present era, the State and private prison companies have seized control of the religious domain in immigrant family detention by defining the place of worship, times of access, and criteria for religious leadership not to protect the detainees' right to religious freedom but rather to constrain it.

Rather than turning to local faith communities that specialize in nonprofit religious care, the State has contracted CoreCivic and GEO Group, both of which specialize in security and prison management, to administer the State's religious care standards in immigrant family detention. The result is a filtering of religious care services through a nonreligious organization that operates under a carceral logic in order to generate profits. This is particularly troubling given that emancipation, freedom, and liberation are hallmarks of many religious traditions, in particular the majority Catholic faith of Central American asylum-seeking families.[67] If containment remains central to the business side of CoreCivic and GEO Group, then we can see how religious practices that call for the freedom of observant noncriminal families from detention would go against these companies' core profit-making agenda. For this reason, these companies seek to implement religious care from the vantage point of carcerality and not religious liberty.

For companies like CoreCivic and GEO Group, concerns about safety, security, and orderly operation end not with state compliance but rather with their wealth production goals. For CoreCivic, the decline in its stock price was an issue at its 2017 annual meeting of stockholders. In its annual report, company leaders attributed declining stocks to its family detention facility in Dilley:

> Although our stock price recovered somewhat once the DOJ [Department of Justice] and DHS [Department of Homeland Security] subsequently extended certain of our contracts and entered into new contracts with us, our stock price also declined based on a reduction of cash flows resulting from a renegotiation and extension of our contract at the South Texas Family Residential Center utilized by ICE to accommodate the influx of Central American female adults with children arriving illegally on the Southwest border while they await the outcome of immigration hearings.[68]

From the angle of "cash flows," CoreCivic's proxy role within ICE's custody operations reveals a system of profit-making that occurs primarily through immigrant containment. Subsumed within this system is religious care to the extent that it also works to fulfill CoreCivic's core business function of immigrant capture. In remaining a profitable business, CoreCivic depends on anti-immigrant legislation—either from Congress or the president's EOs—that leans toward the criminalization and arrest of border crossers and undocumented immigrants. And like the GEO Group, it also relies on the State's willingness to outsource ICE's custody operations to private prison companies. At a meta-level, CoreCivic sees government policies as either facilitating or hindering its cash flows. What this registers is a pursuit of wealth in which entrepreneurial energies and economic resources are rewarded when the ruling ideology and government policies work to criminalize undocumented immigrants.[69] In the Trump era, all sectors of the federal government are operating in unison toward the mass criminalization of mainly black and brown immigrant bodies. Those poised to reap maximum benefit are private prison companies.

In 2016, GEO Group was at twenty-two total US immigrant detention facilities and in 2017 expanded to twenty-six facilities nationwide.[70] Like CoreCivic, the GEO Group relies on criminalizing immigration policies to maximize its investors' profits—for such policies ensure a consistent supply of detainees at its respective facilities.[71] Apart from reaping profits from criminalizing anti-immigrant legislation, the company also increases its cash flows by maintaining low operational costs. Among the company's most deplorable money-saving strategies is forcing detainees to work for sub-minimum wages ($1.00 per day), covering mostly the company's janitorial upkeep and maintenance needs.[72] This forced labor scheme stems from the company's carceral mission of ensuring that detainees remain in its detention facility.

All sectors of the detention facility are attuned to its carceral mission, including its office of religious care. Hence, to curtail religious practices that promote freedom from detention with legal status, CoreCivic and GEO Group hire their own religious care personnel at their respective facilities. As company employees, religious care personnel are beholden to the company's core profit-making system. Posing a threat to this agenda are religious practices and instruction that inspire emancipation. Here the moral conscience and political leanings of religious care personnel are vetted in such a way that these companies ensure the hire of nonthreatening candidates to their profit-making system.

Detention chaplains as company employees

Of primary concern for a borderland hermeneutic is the formulation and standardization of othering mechanisms that render border crossers the nonsacred human other. At stake here are people's livelihoods in the borderlands. For as border history shows us, all discourse devised and deployed by colonizing power strives to repurpose the material lives of borderland people. In the current era of Trump's sacralized public safety, the designated nonsacred human other of the borderlands are black- and brown-bodied people (regardless of whether they are border crossers or border citizens). This ruling ideology has birthed a militarized landscape, factories of human capture, and architecture designed for human suffering. As such, the US-Mexico borderlands serves as the playground for elite power to exploit, ravage, and discard—leaving behind communities of despair, indifference, and with a low sense of self-worth. To disrupt this trajectory, an intervening borderland discourse must emerge and put forth a different understanding of the sacred Other, which in turn can serve as the basis for a life-enriching material reality for border crossers and border communities alike. To achieve this, however, our efforts must begin with dismantling the ruling ideology at the molecular level.

A nexus-site that relies on Trump's sacralized public safety is in the provision of chaplains for privately run immigrant family detention centers. More than just a humanitarian ruse by the elite power structures, this nexus-site renders visible the micro depth to which this assemblage of power has gone to reproduce itself. In privately run immigrant family detention, chaplains are company employees. Although they are hired to fulfill ICE's standards for immigrant detention, their position represents paid labor that ties it to the production goals of the hiring private prison company. Similar to security guards, medical care personnel, case workers, and maintenance staff in the facility, chaplains serve in the interests of the hiring private prison company. From a profit-making standpoint, their employment marks commitment to the company's profit-making goals, which involves them not being an economic liability—such as abusing a detainee, stealing supplies, being late to work, or faking a job injury.

As employees of the private prison company, their religious tradition is also subsumed under the company's hierarchical structure of control and profit-making agenda. This reflects the marketization of religious tradition within the immigrant detention industrial complex. In other words, the affiliated religious tradition of candidate chaplains represents a hiring criterion for the private prison company such that it is vetted for its compatibility. In 2018, CoreCivic advertised its chaplain position at its South Texas Family Residential Center. As stated in its job description, "the Chaplain coordinates all religious services and related activities at the facility and does pastoral work, including pastoral counseling."[73] In terms of credentials, ICE requires that facility chaplains have "the minimum qualifications of clinical pastoral education or equivalent specialized training, and the endorsement of the appropriate religious certifying body."[74] Although these are the state's minimum qualifications, CoreCivic requires many other qualifications in the hiring of detention chaplains. First, the chaplain must have graduated from an accredited college or university with a bachelor's degree in divinity, theology, or religion. Second, the company prefers for its chaplains to have a master's degree from a seminary, school of theology, or university in divinity, theology, biblical studies, or a related field. In addition, the company requires five years full-time pastoral experience and eligibility for denominational endorsement or equivalent certification. In sum, CoreCivic states that the chaplain "must demonstrate knowledge of the principles and methods of conducting religious services, teaching religious studies, administering sacraments, and practices of counseling."[75] As the gatekeeper, the private prison company serves as the arbiter and authenticator of religious credentials to ensure complete loyalty to its profit-making ethos. The transcendent nature of religious tradition and its conferring of spiritual authority do not protect it from this vetting dynamic, for it, too, is subject to privatization.

The concessions religious candidates make in order to be hired as detention chaplains have less to do with the religious diversity of the detainees themselves than the profit-making agenda of the company. Again, it is imperative that like other paid staff, chaplains facilitate profit production in the company's detention facility. Admittedly, the hiring process for detention chaplains requires that they tailor aspects of their religious tradition to fit the profit-making ethos of the private prison company. The ideal candidates, however, are those whose religious tradition already comes with compatible traits such that minimal tweaking is required on the part of the religious candidate. In many ways, the company's leverage over the hiring process reconstitutes the religious tradition by privatizing it for immigrant family detention. Such a dynamic bespeaks the gatekeeping function of the private prison company not only in authenticating religious credentials and pastoral authority of religious candidates, but also in extending the market of chaplaincy to privately run immigrant family detention. An important question, therefore, is which religious tradition has the propensity to being privatized for service in privately run immigrant family detention? Such a religious tradition would need to possess monopolistic-capitalist values, patriotic fervor, and indeed be supportive of Trump's sacralized public safety.

Conclusion

In the US-Mexico borderlands, systems, politics, nature, cultures, the marketplace, religion, ethnicity, gender, and sexuality are encountered in everyday life at distinct nodal points. Here, everyday life in the borderlands represents a constant interfacing dynamic of difference and otherness. Such a way of life gives way to a borderland instinct whereby elite power is always understood as the product of intersecting forces. The colonizing forces that brought forth the US-Mexico border also engendered a counter stance among the colonized that resists their desacralization by interrogating its source.[76] As reflected with the 1899 Zacate Creek residents and the Bible border *corridos*, this stance emerges as an intervening hermeneutic of the borderlands that inspires critical interrogation of the current iterations of State desacralization in the US-Mexico borderlands. Similar to previous conflicts with elite power in the border region, current forms of State desacralization continue to rely on an apparatus of the sacred that includes white supremacist logic, religious nationalism, and official archives. As such, its aims remain the same—the mass annihilation of the black- and brown-bodied border crossers. To interrogate desacralizing power in the spirit of those colonized in the US-Mexico borderlands, activist confrontation, subversive artistry, and clever scrutiny are indispensable modes of action. When applied to the current moment, immigration detention represents the State's meta archive for desacralizing border crossers and in turn sacralizing elite power.

Immigration detention archives border crossers as criminal, stateless, and disposable. Through its religious services this archival process converts into a desacralizing power that justifies the State's violent border security operations. By employing a borderland hermeneutic, this archive can be confronted by offering a counter archive of the lived experiences of border crossers, particularly as they pertain to ideas of the sacred. As a counter archive, the lived experiences of border crossers not only can raise critical awareness about the State's desacralizing agenda but, more importantly, can diminish its impact.

In harnessing the interrogating instincts of a borderland hermeneutic, there is an understanding that desacralizing power is embodied in agents of the State (e.g. Health Inspectors and Texas Rangers). In other words, a borderland hermeneutic knows to focus its interrogating energies on the actual people enacting the State's desacralization of border crossers. For at the human level lie social networks of affiliation, community relationships, government officials, border patrol, doctors, nurses, teachers, clergy, and chaplains. From the human level a borderland hermeneutic then turns its critical gaze to the institutional domain, such as seminaries, churches, schools, health care facilities, and government offices. The critique of these two realms can occur in multiple forms—from formal protests to sacralizing cultural productions. This tandem critique is never final but rather a continual part of the struggle to exist as whole human beings in a region of the world born out of desacralizing elite power.

Notes

1 National Center for Education Statistics, "College Navigator: Liberty University," https://nces.ed.gov/collegenavigator/?q=liberty+university&s=all&id=232557#enrolmt; "Graduating into History," *Liberty Journal* (Summer 2017): 18–31, https://issuu.com/libertyuniversity/docs/lj_summer17_issuu?e=4413175/49598542.
2 "Read President Trump's Liberty University Commencement Speech," *TIME*, May 13, 2017, http://time.com/4778240/donald-trump-liberty-university-speech-transcript/.
3 Gregory A. Smith, "Among White Evangelicals, Regular Churchgoers Are the Most Supportive of Trump," *Fact Tank: News in the Numbers: Pew Research Center*, April 26, 2017, www.pewresearch.org/fact-tank/2017/04/26/among-white-evangelicals-regular-churchgoers-are-the-most-supportive-of-trump/.
4 Andrew Arato and Jean L. Cohen, "Civil Society, Populism, and Religion," *Constellations, An International Journal of Critical and Democratic Theory* 24, no. 3 (September 2017): 292.

5 Nicos Poulantzas, *State, Power, Socialism* (London: Verso, 2000), 228.
6 Chase Peterson-Withorn, "The $4.3 Billion Cabinet: See What Each Top Trump Advisor Is Worth," *Forbes*, July 5, 2017, www.forbes.com/sites/chasewithorn/2017/07/05/the-4-3-billion-cabinet-see-what-each-top-trump-advisor-is-worth/#4d0f74c95dfc; Michelle Goldberg, "Donald Trump, the Religious Right's Trojan Horse," *The New York Times*, January 27, 2017, www.nytimes.com/2017/01/27/opinion/sunday/donald-trump-the-religious-rights-trojan-horse.html; "Trump Taps Hate Group Fellow Ronald Mortensen for Important Post Dealing with Refugees," *Hatewatch, Southern Poverty Law Center*, May 25, 2018, www.splcenter.org/hatewatch/2018/05/25/trump-taps-hate-group-fellow-ronald-mortensen-important-post-dealing-refugees.
7 Poulantzas, *State, Power, Socialism*, 229.
8 Chris Baynes, "US Detaining Hundreds of African Migrants at Border After 'Dramatic Rise' in Arrivals," *Independent*, June 7, 2019, www.independent.co.uk/news/world/americas/us-border-mexico-immigration-africa-trump-congo-angola-a8948241.html; Robbie Feinberg and Bonnie Petrie, "African Migrants Are Becoming a New Face of the U.S. Border Crisis," *NPR*, June 20, 2019, www.npr.org/2019/06/20/733682502/african-migrants-are-becoming-a-new-face-of-the-u-s-border-crisis; Andrew Buncombe, "Honduras: Inside Ground Zero of the Central American Migrant Crisis," *Independent*, July 16, 2019, www.independent.co.uk/news/world/americas/honduras-migrant-crisis-trump-us-mexico-border-immigration-a9006116.html; Andrew Gumbel, "'They Were Laughing at Us': Immigrants Tell of Cruelty, Illness and Filth in US Detention," *The Guardian*, September 12, 2018, www.theguardian.com/us-news/2018/sep/12/us-immigration-detention-facilities.
9 *The White House*, "Remarks of President Donald J. Trump—As Prepared for Delivery: The Inaugural Address," accessed January 20, 2017, www.whitehouse.gov/briefings-statements/the-inaugural-address/.
10 Ibid.
11 Administration of Donald J. Trump, "Remarks at a 'Make America Great Again' Rally in Melbourne, Florida," February 18, 2017, 8, www.govinfo.gov/content/pkg/DCPD-201700130/pdf/DCPD-201700130.pdf.
12 Arato and Cohen, "Civil Society, Populism, and Religion," 291.
13 Paul Bedard, "Pace of Border Wall Construction Doubled, Work on Private Land Begins," *Washington Examiner*, September 9, 2019, www.washingtonexaminer.com/washington-secrets/pace-of-border-wall-construction-doubled-work-on-private-land-begins; Zach Montague, "Pentagon to Send 2,100 More Troops to the Southwestern Border," *The New York Times*, July 17, 2019, www.nytimes.com/2019/07/17/us/politics/troops-border-immigration.html; Molly Hennessey-Fiske, "Tent Courthouses for Migrants to Open Along Texas Border, as Questions Abound," September 9, 2019, www.latimes.com/world-nation/story/2019-09-09/texas-mirgant-tent-courts-mystery?fbclid=IwAR3gfQg439vUW3h5EZgqPi36I92PryWMByvUlkQCTTOKJXb5U75mQijDOAI.
14 The White House, "Remarks by President Trump at the Faith and Freedom Coalition's Road to Majority Conference," accessed June 8, 2017, www.whitehouse.gov/briefings-statements/remarks-president-trump-faith-freedom-coalitions-road-majority-conference/.
15 Ibid.
16 Administration of Donald J. Trump, "Remarks at a 'Make America Great Again' Rally in Pensacola, Florida," accessed December 8, 2017, 12, www.govinfo.gov/content/pkg/DCPD-201700898/pdf/DCPD-201700898.pdf.
17 Robert Barnes, "Supreme Court Says Trump Administration Can Begin Denying Asylum to Migrants While Legal Fight Continues," *The Washington Post*, September 11, 2019, www.washingtonpost.com/politics/courts_law/supreme-

court-says-trump-administration-can-begin-denying-migrants-asylum-while-legal-fight-continues/2019/09/11/94b90da4-d017-11e9-8c1c-7c8ee785b855_story.html?arc404=true.
18 Trump, "Remarks at a 'Make America Great Again' Rally in Pensacola, Florida," 9.
19 Astrid Galvan, "450 Miles of Border Wall by Next Year? In Arizona, It Starts," September 12, 2019, https://apnews.com/a619922781f441c9adaa494f47001429; Haley Willis, Christoph Koettl, Caroline Kim, and Drew Jordan, "Trump Is Having Tent Courthouses Built Along the Border: Here's What They Look Like," *The New York Times, Video,* 2:59, www.nytimes.com/video/us/politics/100000006681200/border-immigration-tent-courthouses.html.
20 Administration of Donald J. Trump, "Remarks at a 'Make America Great Again Rally' in Cedar Rapids, Iowa," accessed June 21, 2017, 11, www.govinfo.gov/content/pkg/DCPD-201700545/pdf/DCPD-201700545.pdf.
21 US Immigration and Customs Enforcement, "Fiscal Year 2017 ICE Enforcement and Removal Operations Report," 15, www.ice.gov/sites/default/files/documents/Report/2017/iceEndOfYearFY2017.pdf.
22 Administration of Donald J. Trump, "Remarks at a 'Make America Great Again' Rally in Youngstown, Ohio," accessed July 25, 2017, 6, www.govinfo.gov/content/pkg/DCPD-201700682/pdf/DCPD-201700682.pdf.
23 David Neiwert, "Racially Incendiary Russian Ads Apparently Had Their Intended Effect," *Hatewatch, Southern Poverty Law Center,* June 6, 2018, www.splcenter.org/hatewatch/2018/06/06/racially-incendiary-russian-ads-apparently-had-their-intended-effect.
24 Donald Trump, "Make America Great Again Rally," filmed May 29, 2018 in Nashville, TN, https://factba.se/transcript/donald-trump-speech-maga-rally-nashville-may-29-2018.
25 Jonathan Blitzer, "How the Trump Administration Got Comfortable Separating Immigrant Kids from Their Parents," *The New Yorker,* May 30, 2018, www.newyorker.com/news/news-desk/how-the-trump-administration-got-comfortable-separating-immigrant-kids-from-their-parents.
26 Sarah Stillman, "When Deportation Is a Death Sentence," *The New Yorker,* January 15, 2018, www.newyorker.com/magazine/2018/01/15/when-deportation-is-a-death-sentence; Mark Townsend, "Women Deported by Trump Face Deadly Welcome from Street Gangs in El Salvador," *The Guardian,* January 13, 2018, www.theguardian.com/global-development/2018/jan/13/el-salvador-women-deported-by-trump-face-deadly-welcome-street-gangs.
27 Roxanne Lynne Doty and Elizabeth Shannon Wheatley, "Private Detention and the Immigration Industrial Complex," *International Political Sociology* 7, no. 4 (December 2013): 426–27.
28 Oliver Laughland and Renée Feltz, "British Firm Aims to Open Immigration Detention Center Near US-Mexico Border," *The Guardian,* June 9, 2016, www.theguardian.com/business/2016/jun/09/texas-mexico-detention-center-serco-obama-administration; Renée Feltz, "Texas Officials Vote Against British Firm's Plans for Immigration Detention Center," *The Guardian,* June 15, 2016, www.theguardian.com/business/2016/jun/15/texas-immigration-detention-center-serco-proposal-mexico-border.
29 Laughland and Feltz, "British Firm Aims to Open Immigration Detention Center Near US-Mexico Border."
30 Ibid; Feltz, "Texas Officials Vote Against British Firm's Plans for Immigration Detention Center."
31 Beatriz Alvarado, "Community Backlash Influenced Family Detention in Jim Wells, Judge Said," *Caller-Times,* June 13, 2016, http://archive.caller.com/news/immigration/jim-wells-leaders-vote-down-planned-family-detention-center--352b652d-1149-1cc3-e053-0100007f49a6-382713431.html/; Molly Hennessy-Fiske,

"A Texas Oil Town Goes Bust: Would Housing Immigrants for the Feds Solve Its Problems?" *Los Angeles Times*, July 16, 2016, www.latimes.com/nation/la-na-oil-town-immigrants-snap-story.html; Feltz, "Texas Officials Vote Against British Firm's Plans for Immigration Detention Center."
32 Alvarado, "Community Backlash Influenced Family Detention in Jim Wells, Judge Said."
33 Mark Reagan, "Another Family Immigration Detention Center May Come to South Texas," *San Antonio Current*, June 8, 2016, www.sacurrent.com/the-daily/archives/2016/06/08/another-family-immigration-detention-center-may-come-to-south-texas.
34 Feltz, "Texas Officials Vote Against British Firm's Plans for Immigration Detention Center."
35 Laughland and Feltz, "British Firm Aims to Open Immigration Detention Center Near US-Mexico Border"; Mark Townsend, "Yarl's Wood: Labour Pledges to Investigate Claims of Sexual Abuse," *The Guardian*, December 13, 2014, www.theguardian.com/uk-news/2014/dec/14/labour-pledges-yarls-wood-centre-investigation; Mark Townsend, "Detainees at Yarl's Wood Immigration Centre 'Facing Sexual Abuse'," *The Guardian*, September 14, 2013, www.theguardian.com/uk-news/2013/sep/14/detainees-yarls-wood-sexual-abuse.
36 Beatriz Alvarado, "Advocates Criticize Duval's Move on Family Detention," *Caller-Times*, July 11, 2016, http://archive.caller.com/news/immigration/duval-county-considers-family-detention-center-375dd7b4-1a13-4ea2-e053-0100007f5bc9-386335001.html/.
37 Ibid.
38 Michael Mulvey, "Statement of the Most Reverend Michael Mulvey, Bishop of Corpus Christi Regarding the Decision by Duval County Commissioners to Move Forward with a Family Detention Facility," *Roman Catholic Diocese of Corpus Christi*, July 14, 2016, https://diocesecc.org/wp-content/uploads/2018/08/MulveyStatement0714-1.pdf.
39 Grassroots Leadership, "Demand Duval County Commissioners Halt Negotiations with Serco Over New Family Detention Camp and Have a Public Hearing!" https://grassrootsleadership.ourpowerbase.net/civicrm/petition/sign?sid=32&reset=1.
40 Grassroots Leadership, "Texas Court Issues Temporary Injunction Prohibiting Licensing of Dilley Family Detention Camp," June 1, 2016, https://grassrootsleadership.org/releases/2016/06/texas-court-issues-temporary-injunction-prohibiting-licensing-dilley-family.
41 University of Michigan Law School, "Final Judgement: Grassroots Leadership, Inc. v. Texas Department of Family and Protective Services (DFPS)," *Civil Rights Litigation Clearinghouse*, December 2, 2016, www.clearinghouse.net/detailDocument.php?id=87018; Fauzeya Rahman, "State Cannot Issue Child Care Licenses for Family Detention Centers, Judgement Finds," *San Antonio Express-News*, December 4, 2016, www.mysanantonio.com/news/local/article/State-cannot-issue-child-care-licenses-for-family-10689616.php.
42 Julián Aguilar, "Immigration Detention Centers Will Continue Operating Despite Judge's Ruling," *The Texas Tribune*, December 6, 2016, www.texastribune.org/2016/12/06/immigration-detention-centers-will-continue-operat/.
43 Beatriz Alvarado, "Judge: Residential Center in San Diego No Longer Being Considered," *Caller-Times*, March 31, 2017, www.caller.com/story/news/local/2017/03/31/judge-residential-center-san-diego-no-longer-being-considered/99890138/.
44 Heather Long, "Private Prison Stocks Up 100% Since Trump's Win," *CNN Business*, February 24, 2017, http://money.cnn.com/2017/02/24/investing/private-prison-stocks-soar-trump/index.html.

45 Exec. Order No. 13,767, 3 C.F.R. 263 (Jan. 25, 2017); Exec. Order No. 13,768 3 C.F.R. 268 (Jan. 25, 2017); Matthew Albence and Derek Benner, "Statement Regarding the Fiscal Year 2019 President's Budget Request," *US Immigration and Customs Enforcement*, April 12, 2018, 2, www.ice.gov/sites/default/files/documents/Speech/2018/180412albenceBenner.pdf.
46 Matt Zapotosky, "Justice Department Will Again Use Private Prisons," *The Washington Post*, February 23, 2017, www.washingtonpost.com/world/national-security/justice-department-will-again-use-private-prisons/2017/02/23/da395d02-fa0e-11e6-be05-1a3817ac21a5_story.html?noredirect=on&utm_term=.caeb87a14865.
47 Samantha Schmidt, "'Utter Chaos': ICE Arrests 114 Workers in Immigration Raid at Ohio Gardening Company," *The Washington Post*, June 6, 2018, www.washingtonpost.com/news/morning-mix/wp/2018/06/06/utter-chaos-ice-arrests-114-workers-in-immigration-raid-at-ohio-gardening-company/?noredirect=on&utm_term=.22f218a1e454; Catherine E. Shoichet, "ICE Raided a Meatpacking Plant: More Than 500 Kids Missed School the Next Day," *CNN*, April 12, 2018, https://edition.cnn.com/2018/04/12/us/tennessee-immigration-raid-schools-impact/index.html.
48 Jeremy Redmon, "Exclusive: A Look Inside Georgia's Newest Immigration Detention Center," *The Atlanta Journal-Constitution*, March 7, 2018, https://politics.myajc.com/news/state--regional-govt--politics/exclusive-look-inside-georgia-newest-immigration-detention-center/MSCIdsHtNOZSOTYyZELDeO/; Bryan Kirk, "ICE Awards Federal Contract to Expand Detention Facility in Conroe," *Patch*, April 19, 2017, https://patch.com/texas/conroe-montgomerycounty/ice-awards-federal-contract-expand-detention-facility-conroe.
49 Consolidated Appropriations Act, 2018, Pub. L. No. 115–141, 132 Stat. 608 (2018); Department of Homeland Security, "Division F—Department of Homeland Security Appropriations Act, 2018," https://docs.house.gov/billsthisweek/20180319/DIV%20F%20HOMELAND%20SOM%20FY18%20OMNI.OCR.pdf.
50 "Division F—Department of Homeland Security Appropriations Act, 2018."
51 Thomas D. Homan, "Stopping the Daily Border Caravan: Time to Build a Policy Wall," US Immigration and Customs Enforcement, May 22, 2018, https://docs.house.gov/meetings/HM/HM11/20180522/108323/HHRG-115-HM11-Bio-HomanT-20180522.pdf.
52 Department of Homeland Security, "Budget Overview: Fiscal Year 2019, Congressional Justification," *US Immigration and Customs Enforcement*, 13–14, www.dhs.gov/sites/default/files/publications/U.S.%20Immigration%20and%20Customs%20Enforcement.pdf.
53 US Immigration and Customs Enforcement, "Family Residential Center Populations FY2013-February 11, 2017," www.ice.gov/doclib/foia/dfs/FRC-FY2013-Feb-2017.xlsx.
54 Albence and Benner, "Statement Regarding the Fiscal Year 2019 President's Budget Request," 4; Homan, "Stopping the Daily Border Caravan," 6.
55 Ryan Devereaux, "1,358 Children and Counting—Trump's 'Zero Tolerance' Border Policy Is Separating Families at Staggering Rates," *The Intercept*, June 8, 2018, https://theintercept.com/2018/06/08/immigration-family-separation-children/; Nila Bala and Arthur Rizer, "Trump's Family Separation Policy Never Really Ended: This Is Why," *NBC News*, July 1, 2019, www.nbcnews.com/think/opinion/trump-s-family-separation-policy-never-really-ended-why-ncna1025376.
56 US Immigration and Customs Enforcement, "Fiscal Year 2017 ICE Enforcement and Removal Operations Report."
57 Noah Lanard, "ICE Just Quietly Opened Three New Detention Centers, Flouting Congress' Limits," *Mother Jones*, July 9, 2019, www.motherjones.com/politics/2019/07/ice-just-quietly-opened-three-new-detention-centers-flouting-congress-limits/; On September 9, 2019, the Department of Homeland Security

102 *The desacralizing power of immigrant detention*

      advertised a contract for Multi-Texas Contract Detention Facilities Solicitation Number: 70CDCR19R00000012, www.fbo.gov/spg/DHS/INS/ICE-OAQ-DM/70CDCR19R00000012/listing.html.
58 Gus Bova, "The Consequence of Trump's New Family Detention Rules," *The Texas Observer*, August 21, 2019, www.texasobserver.org/the-consequence-of-trumps-new-family-detention-rules/.
59 Department of Homeland Security, "Acting Secretary of Homeland Security Kevin K. McAleenan on the DHS-HHS Federal Rule on Flores Agreement," *Speeches*, Released August 21, 2019, www.dhs.gov/news/2019/08/21/acting-secretary-mcaleenan-dhs-hhs-federal-rule-flores-agreement; Michelle Hackman, "U.S. Seeks Longer Detentions for Migrant Families," *The Wall Street Journal*, August 21, 2019, www.wsj.com/articles/trump-administration-unveils-plan-to-hold-migrant-children-in-long-term-detention-with-parents-11566394202; Michael D. Shear and Zolan Kanno-Youngs, "Migrant Families Would Face Indefinite Detention Under New Trump Rule," *The New York Times*, August 21, 2019, www.nytimes.com/2019/08/21/us/politics/flores-migrant-family-detention.html.
60 "Trump Migrant Separation Policy: Children 'in Cages' in Texas," *BBC News*, June 18, 2018, www.bbc.com/news/world-us-canada-44518942.
61 Scott Martelle, "Opinion: The Evidence Is in: Trump's 'Remain in Mexico' Policy Puts Asylum-seekers' Lives at Risk," *Los Angeles Times*, August 30, 2019, www.latimes.com/opinion/story/2019-08-30/remain-in-mexico-dangerous-conditions-asylum-trump-immigration-border.
62 Patricia Clarembaux, "6 de cada 7 familias de inmigrantes que piden asilo en EEUU sí se presentan en la corte, lo que contradice la versión oficial," *Univision Noticias*, June 18, 2019, www.univision.com/noticias/inmigracion/6-de-cada-7-familias-de-inmigrantes-que-piden-asilo-si-se-presentan-en-la-corte-lo-que-contradice-la-version-oficial; Cindy Carcamo, "Las madres inmigrantes que buscan asilo se preparan para afrontar su suerte en la frontera de EE.UU. con México," *Los Angeles Times*, June 25, 2018, www.latimes.com/espanol/eeuu/la-es-en-la-frontera-de-ee-uu-con-mexico-las-madres-inmigrantes-que-buscan-asilo-se-preparan-para-afrontar-20180625-story.html; Sergio Morales Rodas, "'Por mi familia': Guatemalteco solicitante de asilo anhela pasar a Estados Unidos," *Prensa Libre*, April 15, 2019, www.prensalibre.com/guatemala/migrantes/solicitante-guatemalteco-de-asilo-anhela-pasar-a-ee-uu/; Leah Asmelash and Brian Riles, "Madre guatemalteca le pide clemencia a un soldado mexicano en nuevas fotos tomadas en la frontera de Estados Unidos," *CNN*, July 26, 2019, https://cnnespanol.cnn.com/2019/07/26/madre-guatemalteca-le-pide-clemencia-a-un-soldado-mexicano-en-nuevas-fotos-tomadas-en-la-frontera-de-estados-unidos/; Kirk Semple, "'I Didn't Want Them to Go': Salvadoran Family Grieves for Father and Daughter Who Drowned," *The New York Times*, June 28, 2019, www.nytimes.com/2019/06/28/world/americas/rio-grande-drowning-father-daughter.html.
63 US Immigration and Customs Enforcement, "ICE/DRO Residential Standard: Religious Practices," December 21, 2007, 1, www.ice.gov/doclib/dro/family-residential/pdf/rs_religious_practices.pdf.
64 US Immigration and Customs Enforcement, "Report of the ICE Advisory Committee on Family Residential Centers," *US Immigration and Customs Enforcement and Advisory Committee on Family Residential Centers Meeting*, October 7, 2016, 17–18, www.ice.gov/sites/default/files/documents/Report/2016/acfrc-report-final-102016.pdf.
65 US Immigration and Customs Enforcement, "Performance-Based National Detention Standards 2011," accessed December 2016, www.ice.gov/detention-standards/2011.

66 American Civil Liberties Union, "The Rights of Immigrants-ACLU Position Paper," www.aclu.org/other/rights-immigrants-aclu-position-paper.
67 Gregory Lee Cuéllar, "Deportation as a Sacrament of the State: The Religious Instruction of Contracted Chaplains in U.S. Detention Facilities," *Journal of Ethnic Migration Studies* 45, no. 1 (December 2017): 10–11.
68 CoreCivic, "2018 Proxy Statement," accessed March 30, 2017, 20, http://ir.corecivic.com/static-files/0cbd5024-c6da-45a7-8ce2-eed84271599e.
69 David Dayen, "These Private Prison Companies Are Already Profiting Off of Trump's Order on Family Separation," *In These Times*, June 22, 2018, http://inthesetimes.com/article/21234/private-prison-trump-family-separation-immigration-ice; David Dayen, "How Private Contractors Enable Trump's Cruelties at the Border," *In These Times*, June 20, 2018, www.thenation.com/article/private-contractors-enable-trumps-cruelties-border/?print=1.
70 The GEO Group, Inc., "2016 Annual Report," www.snl.com/Interactive/newlookandfeel/4144107/2016-GEO-Annual-Report.pdf.
71 The GEO Group, Inc., "2017 Annual Report," www.snl.com/Interactive/newlookandfeel/4144107/2017-GEO-Annual-Report.pdf.
72 Azadeh Shahshahani, "Why Are For-profit US Prisons Subjecting Detainees to Forced Labor?" *The Guardian*, May 17, 2018, www.theguardian.com/commentisfree/2018/may/17/us-private-prisons-forced-labour-detainees-modern-slavery; Tracy Jan, "These GOP Lawmakers Say It's Okay for Imprisoned Immigrants to Work for a $1 a Day," *The Washington Post*, March 16, 2018, www.washingtonpost.com/news/wonk/wp/2018/03/16/republican-congressmen-defend-1-a-day-wage-for-immigrant-detainees-who-work-in-private-prisons/?utm_term=.2a00abfb4bec; Molly Hennessy-Fiske, "Paid $1 to $3 a Day, Unauthorized Immigrants Keep Family Detention Centers Running," *Los Angeles Times*, August 3, 2015, www.latimes.com/nation/immigration/la-na-detention-immigration-workers-20150803-story.html.
73 This particular job posting is no longer on CoreCivic's website. CoreCivic, accessed June 27, 2018, http://jobs.corecivic.com/ShowJob/Id/247526/Chaplain-Bilingual-(Preferred)/.
74 US Immigration and Customs Enforcement, "ICE/DRO Detention Standard: Religious Practices," December 2, 2008, www.ice.gov/doclib/dro/detention-standards/pdf/religious_practices.pdf.
75 This particular job posting is no longer on CoreCivic's website. CoreCivic, accessed June 27, 2018, http://jobs.corecivic.com/ShowJob/Id/247526/Chaplain-Bilingual-(Preferred)/.
76 Monica Muñoz Martinez, "Recuperating Histories of Violence in the Americas: Vernacular History-Making on the US—Mexico Border," *American Quarterly* 66 (September 2014): 664.

Bibliography

Administration of Donald J. Trump. "Remarks at a 'Make America Great Again Rally' in Cedar Rapids, Iowa." Issued on June 21, 2017. www.govinfo.gov/content/pkg/DCPD-201700545/pdf/DCPD-201700545.pdf.
———. "Remarks at a 'Make America Great Again' Rally in Melbourne, Florida." Issued on February 18, 2017. www.govinfo.gov/content/pkg/DCPD-201700130/pdf/DCPD-201700130.pdf.
———. "Remarks at a 'Make America Great Again' Rally in Pensacola, Florida." Issued on December 8, 2017. www.govinfo.gov/content/pkg/DCPD-201700898/pdf/DCPD-201700898.pdf.

———. "Remarks at a 'Make America Great Again' Rally in Youngstown, Ohio." Issued on July 25, 2017. www.govinfo.gov/content/pkg/DCPD-201700682/pdf/DCPD-201700682.pdf.

Aguilar, Julián. "Immigration Detention Centers Will Continue Operating Despite Judge's Ruling." *The Texas Tribune*, December 6, 2016. www.texastribune.org/2016/12/06/immigration-detention-centers-will-continue-operat/.

Albence, Matthew, and Derek Benner. "Statement Regarding the Fiscal Year 2019 President's Budget Request." *US Immigration and Customs Enforcement*, April 12, 2018. www.ice.gov/sites/default/files/documents/Speech/2018/180412albenceBenner.pdf.

Alvarado, Beatriz. "Advocates Criticize Duval's Move on Family Detention." *Caller-Times*, July 11, 2016. http://archive.caller.com/news/immigration/duval-county-considers-family-detention-center--375dd7b4-1a13-4ea2-e053-0100007f5bc9-386335001.html/.

———. "Community Backlash Influenced Family Detention in Jim Wells, Judge Said." *Caller-Times*, June 13, 2016. http://archive.caller.com/news/immigration/jim-wells-leaders-vote-down-planned-family-detention-center--352b652d-1149-1cc3-e053-0100007f49a6-382713431.html/.

———. "Judge: Residential Center in San Diego No Longer Being Considered." *Caller-Times*, March 31, 2017. www.caller.com/story/news/local/2017/03/31/judge-residential-center-san-diego-no-longer-being-considered/99890138/.

American Civil Liberties Union. "The Rights of Immigrants-ACLU Position Paper." www.aclu.org/other/rights-immigrants-aclu-position-paper.

Arato, Andrew, and Jean L. Cohen. "Civil Society, Populism, and Religion." *Constellations, An International Journal of Critical and Democratic Theory* 24, no. 3 (September 2017): 283–95.

Asmelash, Leah, and Brian Riles. "Madre guatemalteca le pide clemencia a un soldado mexicano en nuevas fotos tomadas en la frontera de Estados Unidos." *CNN*, July 26, 2019. https://cnnespanol.cnn.com/2019/07/26/madre-guatemalteca-le-pide-clemencia-a-un-soldado-mexicano-en-nuevas-fotos-tomadas-en-la-frontera-de-estados-unidos/.

Bala, Nila, and Arthur Rizer. "Trump's Family Separation Policy Never Really Ended: This Is Why." *NBC News*, July 1, 2019. www.nbcnews.com/think/opinion/trump-s-family-separation-policy-never-really-ended-why-ncna1025376.

Barnes, Robert. "Supreme Court Says Trump Administration Can Begin Denying Asylum to Migrants While Legal Fight Continues." *The Washington Post*, September 11, 2019. www.washingtonpost.com/politics/courts_law/supreme-court-says-trump-administration-can-begin-denying-migrants-asylum-while-legal-fight-continues/2019/09/11/94b90da4-d017-11e9-8c1c-7c8ee785b855_story.html?arc404=true.

Baynes, Chris. "US Detaining Hundreds of African Migrants at Border After 'Dramatic Rise' in Arrivals." *Independent*, June 7, 2019. www.independent.co.uk/news/world/americas/us-border-mexico-immigration-africa-trump-congo-angola-a8948241.html.

BBC News. "Trump Migrant Separation Policy: Children 'in Cages' in Texas." June 18, 2018. www.bbc.com/news/world-us-canada-44518942.

Bedard, Paul. "Pace of Border Wall Construction Doubled, Work on Private Land Begins." *Washington Examiner*, September 9, 2019. www.washingtonexaminer.com/washington-secrets/pace-of-border-wall-construction-doubled-work-on-private-land-begins.

Blitzer, Jonathan. "How the Trump Administration Got Comfortable Separating Immigrant Kids from Their Parents." *The New Yorker*, May 30, 2018. www.newyorker.com/news/news-desk/how-the-trump-administration-got-comfortable-separating-immigrant-kids-from-their-parents.

Bova, Gus. "The Consequence of Trump's New Family Detention Rules." *The Texas Observer*, August 21, 2019. www.texasobserver.org/the-consequence-of-trumps-new-family-detention-rules/.

Buncombe, Andrew. "Honduras: Inside Ground Zero of the Central American Migrant Crisis." *Independent*, July 16, 2019. www.independent.co.uk/news/world/americas/honduras-migrant-crisis-trump-us-mexico-border-immigration-a9006116.html.

Carcamo, Cindy. "Las madres inmigrantes que buscan asilo se preparan para afrontar su suerte en la frontera de EE.UU. con México." *Los Angeles Times*, June 25, 2018. www.latimes.com/espanol/eeuu/la-es-en-la-frontera-de-ee-uu-con-mexico-las-madres-inmigrantes-que-buscan-asilo-se-preparan-para-afrontar-20180625-story.html.

Clarembaux, Patricia. "6 de cada 7 familias de inmigrantes que piden asilo en EEUU sí se presentan en la corte, lo que contradice la versión oficial." *Univision Noticias*, June 18, 2019. www.univision.com/noticias/inmigracion/6-de-cada-7-familias-de-inmigrantes-que-piden-asilo-si-se-presentan-en-la-corte-lo-que-contradice-la-version-oficial.

CoreCivic. "2018 Proxy Statement." Accessed March 30, 2017. http://ir.corecivic.com/static-files/0cbd5024-c6da-45a7-8ce2-eed84271599e.

Cuéllar, Gregory Lee. "Deportation as a Sacrament of the State: The Religious Instruction of Contracted Chaplains in U.S. Detention Facilities." *Journal of Ethnic Migration Studies* 45, no. 1 (December 2017): 253–72.

Dayen, David. "How Private Contractors Enable Trump's Cruelties at the Border." *In These Times*, June 20, 2018. www.thenation.com/article/private-contractors-enable-trumps-cruelties-border/?print=1.

———. "These Private Prison Companies Are Already Profiting Off of Trump's Order on Family Separation." *In These Times*, June 22, 2018. http://inthesetimes.com/article/21234/private-prison-trump-family-separation-immigration-ice.

Department of Homeland Security. "Acting Secretary of Homeland Security Kevin K. McAleenan on the DHS-HHS Federal Rule on Flores Agreement." Speeches. Released August 21, 2019. www.dhs.gov/news/2019/08/21/acting-secretary-mcaleenan-dhs-hhs-federal-rule-flores-agreement.

———. "Budget Overview: Fiscal Year 2019, Congressional Justification." US Immigration and Customs Enforcement. www.dhs.gov/sites/default/files/publications/U.S.%20Immigration%20and%20Customs%20Enforcement.pdf.

———. "Division F—Department of Homeland Security Appropriations Act, 2018." https://docs.house.gov/billsthisweek/20180319/DIV%20F%20HOMELAND%20SOM%20FY18%20OMNI.OCR.pdf.

Devereaux, Ryan. "1,358 Children and Counting—Trump's 'Zero Tolerance' Border Policy Is Separating Families at Staggering Rates." *The Intercept*, June 8, 2018. https://theintercept.com/2018/06/08/immigration-family-separation-children/.

Doty, Roxanne Lynne, and Elizabeth Shannon Wheatley. "Private Detention and the Immigration Industrial Complex." *International Political Sociology* 7, no. 4 (December 2013): 426–43.

"Executive Order 13767 of January 25, 2017, Border Security and Immigration Enforcement Improvements." *Code of Federal Regulations* title 3 (2017): 263. www.govinfo.gov/content/pkg/DCPD-201700071/pdf/DCPD-201700071.pdf.

"Executive Order 13768 of January 25, 2017, Enhancing Public Safety in the Interior of the United States." *Code of Federal Regulations* title 3 (2017): 268. www.govinfo.gov/content/pkg/DCPD-201700072/pdf/DCPD-201700072.pdf.

Feinberg, Robbie, and Bonnie Petrie. "African Migrants Are Becoming a New Face of the U.S. Border Crisis." *NPR*, June 20, 2019. www.npr.org/2019/06/20/733682502/african-migrants-are-becoming-a-new-face-of-the-u-s-border-crisis.

Feltz, Renée. "Texas Officials Vote Against British Firm's Plans for Immigration Detention Center." *The Guardian*, June 15, 2016. www.theguardian.com/business/2016/jun/15/texas-immigration-detention-center-serco-proposal-mexico-border.

Galvan, Astrid. "450 Miles of Border Wall by Next Year? In Arizona, It Starts." September 12, 2019. https://apnews.com/a619922781f441c9adaa494f47001429.

The GEO Group, Inc. "2016 Annual Report." www.snl.com/Interactive/newlookandfeel/4144107/2016-GEO-Annual-Report.pdf.

———. "2017 Annual Report." www.snl.com/Interactive/newlookandfeel/4144107/2017-GEO-Annual-Report.pdf.

Goldberg, Michelle. "Donald Trump, the Religious Right's Trojan Horse." *The New York Times*, January 27, 2017. www.nytimes.com/2017/01/27/opinion/sunday/donald-trump-the-religious-rights-trojan-horse.html.

"Graduating into History." *Liberty Journal* (Summer 2017): 18–31. https://issuu.com/libertyuniversity/docs/lj_summer17_issuu?e=4413175/49598542.

Grassroots Leadership. "Demand Duval County Commissioners Halt Negotiations with Serco Over New Family Detention Camp and Have a Public Hearing!" https://grassrootsleadership.ourpowerbase.net/civicrm/petition/sign?sid=32&reset=1.

———. "Texas Court Issues Temporary Injunction Prohibiting Licensing of Dilley Family Detention Camp." *Press Releases*, June 1, 2016. https://grassrootsleadership.org/releases/2016/06/texas-court-issues-temporary-injunction-prohibiting-licensing-dilley-family.

Gumbel, Andrew. "'They Were Laughing at Us': Immigrants Tell of Cruelty, Illness and Filth in US Detention." *The Guardian*, September 12, 2018. www.theguardian.com/us-news/2018/sep/12/us-immigration-detention-facilities.

Hackman, Michelle. "U.S. Seeks Longer Detentions for Migrant Families." *The Wall Street Journal*, August 21, 2019. www.wsj.com/articles/trump-administration-unveils-plan-to-hold-migrant-children-in-long-term-detention-with-parents-11566394202.

Hennessy-Fiske, Molly. "Paid $1 to $3 a Day, Unauthorized Immigrants Keep Family Detention Centers Running." *Los Angeles Times*, August 3, 2015. www.latimes.com/nation/immigration/la-na-detention-immigration-workers-20150803-story.html.

———. "Tent Courthouses for Migrants to Open Along Texas Border, as Questions Abound." September 9, 2019. www.latimes.com/world-nation/story/2019-09-09/texas-mirgant-tent-courts-mystery?fbclid=IwAR3gfQg439vUW3h5EZgqPi36I92PryWMByvUlkQCTTOKJXb5U75mQijDOAI.

———. "A Texas Oil Town Goes Bust: Would Housing Immigrants for the Feds Solve Its Problems?" *Los Angeles Times*, July 16, 2016. www.latimes.com/nation/la-na-oil-town-immigrants-snap-story.html.

Homan, Thomas D. "Stopping the Daily Border Caravan: Time to Build a Policy Wall." *US Immigration and Customs Enforcement*, May 22, 2018. https://docs.house.gov/meetings/HM/HM11/20180522/108323/HHRG-115-HM11-Bio-HomanT-20180522.pdf.

Jan, Tracy. "These GOP Lawmakers Say It's Okay for Imprisoned Immigrants to Work for a $1 a Day." *The Washington Post*, March 16, 2018. www.washingtonpost.com/news/wonk/wp/2018/03/16/republican-congressmen-defend-1-a-day-wage-for-immigrant-detainees-who-work-in-private-prisons/?utm_term=.2a00abfb4bec.

Kirk, Bryan. "ICE Awards Federal Contract to Expand Detention Facility in Conroe." *Patch*, April 19, 2017. https://patch.com/texas/conroe-montgomerycounty/ice-awards-federal-contract-expand-detention-facility-conroe.

Lanard, Noah. "ICE Just Quietly Opened Three New Detention Centers, Flouting Congress' Limits." *Mother Jones*, July 9, 2019. www.motherjones.com/politics/2019/07/ice-just-quietly-opened-three-new-detention-centers-flouting-congress-limits/.

Laughland, Oliver, and Renée Feltz. "British Firm Aims to Open Immigration Detention Center Near US-Mexico Border." *The Guardian*, June 9, 2016. www.theguardian.com/business/2016/jun/09/texas-mexico-detention-center-serco-obama-administration.

Long, Heather. "Private Prison Stocks Up 100% Since Trump's Win." *CNN Business*, February 24, 2017. http://money.cnn.com/2017/02/24/investing/private-prison-stocks-soar-trump/index.html.

Martelle, Scott. "Opinion: The Evidence Is in: Trump's 'Remain in Mexico' Policy Puts Asylum-Seekers' Lives at Risk." *Los Angeles Times*, August 30, 2019. www.latimes.com/opinion/story/2019-08-30/remain-in-mexico-dangerous-conditions-asylum-trump-immigration-border.

Martinez, Monica Muñoz. "Recuperating Histories of Violence in the Americas: Vernacular History-Making on the US—Mexico Border." *American Quarterly* 66 (September 2014): 661–89.

Montague, Zach. "Pentagon to Send 2,100 More Troops to the Southwestern Border." *The New York Times*, July 17, 2019. www.nytimes.com/2019/07/17/us/politics/troops-border-immigration.html.

Mulvey, Michael. "Statement of the Most Reverend Michael Mulvey, Bishop of Corpus Christi Regarding the Decision by Duval County Commissioners to Move Forward with a Family Detention Facility." *Roman Catholic Diocese of Corpus Christi*, July 14, 2016. https://diocesecc.org/wp-content/uploads/2018/08/Mulvey Statement0714-1.pdf.

National Center for Education Statistics. "College Navigator: Liberty University." https://nces.ed.gov/collegenavigator/?q=liberty+university&s=all&id=232557#enrolmt.

Neiwert, David. "Racially Incendiary Russian Ads Apparently Had Their Intended Effect." *Hatewatch, Southern Poverty Law Center*, June 6, 2018. www.splcenter.org/hatewatch/2018/06/06/racially-incendiary-russian-ads-apparently-had-their-intended-effect.

Peterson-Withorn, Chase. "The $4.3 Billion Cabinet: See What Each Top Trump Advisor Is Worth." *Forbes*, July 5, 2017. www.forbes.com/sites/chasewithorn/2017/07/05/the-4-3-billion-cabinet-see-what-each-top-trump-advisor-is-worth/#4d0f74c95dfc.

Poulantzas, Nicos. *State, Power, Socialism*. London: Verso, 2000.

Rahman, Fauzeya. "State Cannot Issue Child Care Licenses for Family Detention Centers, Judgement Finds." *San Antonio Express-News*, December 4, 2016. www.mysanantonio.com/news/local/article/State-cannot-issue-child-care-licenses-for-family-10689616.php.

"Read President Trump's Liberty University Commencement Speech." *TIME*, May 13, 2017. http://time.com/4778240/donald-trump-liberty-university-speech-transcript/.

Reagan, Mark. "Another Family Immigration Detention Center May Come to South Texas." *San Antonio Current*, June 8, 2016. www.sacurrent.com/the-daily/archives/2016/06/08/another-family-immigration-detention-center-may-come-to-south-texas.

Redmon, Jeremy. "Exclusive: A Look Inside Georgia's Newest Immigration Detention Center." *The Atlanta Journal-Constitution*, March 7, 2018. https://politics.myajc.com/news/state--regional-govt--politics/exclusive-look-inside-georgia-new est-immigration-detention-center/MSCIdsHtNOZSOTYyZELDeO/.

Rodas, Sergio Morales. " 'Por mi familia': Guatemalteco solicitante de asilo anhela pasar a Estados Unidos." *Prensa Libre*, April 15, 2019. www.prensalibre.com/guatemala/migrantes/solicitante-guatemalteco-de-asilo-anhela-pasar-a-ee-uu/.

Schmidt, Samantha. " 'Utter Chaos': ICE Arrests 114 Workers in Immigration Raid at Ohio Gardening Company." *The Washington Post*, June 6, 2018. www.washingtonpost.com/news/morning-mix/wp/2018/06/06/utter-chaos-ice-arrests-114-workers-in-immigration-raid-at-ohio-gardening-company/?noredirect=on&utm_term=.22f218a1e454.

Semple, Kirk. " 'I Didn't Want Them to Go': Salvadoran Family Grieves for Father and Daughter Who Drowned." *The New York Times*, June 28, 2019. www.nytimes.com/2019/06/28/world/americas/rio-grande-drowning-father-daughter.html.

Shahshahani, Azadeh. "Why Are For-profit US Prisons Subjecting Detainees to Forced Labor?" *The Guardian*, May 17, 2018. www.theguardian.com/commentisfree/2018/may/17/us-private-prisons-forced-labour-detainees-modern-slavery.

Shear, Michael D., and Zolan Kanno-Youngs. "Migrant Families Would Face Indefinite Detention Under New Trump Rule." *The New York Times*, August 21, 2019. www.nytimes.com/2019/08/21/us/politics/flores-migrant-family-detention.html.

Shoichet, Catherine E. "ICE Raided a Meatpacking Plant: More Than 500 Kids Missed School the Next Day." *CNN*, April 12, 2018. https://edition.cnn.com/2018/04/12/us/tennessee-immigration-raid-schools-impact/index.html.

Smith, Gregory A. "Among White Evangelicals, Regular Churchgoers Are the Most Supportive of Trump." *Fact Tank: News in the Numbers: Pew Research Center*, April 26, 2017. www.pewresearch.org/fact-tank/2017/04/26/among-white-evan gelicals-regular-churchgoers-are-the-most-supportive-of-trump/.

Southern Poverty Law Center. "Trump Taps Hate Group Fellow Ronald Mortensen for Important Post Dealing with Refugees." *Hatewatch*, May 25, 2018. www.splcenter.org/hatewatch/2018/05/25/trump-taps-hate-group-fellow-ronald-mortensen-important-post-dealing-refugees.

Stillman, Sarah. "When Deportation Is a Death Sentence." *The New Yorker*, January 15, 2018. www.newyorker.com/magazine/2018/01/15/when-deportation-is-a-death-sentence.

Townsend, Mark. "Detainees at Yarl's Wood Immigration Centre 'Facing Sexual Abuse'." *The Guardian*, September 14, 2013. www.theguardian.com/uk-news/2013/sep/14/detainees-yarls-wood-sexual-abuse.

———. "Women Deported by Trump Face Deadly Welcome from Street Gangs in El Salvador." *The Guardian*, January 13, 2018. www.theguardian.com/global-development/2018/jan/13/el-salvador-women-deported-by-trump-face-deadly-welcome-street-gangs.

———. "Yarl's Wood: Labour Pledges to Investigate Claims of Sexual Abuse." *The Guardian*, December 13, 2014. www.theguardian.com/uk-news/2014/dec/14/labour-pledges-yarls-wood-centre-investigation.

Trump, Donald. "Make America Great Again Rally." Filmed May 29, 2018 in Nashville, TN. https://factba.se/transcript/donald-trump-speech-maga-rally-nashville-may-29-2018.

University of Michigan Law School. "Final Judgement: Grassroots Leadership, Inc. v. Texas Department of Family and Protective Services (DFPS)." *Civil Rights Litigation Clearinghouse*, December 2, 2016. www.clearinghouse.net/detailDocument.php?id=87018.

US Immigration and Customs Enforcement. "Family Residential Center Populations FY2013-February 11, 2017." www.ice.gov/doclib/foia/dfs/FRC-FY2013-Feb-2017.xlsx.

———. "Fiscal Year 2017 ICE Enforcement and Removal Operations Report." www.ice.gov/sites/default/files/documents/Report/2017/iceEndOfYearFY2017.pdf.

———. "ICE/DRO Residential Standard: Religious Practices." December 21, 2007. www.ice.gov/doclib/dro/family-residential/pdf/rs_religious_practices.pdf.

———. "ICE/DRO Detention Standard: Religious Practices." December 2, 2008. www.ice.gov/doclib/dro/detention-standards/pdf/religious_practices.pdf.

———. "Performance-Based National Detention Standards 2011." December 2016. www.ice.gov/detention-standards/2011.

———. "Report of the ICE Advisory Committee on Family Residential Centers." *US Immigration and Customs Enforcement and Advisory Committee on Family Residential Centers Meeting*. October 7, 2016. www.ice.gov/sites/default/files/documents/Report/2016/acfrc-report-final-102016.pdf.

The White House. "Remarks of President Donald J. Trump—As Prepared for Delivery: The Inaugural Address." Issued on January 20, 2017. www.whitehouse.gov/briefings-statements/the-inaugural-address/.

———. "Remarks by President Trump at the Faith and Freedom Coalition's Road to Majority Conference." Issued on June 8, 2017. www.whitehouse.gov/briefings-statements/remarks-president-trump-faith-freedom-coalitions-road-majority-conference/.

Willis, Haley, Christoph Koettl, Caroline Kim, and Drew Jordan. "Trump Is Having Tent Courthouses Built Along the Border: Here's What They Look Like." *The New York Times*. Video, 2:59. www.nytimes.com/video/us/politics/100000006681200/border-immigration-tent-courthouses.html.

Zapotosky, Matt. "Justice Department Will Again Use Private Prisons." *The Washington Post*, February 23, 2017. www.washingtonpost.com/world/national-security/justice-department-will-again-use-private-prisons/2017/02/23/da395d02-fa0e-11e6-be05-1a3817ac21a5_story.html?noredirect=on&utm_term=.caeb87a14865.

5 Caring for the sacred Other

The forces operating to render black- and brown-bodied people the nonsacred other in the US-Mexico borderlands recruit from a versatile assemblage of rhetoric, networks, technologies, and mechanisms. Ending their devouring bite on border crossers and border communities, however, requires an intervening system of sacralization. This oppositional way of truth-making has always been present in the US-Mexico borderlands; since its inception in 1848, border crossers and border communities alike have resisted and struggled against their desacralization by elite power.[1] When viewed as the product of colonization, the borderlands represent a traumatic and yet creative social reality.

Kept at the fore in the US-Mexico borderlands are signs of domination across the physical landscape (e.g. landownership). Nevertheless, parallel with this mastery are counter modes of truth-making that the subjugated people of the borderlands devise amid the master's bordering violence. At this creative juncture, there are ways of knowing and being that flow adversely to those imposed by elite power structures. These ways are lifegiving because they undermine the desacralizing and eradicating schemes of elite power that operate within the social, political, and economic domains of the US-Mexico borderlands. The plurality of the borderlands points to multiple hermeneutics, yet here I focus on a singular borderland hermeneutic in which the target domain is the sacred Other. In terms of process, the proposed borderland hermeneutic draws from a multiplicity of hermeneutics of the borderlands but for a singular purpose: the re-sacralization of the border-crossing Other. Indeed, this single attempt at a borderland hermeneutic does not imply an all-in-one, but rather one of many hermeneutical fronts in need of activist reinforcement.[2] Such an endeavor is always provisional and never claims any set point of arrival or, as Luis D. Léon describes, is always working toward a hermeneutics of the borderlands.[3] For at the nexus of the sacred and the human Other is nefarious elite power rendering black- and brown-bodied people of the borderlands as the region's primary public enemy.

In this season of the US-Mexico borderlands, those bearing the brunt of elite power's othering assaults are migrant border crossers.[4] Rather than allowing its bordering violence to dictate life on the borderlands, can a borderland hermeneutic of care and healing be offered instead? Such an approach would not only need to ascribe sacred value to migrant border crossers but, more importantly, to assemble into actual care practices of healing for them. By turning to care of migrant border crossers, the proposed borderland hermeneutic is concerned first and foremost with the region's most vulnerable Other.[5]

Marking the current contours of state care for migrant border crossers is a desacralizing care system in which diagnosis and treatment of trauma occurs within a framework of racializing criminality and wealth production for the elite class. Such a scheme triggers a trajectory of care practices that begin with their arrest and then imprisonment. Here, state care follows a carceral logic and as such offers sedative relief to deeply inflicted social wounds. Defined as "criminal aliens," migrant border crossers are denied their human fullness and, as such, their personhoods remain racialized, criminalized, and commoditized throughout the State's caring operations.

It is worth repeating that the State's sacred apparatus sets the value threshold of migrant border crossers well below their human fullness. In othering migrant border crossers, the State relies on a repertoire of desacralizing categories—"illegal," "alien," and "criminal," to name a few. These objectifying labels translate into a carceral system of care that depletes any sense of hope of recovery or wellness in migrant border crossers.[6] Indeed, it is in the area of migrant care that the State's hermeneutic of the sacred comes into full view. Implied in human care is a certain degree of ascribed sanctity to human sufferers, enough so that their lives are worth sustaining. Yet care of the desacralized other begins with the lowest valuing of human life and hence is prone to providing only limited relief. For the State, caring for migrant border crossers does not aim for their wholeness but rather for the wholeness of its sacralized public good. Therefore, care of the State's desacralized other actually translates into torture for migrant border crossers, not healing. This may seem to contradict traditional notions of human care; however, under the State's desacralizing scheme this type of human care makes complete sense. As the State's desacralized, migrant border crossers are diagnosed as the disease of the public good and hence cared for through a carceral system. Their care then comes in the form of arrests, detention, and deportation, for only the State's sacralized public good is deserving of wholeness and wellness. This carceral approach to migrant pain and trauma reflects less genuine migrant care than care for the State's sacred apparatus. In other words, caring for the State's sacred occurs through desacralized forms of "care" of migrant border crossers. This dynamic in which migrant torture represents a mode of human care is made possible through the State's investments in the sacred. As argued in previous chapters, the sacred serves as an effective social force for elite power precisely because it exonerates the most egregious and inhumane acts of violence. From the sacred, elite power is able to construct an inverted world in which migrant torture is an integral part of human care and the true sufferers are the sacralized members of the State. Moreover, this inverted world is not isolated to migrants but rather extends to border communities due to their common physiognomy with many black- and brown-bodied border crossers.[7] Ultimately, the dehumanizing care of racially criminalized border crossers serves as a template for all black- and brown-bodied citizens in the US-Mexico borderlands. These insidious ripple effects are what link migrant border crossers to the border community under a hegemonic regime that seeks to subjugate and devour all people deemed nonsacred by the State.

Given that this elite project thrives on the desacralization of the human Other, a borderland hermeneutic of healing care must assert a different valuing system of black- and brown-bodied people. In the US-Mexico borderlands, *curanderismo* (from the Spanish verb *curar*, which means "to heal" or "to cure") represents an abiding practice of healing care, particularly for the disenfranchised poor.[8] Endowed with a different valuing system, *curanderismo* begins with a generous valuation of all life forms and their contexts of origin while also cherishing that which is other to the earth and human beings, as with the spirit realm.[9] In privileging what is other to our earthly reality (the metaphysical), *curanderismo* represents a praxis that inhabits otherness in order to sacralize otherness. For those deemed the nonsacred other, this mode of human care can be particularly effective, largely because their otherness serves as a source of healing and not as an object through which elite power reproduces itself. As reflected previously, state modes of human care are designed to treat the desacralized human other as the disease of the public good. In the case of migrant border crossers, their desacralization gives way to a carceral system of care that aims to objectify their otherness for wealth production.[10] Designated as the nonsacred other of the public good, migrant border crossers are not meant to be whole or well but rather to be the State's emblem of social sickness, cultural deformity, and chronic criminality. Through the State's sacred apparatus, the nonsacred migrant other is treated as a social cancer and hence is arrested, detained, and deported. Here, their otherness is their demise. Destined for eradication, there is little that state-sponsored forms of human care can do to reverse the wretched plight of migrant border crossers, due in large part to their dependence on migrant otherness as disease of the public good. Care in the genuine sense of the word registers here as a minimalist approach to migrant wellness, with the bulk of the State's energies and resources expended primarily on migrant custody.[11] Yet for *curanderismo*, otherness is not the disease but rather the healing agent. This conceptualization of otherness translates into modes of human care in which otherness is sacralized. Hence the energies and resources expended through *curandera* care are at maximum levels such that healing, wellness, and wholeness are attainable outcomes for the wounded Other. By calibrating a borderland hermeneutic to a *curandera* valuing system, the aim here is to replace the State's hermeneutic of the sacred—which destines migrant border crossers

Caring for the sacred Other 113

for permanent trauma—with an "Other" vision of healing care that elevates the intrinsic sacredness of all migrant border crossers. As for the otherness that defines *curanderismo*, Anzaldúa provides this fitting description:

> Chamanas, curanderas, artistas, and spiritual activists, like nepantleras, are liminal people, at the thresholds of form, forever betwixt and between. They move among different realities and psychic states, journeying beyond the natural order or status quo and into other worlds. Often curanderas express an oppositional worldview. For them, life is a struggle between forces of good and evil, and their lives and therapeutic philosophies have an adversarial quality. They mediate between life-giving and life-taking forces, bring the opposites together in some meaningful fashion. They seem to perform a balancing act by standing above the contest and mastering both sides.[12]

The ways in which *curandera* care sacralizes otherness is to inhabit it in the form of a truth-making position or, as Anzaldúa describes, a liminal position that is "forever betwixt and between." Here difference, opposition, and resistance reflect what *curandera* care seeks to achieve—which is to privilege otherness as the primary healing agent. With otherness integral to the therapeutic philosophy of *curandera* care, the ideal patient is the desacralized migrant other. For from and through otherness, *curandera* care comes to migrant border crossers not in the form of a carceral system, as reflected in state modes of migrant care, but rather in a form that seeks their longevity of life. *Curanderas* harness otherness—as Anzaldúa indicates moving among "different realities and psychic states, journeying beyond the natural order or status quo and into other worlds"—in order to care for otherness. In contrast to state modes of migrant care, the desacralized other is used to care for the State's sacralized public good, as seen in the arrest, detainment, and deportation of migrant border crossers. Among the questions informing this chapter include: what is modeled in *curandera* care in terms of how it sacralizes otherness? How does the practice of *curanderismo* translate into a healing epistemology of otherness for migrant border crossers? In the words of Anzaldúa, essential to *curandera* practice is to "perform a balancing act by standing above the contest and mastering both sides." In the end, this chapter aims to theorize on this aspect of *curandera* practice, such that our notions of otherness are able to stand above the State's desacralization of migrant border crossers and its sacralized public good in ways that master both sides.

State inventions of the sacred

In ascribing a higher worth to certain humans over others, the State relies on inventions of the sacred in which national sovereignty, citizenship, and security are linked to the divine. These constructions of religious nationalism reflect the magnetic nature of "the sacred" in mobilizing a body politic for the benefit of elite power. The sacred—at least in the religious sense of the term—is expressed in multiple cultural forms and ethnic varieties; yet as it pertains to the US-Mexico borderlands, the State has found it useful for reproducing wealth and justifying eradicating forms of violence. Indeed, the ascribed authority given to the realms of the divine and sacred is not a State invention, but rather endemic to the human experience. What is a State invention, however, is the current version of religious nationalism that invests in the authoritative currency of the sacred to create vilifying notions of migrant border crossers. Within a monopoly capitalist context, the material effects of this invention of the sacred bolster its authority as a profitable system of belief and lucrative moral framework. The ensuing social reality is a reproduction of elite power at the expense of dehumanized migrant border crossers. If, under the State's inventions of the sacred, migrant border crossers represent the desacralized human other, then a counter measure would be to begin with the valuation of migrant border crosser as the sacred human Other. It is precisely the latter strategy that I am trying to bring to the fore through the valuing framework of borderlands *curanderismo*.

The State's reliance on the sacred to desacralize migrant border crossers renders them foes of the body politic and hence the divine realm. The transcendence of their vilification raises the moral stakes, particularly among religious nationalists, regarding their elimination from the body politic. Thus, to redress the plight of migrant border crossers solely from a social or political vantage point would not have lasting effects given that their dehumanization also stems from the State's reliance on religious belief and elite notions of the sacred. As such, the sacred must serve as a hermeneutical focal point for those seeking to better the lives of migrant border crossers. It represents a major site of epistemological and activist struggle largely because of its instrumentalization by the State (often with the assistance of the Christian church) to devastate the lives of migrant border crossers. A crucial first step is to invert the sacralization regime of the State, such that the hermeneutical starting point is the migrant border crosser as the sacred Other. Underlying this initial strategy is not a rejection of the sacred as an irrelevant domain for social change but rather an inversion of the State's economy of the sacred to actualize a different material reality for migrant border crossers. For the State, the authoritative weight of the sacred is commensurate to its effectiveness in reproducing elite power. Here its public currency is in flux and as such places its rhetoric, symbols, and religious alliances under constant negotiation. In the current era, the State has strengthened the public value of the sacred as a source for realizing a spectrum of inequalities that primarily benefit elite power. Rather than dismiss the public currency of the sacred under the State, how can this currency and hence authority be harnessed and redirected in ways that bring dignity and material benefit to migrant border crossers?

Implied in a humanitarian valuation of humans is an emphasis on our earthly worth with minimal attention to our transcendent worth. For the State, the sacred inspires a transcendent valuation of humans, hence enabling the construction of broad thresholds for ensuring its reproduction. Through the sacralization of people, places, and events, the threshold for their existence is imagined beyond this earthly existence, thereby securing their permanence within society. With the power to inspire the political imagination toward a transcendent valuation of humans—and thereby effect social reality—is also a function of desacralization. Where sacralization affords the State permanence in positive ways, desacralization gives life to elite power through broad thresholds of violence. Here, the political imagination is inspired to construct an expansive playing field within which to perform a kind of transcending violence against the State's desacralized other. In other words, what desacralization ultimately sanctions is not only genocide, but complete erasure of any earthly trace. For any intervening human valuation system, the sacred is still a worthwhile investment in that, if invested differently, it has the power to inspire the political imagination to create life-giving permanence of those desacralized under the State's sacred apparatus. The key benefit is the setting of the threshold beyond the social realms and into the otherworldly such that the imagined value of people like migrant border crossers transcends the earth-bound logic of racial criminalization. In imagining migrant border crossers as the sacred Other, the resulting social reality should be one of life-giving permanence.

As the State has shown, elite power has much to gain when the sacred is applied to humans—either to sanctify or to demonize them. Ironically, in applying the sacred to people, the State admits to its power to inspire the political imagination of the transcendent intrinsic worth of humans. In many ways, this sacred-to-human application subtends the public currency of the sacred, for without such a linkage it would have minimal rhetorical sway in a majority Christian body politic. For the US-Mexico borderlands, what is problematic about the State's sacred-to-human scheme is the population imagined to have transcendent criminality such that their social reality is permanently traumatic. The counter aim, therefore, is to reallocate the human aspect of the State's economy of the sacred to benefit those deemed public enemies both here on earth and beyond. In the US-Mexico borderlands, the State's number one public enemy under its sacred apparatus are mainly black- and brown-bodied migrant border crossers.[13]

Although the State's investments in the sacred have in view the human domain, they are resourced by a complex assemblage of stakeholders that include white nationalists, monopoly capitalists, and what I call "franchising US evangelicalism." These linkages require that the sacred be conveyed through religious nationalist tropes that exalt US citizenship, government, law, and border security as divinely good. Those relied upon to ensure that such exaltation is realized in the human domain are the people within the human care sector, such as clergy, nurses, doctors, therapists, social workers, humanitarians, educators, and police. Through this vast network of state agents within the human care sector, the State is able to apply its invention of the sacred in ways that reproduce its stakeholders' power and privilege. Hence, not turning our critical gaze to the sacred leaves this front open for the State to instrumentalize and harness it in ways that continue to render migrant border crossers nonhuman others. Hence, rather than abandon the sacred as a futile concept, does its raised public currency under the State index the site where our critical gaze should turn in order to improve the social and material realities of migrant border crossers? Of concern in this chapter is not so much critiquing how the ruling economy of the sacred is working to ravage and annihilate the lives of migrant border crossers. Rather, I seek to offer a valuing framework that draws upon the healing care practices of *curanderismo* as a counter strategy that renders migrant border crossers as the sacred Other and not transcending enemies of the State.

Sacralizing the human other through *curandera* praxis

In stark contrast to the State's human care regime, *curanderismo* in the US-Mexico borderlands resorts to healing care practices that defy the racializing logic subtending Western scientific objectivity by first privileging minoritized bodies as worthy of healing touch, transcendent worth, symbolic interchange, historical connectedness, and sacralized spaces. In this way, the standards for care do not default to a white male heterosexual able bodied; rather, minoritized bodies are understood to be intrinsically sacred from the outset.[14] As a result, *curanderismo*, or what Luis D. Léon calls "*curandera* praxis,"[15] does not operate within a matrix in which pained minoritized bodies are measured, weighed, and calibrated according to Western social ideals. In many ways, this attempt to standardize minoritized bodies is for *curandera* praxis a contributing factor to their pain and trauma.[16] For this reason, borderlands *curandera* praxis does not view pained minoritized bodies as a deviation from the Western social ideal but rather as a person with agency, discernment, transcendence, and symbolic awareness, as well as someone with a social critique.[17] In turning to *curandera* praxis as a theoretical source for a borderland hermeneutic of the sacred, the focus lies less on ingredients, rituals, and folklore than on the rhetorical meaning of *curandera* instincts, intuitions, and conceptualizations of the pained human Other as expressed through sacralizing performances and the production of sacred spaces.

Borderlands *curandera* praxis functions innately as a counter episteme in that it sacralizes minoritized bodies in domains that are intentionally set apart from state-sponsored human care systems. Defined as a backward logic within an empiricist framework, *curandera* praxis privileges marginality—both in terms of diagnosing pain and healing strategies.[18] Unlike the dominant institutions of human care, which are mostly under the watchful gaze of the State, *curandera* praxis admits to a mode of care that harnesses marginality in ways that displaces elite power spatially and conceptually. Instead of state-sponsored institutions controlling the domain of care, *curandera* praxis commands the healing moment by sacralizing marginality, from the physical to the metaphysical. This renders human otherness as the sacred portal through which healing care is made possible. To resemble the logics inherent within state-sponsored human care systems is not the aim of *curandera* praxis, for to do so only nullifies the healing process. Otherness, both in terms of a minoritized body and a counter logic of care, frames the sacralizing process of *curandera* praxis.

Through a carefully constructed web of inversions, otherness is made sacred, hence unleashing a healing reversal process of the elite forces that weaponize otherness to desacralize and hence render minoritized bodies permanent social outcasts. By sacralizing otherness, *curandera* praxis converts elite power's source of control (othering) into a source of healing. As much as this is an indictment on the State's dehumanizing modes of human care, what is extraordinary about *curanderismo* is how embodying otherness makes possible a sacralizing praxis of healing care that relies on different ways of being and knowing (in Anzaldúa's words, "an oppositional worldview").[19] In essence, the more outlandish or irrational its practices appear to the Western scientific gaze, the more it is able to provide healing care to pained, minoritized bodies. By remaining an "Other" to the Western scientific gaze, *curandera* praxis avoids being infiltrated by its desacralizing logics. Thus, intrinsic to its care instincts is a profound care for otherness, both in terms of other therapeutic philosophies and the wounded human Other. This care for otherness invests heavily in the sacred largely because it is synonymous with otherness. For *curandera* praxis, the sacred is that which transcends this world (other worldly) and as such is able to interface in healing ways with human otherness. With the sacred registering the highest designation of worth, its intrinsic otherness serves to elevate the worth of human otherness to a transcendent level. This valuing dynamic of otherness constitutes the sacralizing process of *curandera* praxis. In conferring transcendent value to the human Other, *curandera* praxis also destines new thresholds for minoritized bodies to fulfill. Destined for them is not the threshold of eradication violence as set by the State, but rather a life of healing and self-confidence.

Although the wounds of othering are cared for within *curandera* praxis, what is ultimately sacralized is the inherent otherness that constitutes all human beings. This form of otherness is not state-induced but rather natural to our earthly existence. This is otherness as it pertains to our individual uniqueness as human beings, recognizing that no one human is exactly the same and that humans contain spirits. Under the State's othering regime in the US-Mexico borderlands, there is the standard human being, white male heterosexual able bodied, and the other nonwhite human beings. In the former, their natural otherness is replaced with sacralized notions of homogeneity such that those possessing whiteness are understood to be the definitive standard of measurement for the entire human race. As the standard human, they can never be the human other, for this is solely the function of nonwhite human beings. It is here that *curandera* praxis offers a counter framework of otherness—one where the sacred is not a standardized human being but rather otherness as a trait of all human beings.

For *curandera* praxis, all humans are deserving of sacralization precisely because of our intrinsic otherness. Any manufactured system of othering—as reflected with the State and migrant border crossers—creates artificial otherness, often for the purpose of reproducing elite power. As gleaned from *curandera* praxis, artificial othering fragments selfhood—that is, the person's natural otherness—and causes social wounds like inferiority complex and *sustos* (loss of soul).[20] What is instructive about *curandera* praxis as an approach to human care is how it harnesses the otherness of the sacred (other worldly) to sacralize what is naturally other in the person. Yet incongruent with this approach is the manufacturing of othering to create abiding social wounds, as reflected in the State's desacralization of migrant border crossers. *Curandera* care tends to this type of wounding by desacralizing the othering strategies that create the wounds and yet sacralizes the wounds themselves. Within *curandera* praxis, what is not worth sacralizing are those forces that diminish a sense of self-worth in the person, the kind that lower the person's morale and eats away at a person's confidence in a better future. These forces are desacralized, while what is sacralized are the aspects of the wounded Other that are unique to them, which include the wounds themselves as well as their bodies, minds, and spirits.

In the case of the malicious othering that the State has used to wound migrant border crossers, *curandera* praxis models a conceptualization of otherness that practitioners of human care at the US-Mexico border would be wise to consider. First of all, it invests in the otherness of the sacred in order to confer transcendent value to the intrinsic otherness in all people. This sets the threshold of human care to a level commensurate with their sacred value, which again begins with their embodied otherness. Hence rather than expending minimal energies and resources on migrant border crossers because they are other, practitioners would be led to provide maximum care resources for them on the basis that they each bear distinct social wounds and possess one-of-a-kind bodies, minds, and spirits. With transcendent value, the thresholds for migrant livelihood, well-being, and wholeness are also raised to a more permanent level. Indeed, at the US-Mexico border, migrant border crossers are in desperate need of this empowering type of valuation, for the chronic wounds they have amassed from the State's desacralizing modes of othering are raising the human death toll.[21]

In large part, borderlands *curanderismo* as a human care approach emerged as a response to the social and physical wounds caused by desacralizing modes of othering (in *curandera* terminology *mal ojo, sustos*).[22] Although *curandera* praxis sacralizes the otherness in all humans, it ultimately exists to care for the wounds of people artificially othered by elite power, like migrant border crossers. By sacralizing them, *curandera* praxis assigns their otherness the highest value, resulting in a heightened sense of belonging. Achieving this goal requires a trans-epistemological process involving symbolic connections, spatial arrangements, scents, touch, sounds, tastes, memories, and texts that together communicate to minoritized bodies that they are sacred.[23] In the words of Anzaldúa, "they (*curanderas*) move among different realities and psychic states, journeying beyond the natural order or status quo and into other worlds."[24]

Cure as a counter-othering space

In opposition to their inferior ranking by elite power, *curandera* praxis assigns sacred worth to minoritized bodies within its curing spaces. Subtending these spaces are counter-othering tactics that privilege the unique imagination, senses, and instincts of minoritized bodies. Thus, the notion of cure as an othering space points to a contextualized form of human care that attends to the social and physical wounds of minoritized bodies by first displacing state-sponsored minoritization processes. In minoritizing certain segments of the population, the State relies on affective networks of affiliation and institutions, or in what Foucault describes as individualizing and totalizing forms of power.[25] Thus, accompanying *curandera* praxis are counter modes of human care that seek to desacralize the State and its minoritizing agenda, thereby introducing a curing space for minoritized bodies.[26]

To render the State as a desacralized other, *curandera* praxis fosters curing spaces within *el barrio* (neighborhood), which, as Virgilio Elizondo rightly argues, not only represents the residence of US society's out-groups, but also the place where they experience belonging and participation.[27] *El barrio* registers the minoritizing effects of elite power, marking clearly the systemic and orchestrated negation of social, economic, and political privileges for populations marked as the nonwhite human Other. Nevertheless, the othering mechanisms that relegate *el barrio* to the periphery of elite society are reconstituted within *curandera* praxis to produce curing spaces for wounded minoritized bodies. In this way, borderlands *curandera* praxis resists the desired outcome of state-sponsored minoritization, which as seen in chapter 2 pertains to the eradication of brown-bodied communities. In spaces othered by the State, *curandera* praxis creates curing spaces in the very place where the community's social wounds occur. Marginalized from dominant US society, these communities lie outside the primary flows of wealth production and economies of material privilege. Hence, by creating curing spaces within *el barrio*, *curandera* praxis sacralizes the community's lived spaces of social wound. This inversion of wounding social spaces subverts the nefarious aims of elite power, which is to ensure the community's submission to dominant US society. The emotional and mental toll of marginalization exasperate the community's sense of inferiority and worthlessness.

Yet within the curing spaces of *curandera* praxis, the spaces meant for social wound convert into sacralized spaces of healing and empowerment.

The curing spaces within *curandera* praxis are careful to reflect ways of knowing that differ from state-sponsored logics of human care. To achieve this, it cuts across a matrix of epistemological domains, or as León describes, "a variety of ancient Mexican healing systems that arise from the religious matrix articulated in colonialism."[28] This trans-epistemological interchange of *curandera* praxis, which is nonlinear and nonhierarchical, gives shape to curing spaces that oppose state-sponsored minoritizing logics by conveying a deep sense of belonging to injured minoritized bodies. For the State, human care is driven by a monopoly capitalist market system that forces knowledge exchange, prognosis, and ensuing treatment of injury to be dispensed according to an inflated price scale. Thus, care within state-sponsored spaces (e.g. hospitals, clinics, prisons, detention centers, etc.) exacerbates the injury of minoritized bodies through a system of perpetual indebtedness. Ultimately, these spaces produce commoditized, minoritized bodies that enrich society's elite class. Indeed, curing minoritized bodies is always provisional within state-sponsored spaces of human care precisely because they prioritize elite market systems. By conflating a surplus of spaces, supplies, and medical expertise with cure, elite power is able to deflect from the insidious processes that fragmentize and individualize minoritized bodies. As for the curing spaces of *curandera* praxis, the surplus lies not in medical machinery but in the ways in which it prioritizes minoritized bodies. Distinctive here is how space is produced for the human Other rather than for the reproduction of elite power. To separate cure from the latter economic system, *curandera* praxis fills its curing spaces with non-commoditizing objects (e.g. candles, eggs, oils, lemons, incense, glasses of water, crosses, herbs, etc.) and capacitating configurations (e.g. altars) that acknowledge the intelligibility of the injured human Other.

An essential function of the curing spaces of *curandera* praxis is to draw minoritized bodies closer to the curing process, or what León identifies as "proximity and similarity."[29] In contrast to state-sponsored spaces of human care, which work diligently to confound minoritized bodies, the curing spaces of *curandera* praxis make healing accessible outside of a surplus of medical commodities and exclusionary expert networks.[30] Rather than relying on profit-driven spaces, *curandera* praxis attunes its curing spaces to the specific intelligibility of the injured minoritized body. Such a maneuver recognizes the construction of space as giving worth to the injured minoritized body rather than medical commodities and positivistic procedures. In prioritizing the embodied injury—which is social, physical, and spiritual in nature—*curandera* curing spaces accommodate for the fullness and fluxes of context.[31] The aim is less about sterilizing the curing space as to render it unfamiliar to a wounded minoritized body than cultivating an atmosphere that conveys a strong sense of connection and belonging. The othering performed in sterile spaces reinforces the wounds of desacralizing otherness that minoritized bodies endure in dominant society. Here, they are removed from what is familiar and as such produce provisional relief. By mirroring the othering endured in dominant society, the sterile curing spaces created by state-sponsored modes of care only treat the physical pain—albeit temporarily. Yet, the elite power undergirding the production of these spaces inevitably perpetuates the deeply rooted social wounds that afflict all minoritized bodies. What sterile curing spaces and minoritized bodies have in common is that both are constructions of elite power. Sterile spaces therefore contradict their intended purpose by caring for both the physical and social wounds of minoritized bodies. Their affiliations with elite power hinder that latter result, for to heal their social wounds destabilizes a key strategy in the reproduction of elite power. Within *curandera* praxis, the curing spaces are made familiar in ways that address both the physical and social wounds of minoritized bodies. To render curing spaces familiar to injured minoritized bodies, *curandera* praxis avoids bureaucratic processes for ordering bodies and objects, for such an approach reflects rigid state disciplinary practices that reinforce their minoritization. Instead, these curing spaces move from the *curandera*'s workroom to the homes of injured minoritized bodies, revealing a spectrum of embodied trans-connectedness across multiple ways of knowing.[32]

As for the objects in its curing spaces, *curandera* praxis engenders a sacred imaginary (e.g. altars, saint statues, crucifixes, candles, incenses, perfumes, and oils) that elevates a sense of self-worth and hope of a better future. Different from the medical machinery within state-sponsored spaces, all of which commoditize injured bodies, *curandera* praxis chooses from a specific repertoire of objects for the sole purpose of sacralizing its curing spaces and those who inhabit them. Objects that sacralize rather than commoditize prompt a type of healing that is free from economic indebtedness and financial servitude to the elite class. This is where simplicity and resourcefulness affirm an economic awareness for *curandera* praxis, especially as it pertains to the affordability of healing care for minoritized bodies. In the US-Mexico borderlands, injury, anxiety, and trauma are rooted within elite economic structures that exhaust, ravage, and eradicate minoritized bodies.[33] In this context, low-wages, an abiding racial logic, and chronic poverty make state-sponsored healing care economically unfeasible for many black- and brown-bodied communities in the border region.[34] Marginalized from the economies of privilege that afford the dominant culture access to higher-wage employment and hence better quality of life, minoritized bodies encounter lifelong social wounds that they simply cannot afford to heal.

Therefore, object selection for *curandera* praxis stems not from a consumerist impulse but from an ethic of care that prioritizes a sense of belonging for injured minoritized bodies. In using mainly household items and native plants, *curandera* praxis enables healing without financial indebtedness. Here the affordability of care admits to *curanderismo*'s commitment to healing minoritized bodies, for it realizes that lower costs equate to lower anxieties, which is necessary for healing to occur. As part of the sense of belonging that *curandera* praxis strives to create, its affordability in turn displaces the economy of privilege that undergirds state-sponsored modes of human care. In caring for minoritized bodies, their healing is put within their reach—economically, materially, socially, and culturally.

It is this sense of belonging (such that spaces, movements, objects, and costs privilege the healing needs of minoritized bodies) that *curandera* praxis operates as a counter-othering strategy of state-sponsored systems of human care. To the State, the counter-othering tactics of these curing spaces are assigned inferior status precisely because their sources are from people it has deemed unintelligent, subhuman, and disposable. This undervaluing of *curandera* praxis, however, is exploited by *curanderas* in that it allows them to construct curing spaces away from any state influence. Characterized as folkish charlatans, the State is under the false impression that their curing spaces are fraudulent. As such, *curanderas* are conversely free to construct a sacralizing world in which minoritized bodies are decriminalized, deracialized, and decolonized. Within state-sponsored spaces of human care, surveillance and commodification of the body are intrinsic functions of their design; whereas for *curandera* praxis, the aim of its curing spaces is not to reproduce elite power structures, but rather to sacralize minoritized bodies.[35] In essence, *curandera* praxis is not only forced into a marginalized position as a human care approach; it is also intentional in preserving this position in order to heal minoritized bodies. Although othered by the State's human care apparatus, *curandera* praxis engages in a counter-othering tactic that desacralizes state-sponsored modes of human care. From its object selection to its curing spaces, *curandera* praxis desacralizes the profit-driven industry of state-sponsored human care. Ultimately, what is deemed sacred within *curandera* praxis is the healing of minoritized bodies. Such a mission requires the absence of state-sponsored modes of human care largely because the value system that undergirds them is the source of social wound for minoritized bodies. Hence *curandera* praxis sacralizes their otherness by othering the economic and social forces that contribute to their suffering.

The *corpo*-reality of minoritized bodies

Sacralizing minoritized bodies within *curandera* praxis serves as an indictment on how the State has abandoned certain people to a place of abject scarcity. Their destitution intimates a state-sponsored diagnosis that black- and brown-bodied people are biological defects and hence incapable of embodying the social ideal of white heterosexual masculinity. What is "*corpo*-reality" (my hyphenation seizes upon the two words in corporeality, *corpo* from the Latin word for "body" and reality for "real life") for minoritized populations is ascribed to a state of illegality, criminality, disease, ignorance, and inferiority. These desacralizing states of existence foreclose on any human sense of presence for minoritized bodies within the body politic.

As minoritized bodies, their struggle for meaningful earthly existence poses a threat to the desired aims of the State, which involve their negation from the body politic. Their severing from wealth and well-being occurs on the flesh and within carceral spaces. This *corpo*-reality of negation is solidified in the State's sacralized archives. Like their bodies, their memory is mangled within the official archives of the State such that their earthly witness is present only as a public menace. From a negated reality in the body and in public memory, the State sanctions violence against minoritized bodies in perpetuity. Represented by the State as an enemy, the full humanity of minoritized bodies is rendered unseen within the body politic. The implications are catastrophic in that their invisibility prevents the delivery of state-distributed recourses. In this way, their material scarcity is the symptom of their negated *corpo*-realities within the body politic, all of which points to the crisis of presence. Although present as public menaces, minoritized bodies never fully enjoy a state of real presence or *corpo*-reality.

Within *curandera* praxis, the state of a negated *corpo*-reality for minoritized bodies, both to self and to society, is diagnosed as *susto*, which is understood to be the loss of soul or not being fully present in the body.[36] *Susto*, therefore, identifies a frightened, violated, or enslaved minoritized body such that the body lacks real presence.[37] Without *corpo*-reality, minoritized bodies enter a self-destructive state, or what *curandera* Elena Avila refers to as "internalized oppression."[38] Indeed, the processes of minoritization used by elite power to render black- and brown-bodied people invisible to self and the body politic align with what Avila terms "immense *susto*."[39] For her, this type of *susto* involves a violent large-scale event like the imperial conquest of a people and their systemic colonization.[40] The expansive loss of *corpo*-reality under a large-scale *susto* admits to technologies of elite power that violently impose their will upon an entire demographic in ways that leave them culturally destroyed and physically enslaved. Meeting the criterion of a large-scale *susto* is state-sponsored desacralization of mainly black- and brown-bodied people at the US-Mexico border. Like early European colonialism, the State produces its desacralizing power from investments made to the sacred, which in the current era consists of white supremacy, US evangelicalism, and the border-sovereignty-citizenship triplex. The goal of their desacralization is not only the denial of any real presence to self but more importantly their exploitation and then eradication. Framing this as a large-scale *susto* admits to the mass scale of this type of social wounding as well as marks the depths to which it is able to go in destroying a sense of personhood (loss of soul). The mechanics to a *susto* of this scale dissects into networks, institutions, procedures, techniques, spaces, and rhetorics that all operate in unison to demolish the real presence of black- and brown-bodied people.

Casted as innately deviant, minoritized bodies are not only denied meaningful *corpo*-reality but are also made to detest themselves largely because being present in their bodies means being an enemy of the public good. Herein lies the nefarious depths of the *susto*, a fear of self. For what the State's desacralization reflects back to dark-skinned bodies is that their bodies are irreparable and therefore require a lifetime of whitening alterations to hair, body, speech, and culture. This engenders a series of self-hating habits that aim to hide, disguise, or eliminate those physical and cultural attributes that are the cause of fright for white society. With the large-scale *susto* of State desacralization, black- and brown-bodied people are not only a detestable curse to the body politic, but in addition their presence is a curse to themselves. Under the topic of "Healing *sustos* and breaches in reality," Anzaldúa describes the full magnitude of this type of *susto* as follows:

> For racialized people, managing losses, the trauma of racism, and other colonial abuses affect our self-conceptions, our very identity, fragmenting our psyches and pitching us into states of nepantla. During or after any trauma (including individual and group racist acts), you lose parts of your soul as an immediate strategy to minimize the pain and to cope—*hecho pedazos*, you go into a state of *susto*.[41]

This form of large-scale *susto*, as conceived within *curandera* care, rightly registers the traumas of racism and colonizing power at the level of the sacred (as indicated in the notion of loss of the soul). As discussed in previous chapters, the State's criminally racializing logic is not a stand-alone force for inflicting social wounds, nor does it suffice in fulfilling elite power's ultimate ambitions of permanent domination. Within the State's sacred apparatus, it represents one of many other socially traumatizing forces that in their entirety fall more accurately under desacralizing power. In diagnosing *susto*, *curandera* care admits to the full measure of the social wound, so much so that the person's soul is among the domains treated. As desacralized bodies, *curandera* care turns to sacralizing rituals and spaces to heal the traumatizing malady of *susto*.

In curing *susto*, *curanderas* use sacralized ritual cleansings (*limpias*) and curing spaces to call the frightened soul back into the body.[42] Robert T. Trotter and Juan Antonio Chavira describe the healing process as follows:

> The healer [*el que cura*] sweeps the patient with the broom, saying the Apostles' Creed three times. At the end of each Creed, the healer whispers in the patient's ear, "Come, don't stay there" [*Vente no te quedes allí*]. The patient responds, "I am coming" [*Aquí vengo*]. The sick person must perspire and is then given some tea of *yerba anis* to drink. The healer then places a cross of holy palm on the patient's head and asks Almighty God, in the name of the Holy Trinity, to restore the patient's spiritual strength.[43]

The investments that the *curandera* makes in the sacred privilege the wounded minoritized body.

Ritual, space, and religious discourse are used to construct a sacralizing counter force that seeks to restore the patient's frightened personhood (or as Christina Garcia Lopez describes "calling back the soul").[44] It is through the sacred that the *curandera* calls to the wounded patient, "come, don't stay there." Where minoritized bodies in the US-Mexico borderlands find themselves is in a desacralized state of *susto*, fragmented and tormented beyond recognition. This condition not only goes underdiagnosed in state-sponsored spaces of human care; the extent of this type of wounding is even underestimated within critical theory, particularly the kind that hold a bias toward the sacred and spiritual phenomena. The trans-epistemological instincts of *curandera* care know to treat socially wounded minoritized bodies through the sacred, for this is the full extent of the wound. In other words, the racially criminalized self is not only suffering physically and mentally; this type of wounding also points to a transcendent devaluing on the self that reaches to the soul. The result of this condition is complete eradication of all traces of self, personhood, and soul to the patient and the body politic. This is the severity of the loss, hence the diagnosis of a frightened soul. It is "there"—a place of complete disconnect—that desacralizing power seeks to take minoritized bodies. Yet within *curandera* care, their lostness to self and to those around them is remedied through a sacralizing process that calls back body, mind, and soul to a place of self-awareness, self-dignity, and self-worth.

Making present minoritized bodies

In curing minoritized bodies from *susto*, *curandera* praxis relies on a series of ritual sweepings of the body called *barridas*.[45] Through this care practice, minoritized bodies are touched not with the intention of measuring pain as to commoditize it but rather to acknowledge the life forces present within and around their violated bodies. An egg, lemon, and bushel of herbs are used in the *barrida* (sweeping) cleansing ritual in order to extract the desacralizing forces that are causing a loss of real presence of a minoritized person's body.[46] In addition to the staple *barrida* ritual, *curandera* praxis in the US-Mexico borderlands registers a variety of original treatments for *susto* that are unique to particular *curanderas*. Among them is the practice of the *curandera* whispering to the person, "*vente no te quedes allí*" (come, don't stay there) to which the person responds, "*aquí vengo*" (I am coming).[47] Another includes the *curandera* drawing an outline of the body in the dirt three times a day. Drawing from the research of Brett Hendrickson: "the patient lies on a dirt floor while I [Doña Juanita] use a knife to cut an outline of his body in the ground. When he rises, I take dirt from the lines cut in the ground and mix it with water for him to drink. This I do three times a day for nine days."[48] These additional practices that accompany the standard *barrida* treatment for *susto* reinforce the primary aim of *curandera* praxis—making present minoritized bodies within the realm of the sacred. Whether it be tasting the very dirt that outlined the entire body or summoning the lostness inside the person, the sacred permeates the curing process of making the person present to self-personhood-soul.

As the curing space sacralizes minoritized bodies, the *barrida* ritual affirms their life-emitting *corpo*-reality. Present as sacred bodies, *curandera* praxis reverses the State's desacralizing mission for black- and brown-bodied people in the US-Mexico borderlands. The ritual movements, organic materials, and spiritual invocations of the *barrida* not only suggest a starkly different logic from the one in use within state-sponsored modes of human care, but also their use within the *curandera*'s curing space guide minoritized bodies toward a state-denied status of *corpo*-reality. Through *curandera*'s sweeping touches across the body, the *barrida* ritual connects the body to immediate life forces rather than an eradicating system of commodification and exploitation.

For *curandera* praxis, the immediate life forces in the body are interrelated with broader life forces of the natural and spiritual worlds. As Christina Garcia Lopez indicates, "the epistemological worldview that conceives of susto and its ritual cure (*limpia*) is predicated upon intersubjectivity, in that it recognizes a flow and transference of energy that can cause illness as well as healing."[49] This connectional conceptualization of the body understands life as an accessible power to all living beings despite their intrinsic otherness to each other. The interconnectedness of life links the body to resources of healing and care that are freely accessible simply by virtue of being alive. Within the State's desacralizing mission, however, the dark-skinned Other is displaced from life's proximity and then subjected to a commoditizing system that regulates how they are to live in the body. In the US-Mexico borderlands in particular, minoritized bodies, like migrant border crossers, are made present as performers of criminality, hosts of disease, and bearers of poverty. Added to the State's desacralizing mission, these domains of presence bear a transcendent value and as such destines them to a state of permanent eradication.

Through its curing spaces and *barridas*, *curandera* praxis treats the *susto* at the nexus of a trans-epistemological matrix in which the body is made present as a sacred life and hence deserving of a dignified earthly existence. This disrupts the State's efforts to commoditize minoritized bodies as criminal nonbeings in order to legitimate the mass production of weapons, prisons, security technologies, and behavior-altering pharmaceuticals. For *curandera* praxis, the aim is to connect the displaced sel-personhood-soul to what the State has sought to deny, the proximity of life and a sacralized presence. To touch the entire body with herbs, an egg, and a lemon is to connect the body with organic materials that participate in the same life source as the body. Different from the manufactured human care instruments used to measure, examine, and calibrate minoritized bodies, *curandera* praxis connects their socially wounded bodies to the proximity of life without any incurred debt. In this way, the minoritized body emerges from the curing space of *curandera* praxis as being present not to the State but to life in a sacralized body.

Conclusion

The current state-sponsored regimes of human care in the US-Mexico borderlands have been inadequate in curing the social wounds of black- and brown-bodied people, particularly those who are migrant border crossers. Guarded in this context is a proximity to life's resources and the conferring of a sacralized presence. Here, state-sponsored modes of human care assemble into an elaborate complex of interlocking agents, institutions, instruments, and technologies, all of which desacralize dark-skinned people for the benefit of those sacralized by elite power. What is grossly evil is how this elite complex of control is able to convince the body politic that certain humans are unworthy of full access to life's resources solely on the basis of their darker skin color. Yet even more nefarious is how the State's desacralizing mission renders minoritized bodies enemies to themselves and as such incites self-hating habits that are self-effacing.

While the US-Mexico borderlands represent a major site of state-sponsored human desacralization, this region also offers multiple counter logics as a defense against the State's agenda of eradicating violence. Since the formation of the US-Mexico border in the nineteenth century, the people deemed the nonsacred other in the region have shown their humanity through acts of resistance and activism rather than through the passive embrace of what elite power has destined for them. Among the abiding acts of resistance to state-sponsored regimes of human care in the borderlands is *curandera* praxis. Unique to this borderlands approach to human care is a sacralizing response to the minoritized bodies desacralized as enemies of the public good. *Curandera* care inhabits otherness as the initial step to sacralizing those deemed the nonsacred other. Such otherness is reflected in the curing spaces it constructs as well as the counter-intuitive ways it diagnoses social wounds. In many ways, *curandera* care embodies otherness in order to heal the human Other. Its otherness coincides with an essential characteristic of the sacred, hence the instincts of *curanderas* are led to include the transcendent realms in their diagnosis of trauma and physical ailments. This transcendence is not only the source of otherworldly life forces, it also indexes the ambitions of the State's desacralizing power.

In caring for the desacralized human Other in the US-Mexico borderlands, *curandera* praxis indicts state-constructed spaces for human care. This indictment points to the commoditization of injured minoritized bodies that occurs within state spaces of human care (e.g. detention centers, prisons, hospitals, public clinics, retirement homes, etc.). To counter this process, *curandera* praxis offers curing spaces that privilege the well-being of injured minoritized bodies by sacralizing them. Such an approach limits the curing space to objects, movements, and speech that contribute to the sacralization of the human Other. In what appears to the State as a folkish inferior practice, the objects selected for the *curandera's* curing space are careful not to contribute to the commoditization of the injured minoritized body. Counter to State objectives, which consist of the reproduction of elite wealth, *curandera* praxis operates outside a monopoly capitalist framework, privileging instead the cure and empowerment of injured minoritized bodies. The curing spaces of *curandera* praxis admits to a human-care approach that seeks to de-minoritize, decriminalize, deracialize, and de-commoditize the human Other. To achieve this, *curandera* praxis relies on different ways of conceptualizing injury, cure, and the body in order to facilitate healing of minoritized bodies.

In the current era, black- and brown-bodied border crossers are being ravaged by state-sponsored regimes of human care. In contrast to a *curandera* approach, they are desacralized beyond any human recognition as to render them objects of state-sanctioned violence. Their care occurs primarily in carceral spaces that have commoditized their state-imposed criminality. Left with abject scarcity, they are converted into raw fuel that propels elite economic structures to the status of global dominance. Desacralized black- and brown-bodied border crossers make possible an expanding prison industrial complex, marketized masculine sensuality (as in human sex trafficking), and the human organ supply market.

With borderlands *curanderismo*, minoritized people are granted access to organic strategies of human care that intuit the desacralizing effects of the State's sacred apparatus. By drawing on this approach to human care, medical professionals, clergy, and humanitarians are given a diagnosing framework that instinctually privileges the geography, relationships, and materiality of minoritized bodies in ways that render them sacred domains. From a *curandera* care approach, those socially wounded by the State's desacralizing mission are placed in curing spaces that sacralizes their body, memory, instincts, and sense of agency. As the sacred human Other, they are made present to life in ways that confer to them permanent transcendent value. In the end, their presence projects a life span of well-being rather than ensures the reproduction of elite power.

For those seeking to provide care for the human Other in the US-Mexico borderlands, they must pivot to the domain of the sacred in their diagnosis of their lived trauma. Such a pivot does not imply the privileging of religious belief as the primary mode of care, but rather the pursuit of the full magnitude of the wounds minoritized bodies bear. By turning to the sacred, as reflected in *curandera* praxis, human care providers encounter investments in the sacred that elite power has made in order to wound minoritized bodies. Through the domain of the sacred, human care providers register more accurately the extent of their wounds as well as their intended purpose. The sacred also proves instrumental in conferring transcendent worth to minoritized bodies, a valuation potential that the State has exploited and yet is unavailable to reason-based care systems. It is not enough to designate the human worth of minoritized bodies at the socio-physical level; their current plight requires that their threshold of human value be set to the metaphysical level—and hence out of reach from the State's desacralizing mission.

Notes

1 See Bullock Texas State History Museum, "Life and Death on the Border 1910–1920: Texans Had Divergent Reactions to Revolution in Mexico," 2016, www.thestoryoftexas.com/visit/exhibits/life-and-death-on-the-border-1910-1920; Miguel Antonio Levario, *Militarizing the Border: When Mexicans Became the Enemy* (College Station, TX: Texas A&M University Press, 2015).
2 Gloria Anzaldúa, *Borderlands/La Frontera: The New Mestiza* (San Francisco: Spinsters/Aunt Lute, 1987); Ramón Saldívar, *The Borderlands of Culture: Américo Paredes and the Transnational Imaginary* (Durham, NC: Duke University Press, 2006); Héctor Calderón and José David Saldívar, *Criticism in the Borderlands: Studies in Chicano Literature, Culture, and Ideology* (Durham, NC: Duke University Press, 1991); Carl Gutiérrez-Jones, *Rethinking the Borderlands: Between Chicano Culture and Legal Discourse* (Berkeley, CA: University of California Press, 1995); José David Saldívar, *Border Matters: Remapping American Cultural Studies* (Berkeley, CA: University of California Press, 1997); Rosa Linda Fregoso, *Mexicana Encounters: The Making of Social Identities on the Borderlands* (Berkeley, CA: University of California Press, 2003); Luis D. León, *La Llorona's Children: Religion, Life, and Death in the U.S.-Mexican Borderlands* (Berkeley, CA: University of California Press, 2004), 261–62.
3 Luis D. León, "Metaphor and Place: The U.S.-Mexico Border as Center and Periphery in the Interpretation of Religion," *Journal of the American Academy of Religion* 67 (2015): 543–45.
4 Frank Laczko, Ann Singleton, and Julia Black, eds., "Fatal Journeys, Volume 3, Part 1: Improving Data on Missing Migrants," *International Organization for Migration*, 77–91, http://publications.iom.int/system/files/pdf/fatal_journeys_volume_3_part_1.pdf.
5 Matt Smith and Aura Bogado, "Immigrant Children Forcibly Injected with Drugs at Texas Shelter, Lawsuit Claims," *The Texas Tribune*, June 20, 2018, www.texastribune.org/2018/06/20/immigrant-children-forcibly-injected-drugs-lawsuit-claims/; Clark Mindok, "Startling Increase in Physical and Sexual Abuse of Child Immigrants by US Border Patrol, New Report Alleges," *The Independent*, May 23, 2018, www.independent.co.uk/news/world/americas/child-sex-abuse-us-border-patrol-physical-central-america-trump-a8365966.html; Kevin Loria, "Trump Now Claims Migrant Children Will Be Reunited with Their Families: Here Are the Lifelong Psychological Consequences These Kids Face," *Business Insider*, June 21, 2018, http://uk.businessinsider.com/how-family-separation-and-detention-affect-children-2018-6.
6 The Associated Press, "Detained Immigrants Sue Over Conditions, Medical Care," *NBC News*, August 20, 2019, www.nbcnews.com/news/us-news/detained-immigrants-sue-over-conditions-medical-care-n1044316; Simon Romero et al., "Hungry, Scared and Sick: Inside the Migrant Detention Center in Clint, Tex," *The New York Times*, July 9, 2019, www.nytimes.com/interactive/2019/07/06/us/migrants-border-patrol-clint.html.

7 Dan Solomon, "The Trump Administration Is Targeting Latino Texans Who Are U.S. Citizens," *Texas Monthly*, August 31, 2018, www.texasmonthly.com/politics/its-not-just-about-immigrants-anymore/.
8 See original source material in the *Curanderismo Collection* of the Border Studies Archive at the University of Texas Rio Grande Valley, www.utrgv.edu/bsa/en-us/collections/traditional-mexican-american-folklore/curanderismo/index.htm; Robert T. Trotter and Juan Antonio Chavira, *Curanderismo: Mexican American Folk Healing* (Athens, GA: University of Georgia Press, 1997), 44–43.
9 León, *La Llorona's Children*, 133–34.
10 News Hour, "Detained Migrant Children Suffer 'Trauma After Trauma,' Say Pediatric Experts," *PBS*, September 17, 2019, www.pbs.org/newshour/show/detained-migrant-children-suffer-trauma-after-trauma-say-pediatric-experts; Laura Santhanam, "How Detention Causes Long-term Harm to Children," *PBS*, August 22, 2019, www.pbs.org/newshour/health/how-detention-causes-long-term-harm-to-children.
11 Elizabeth Hlavinka, "Physicians Struggle to Care for Migrants on U.S.-Mexico Border," *MedPage Today*, September 17, 2019, www.medpagetoday.com/publichealthpolicy/generalprofessionalissues/82203.
12 Gloria Anzaldúa, *Light in the Dark/Luz en lo Oscuro: Rewriting Identity, Spirituality, Reality* (Durham, NC: Duke University Press, 2015), 31.
13 US Customs and Border Protection, "U.S. Border Patrol Nationwide Apprehensions by Citizenship and Sector in FY2007," www.cbp.gov/sites/default/files/assets/documents/2018-Jul/usbp-nationwide-apps-sector-citizenship-fy07-fy17.pdf; Victoria Macchi, "At US-Mexico Border, Africans Join Diversifying Migrant Community," *VOA*, August 31, 2019, www.voanews.com/usa/us-mexico-border-africans-join-diversifying-migrant-community; Rick Jervis, "At US-Mexico Border, Migrants from Africa, Haiti Wait to Seek Asylum," *USA Today*, June 4, 2019, www.usatoday.com/story/news/nation/2019/06/04/african-migrants-border-trump-immigration-nuevo-laredo-congo/1319996001/; Adolfo Flores, "A Teen Girl Forced to Wait in Mexico Under Trump's Asylum Policies Nearly Drowned While Waiting to Cross," *BuzzFeed News*, September 16, 2019, www.buzzfeednews.com/article/adolfoflores/trump-asylum-policy-mexico-mpp-remain-rio-grande-dangers.
14 León, *La Llorona's Children*, 249; Elizabeth De La Portilla, *They All Want Magic: Curanderas and Folk Healing* (College Station, TX: Texas A&M University Press, 2009), 52–54; Renoldo J. Maduro, "Curanderismo: Latin American Folk Healing," Ways of Healing, Ancient and Modern, Conference, San Francisco, CA, January 1976, 871; The University of Texas Rio Grande Valley, "Los Que Curan," published in 2012 at *Border Studies Archive: Curanderismo Collection, Video*, 40:15, www.utrgv.edu/bsa/en-us/collections/traditional-mexican-american-folklore/curanderismo/index.htm.
15 León, *La Llorona's Children*, 135.
16 Maduro, "Curanderismo," 2; Ari Kiev, *Curanderismo: Mexican-American Folk Psychiatry* (New York: Free Press, 1968), 17; Trotter and Chavira, *Curanderismo*, 99, 164–65.
17 Trotter and Chavira, *Curanderismo*, 61.
18 Ibid., 2–3.
19 Anzaldúa, *Light in the Dark/Luz en lo Oscuro*, 31.
20 Trotter and Chavira, *Curanderismo*, 89–90.
21 Sarah Stillman, "When Deportation Is a Death Sentence," *The New Yorker*, January 8, 2018, www.newyorker.com/magazine/2018/01/15/when-deportation-is-a-death-sentence; Natascha Elena Uhlmann, "The US Government Deliberately Made the Desert Deadly for Migrants," *The Guardian*, December 29, 2018, www.theguardian.com/commentisfree/2018/dec/29/the-us-government-deliberately-made-the-desert-deadly-for-migrants; Hannah Rappleye and

Lisa Riordan Seville, "24 Immigrants Have Died in ICE Custody During the Trump Administration," *NBC News*, June 9, 2019, www.nbcnews.com/politics/immigration/24-immigrants-have-died-ice-custody-during-trump-administration-n1015291; Adolfo Flores, "More Immigrant Children Are Dying at the Border as the Trump Administration Sends People Back to Mexico," *BuzzFeed News*, September 20, 2019, www.buzzfeednews.com/article/adolfoflores/immigrant-children-dying-united-states-mexico-trump.
22 Trotter and Chavira, *Curanderismo*, 90–92.
23 Ibid., 83, 150–54.
24 Anzaldúa, *Light in the Dark/Luz en lo Oscuro*, 31.
25 Anneleise Victoria Azua, "Borderlands Curanderismo: Folk Healing in the Rio Grande Valley," master's report, the University of Texas at Austin, 2016, 43, https://repositories.lib.utexas.edu/bitstream/handle/2152/41584/AZUA-MASTERSREPORT-2016.pdf?sequence=1&isAllowed=y; Michel Foucault, "The Subject and Power," *Critical Inquiry* 8, no. 4 (Summer 1982): 782.
26 Daniel Alegria, Ernesto Guerra, Cervando Martinez Jr., et al., "El Hospital Invisible: A Study of Curanderismo," *Arch Gen Psychiatry* 34, no. 11 (1977): 1356.
27 Virgilio Elizondo, *Galilean Journey: The Mexican-American Promise*, 24; Alegria et al., "El Hospital Invisible," 1356; Azua, "Borderlands Curanderismo," 24, 39–41; Trotter and Chavira, *Curanderismo*, 1–2; The University of Texas Rio Grande Valley, "Los Que Curan."
28 Alegria et al., "El Hospital Invisible," 1356; Trotter and Chavira, *Curanderismo*, 26, 45.
29 León, *La Llorona's Children*, 135.
30 Trotter and Chavira, *Curanderismo*, 2.
31 Ibid., 150, 164.
32 See *Curanderismo Collection* of the Border Studies Archive at the University of Texas Rio Grande Valley; Trotter and Chavira, *Curanderismo*, 150.
33 Maduro, "Curanderismo," 869.
34 Gaby Galvin, "Battle on the Border," *U.S. News*, May 16, 2018, www.usnews.com/news/healthiest-communities/articles/2018-05-16/a-battle-for-community-health-in-texas-rio-grande-valley; Gaby Galvin, "On the Border, Out of the Shadows," *U.S. News*, May 16, 2018, www.usnews.com/news/healthiest-communities/articles/2018-05-16/americas-third-world-border-colonias-in-texas-struggle-to-attain-services.
35 Dona Maria, "Interview with Curandero_10," recorded November 21, 1974, audio, 57:02, https://cdm16775.contentdm.oclc.org/digital/collection/p16775coll3/id/55/rec/29; Alegria et al., "El Hospital Invisible," 1356; Octavio Ignacio Romano V., "Charismatic Medicine, Folk-Healing, and Folk-Sainthood," *American Anthropologist* 67, no. 5 (October 1965): 1153; Azua, "Borderlands Curanderismo," 40.
36 Trotter and Chavira, *Curanderismo*, 90; Jennifer Koshatka Seman, "The Politics of Curanderismo: Santa Teresa Urrea, Don Pedrito Jaramillo, and Faith Healing in the U.S.-Mexico Borderlands at the Turn of the Twentieth Century," PhD diss., Southern Methodist University, 2015, 6.
37 Trotter and Chavira, *Curanderismo*, 90.
38 Elena Avila and Joy Parker, *Woman Who Glows in the Dark: A Curandera Reveals Traditional Aztec Secrets of Physical and Spiritual Health* (New York: Jeremy P. Tarcher/Putnam, 2000), 28; Kiev, *Curanderismo*, 118.
39 Avila and Parker, *Woman Who Glows in the Dark*, 28.
40 Ibid.
41 Anzaldúa, *Light in the Dark/Luz en lo Oscuro*, 87.
42 Christina Garcia Lopez, *Calling the Soul Back: Embodied Spirituality in Chicanx Narrative* (Tucson: The University of Arizona Press, 2019), 5.
43 Trotter and Chavira, *Curanderismo*, 90–91.

44 Lopez, *Calling the Soul Back*, 11.
45 De La Portilla, *They All Want Magic*, 123; Trotter and Chavira, *Curanderismo*, 82.
46 Ibid.
47 Trotter and Chavira, *Curanderismo*, 90–91.
48 Brett Hendrickson, *Border Medicine: A Transcultural History of Mexican American Curanderismo* (New York: New York University Press, 2014), 126.
49 Lopez, *Calling the Soul Back*, 33.

Bibliography

Alegria, Daniel, Ernesto Guerra, Cervando Martinez Jr., and George G. Meyer. "El Hospital Invisible: A Study of Curanderismo." *Arch Gen Psychiatry* 34, no. 11 (1977): 1354–57.

Anzaldúa, Gloria. *Borderlands/La Frontera: The New Mestiza*. San Francisco: Spinsters/Aunt Lute, 1987.

———. *Light in the Dark/Luz en lo Oscuro: Rewriting Identity, Spirituality, Reality*. Durham, NC: Duke University Press, 2015.

The Associated Press. "Detained Immigrants Sue Over Conditions, Medical Care." *NBC News*, August 20, 2019. www.nbcnews.com/news/us-news/detained-immigrants-sue-over-conditions-medical-care-n1044316.

Avila, Elena, and Joy Parker. *Woman Who Glows in the Dark: A Curandera Reveals Traditional Aztec Secrets of Physical and Spiritual Health*. New York: Jeremy P. Tarcher/Putnam, 2000.

Azua, Anneleise Victoria. "Borderlands Curanderismo: Folk Healing in the Rio Grande Valley." Master's Report, the University of Texas at Austin, 2016. https://repositories.lib.utexas.edu/bitstream/handle/2152/41584/AZUA-MASTERSREPORT-2016.pdf?sequence=1&isAllowed=y.

Bullock Texas State History Museum. "Life and Death on the Border 1910–1920: Texans Had Divergent Reactions to Revolution in Mexico." 2016. www.thestoryoftexas.com/visit/exhibits/life-and-death-on-the-border-1910-1920.

Calderón, Héctor, and José David Saldívar. *Criticism in the Borderlands: Studies in Chicano Literature, Culture, and Ideology*. Durham, NC: Duke University Press, 1991.

De La Portilla, Elizabeth. *They All Want Magic: Curanderas and Folk Healing*. College Station, TX: Texas A&M University Press, 2009.

Elizondo, Virgilio. *Galilean Journey: The Mexican-American Promise*. Maryknoll, NY: Orbis Books, 2003.

Flores, Adolfo. "More Immigrant Children Are Dying at the Border as the Trump Administration Sends People Back to Mexico." *BuzzFeed News*, September 20, 2019. www.buzzfeednews.com/article/adolfoflores/immigrant-children-dying-united-states-mexico-trump.

———. "A Teen Girl Forced to Wait in Mexico Under Trump's Asylum Policies Nearly Drowned While Waiting to Cross." *BuzzFeed News*, September 16, 2019. www.buzzfeednews.com/article/adolfoflores/trump-asylum-policy-mexico-mpp-remain-rio-grande-dangers.

Foucault, Michel. "The Subject and Power." *Critical Inquiry* 8, no. 4 (Summer 1982): 777–95.

Fregoso, Rosa Linda. *Mexicana Encounters: The Making of Social Identities on the Borderlands*. Berkeley, CA: University of California Press, 2003.

Galvin, Gaby. "Battle on the Border." *U.S. News*, May 16, 2018. www.usnews.com/news/healthiest-communities/articles/2018-05-16/a-battle-for-community-health-in-texas-rio-grande-valley.

———. "On the Border, Out of the Shadows," *U.S. News*, May 16, 2018. www.usnews.com/news/healthiest-communities/articles/2018-05-16/americas-third-world-border-colonias-in-texas-struggle-to-attain-services.

Gutiérrez-Jones, Carl. *Rethinking the Borderlands: Between Chicano Culture and Legal Discourse*. Berkeley, CA: University of California Press, 1995.

Hendrickson, Brett. *Border Medicine: A Transcultural History of Mexican American Curanderismo*. New York: New York University Press, 2014.

Hlavinka, Elizabeth. "Physicians Struggle to Care for Migrants on U.S.-Mexico Border." *MedPage Today*, September 17, 2019. www.medpagetoday.com/publichealthpolicy/generalprofessionalissues/82203.

Jervis, Rick. "At US-Mexico Border, Migrants from Africa, Haiti Wait to Seek Asylum." *USA Today*, June 4, 2019. www.usatoday.com/story/news/nation/2019/06/04/african-migrants-border-trump-immigration-nuevo-laredo-congo/1319996001/.

Kiev, Ari. *Curanderismo: Mexican-American Folk Psychiatry*. New York: Free Press, 1968.

Laczko, Frank, Ann Singleton, and Julia Black, eds. "Fatal Journeys, Volume 3, Part 1: Improving Data on Missing Migrants." *International Organization for Migration*. http://publications.iom.int/system/files/pdf/fatal_journeys_volume_3_part_1.pdf.

León, Luis D. *La Llorona's Children: Religion, Life, and Death in the U.S.-Mexican Borderlands*. Berkeley, CA: University of California Press, 2004.

———. "Metaphor and Place: The U.S.-Mexico Border as Center and Periphery in the Interpretation of Religion." *Journal of the American Academy of Religion* 67 (2015): 541–71.

Levario, Miguel Antonio. *Militarizing the Border: When Mexicans Became the Enemy*. College Station, TX: Texas A&M University Press, 2015.

Lopez, Christina Garcia. *Calling the Soul Back: Embodied Spirituality in Chicanx Narrative*. Tucson: The University of Arizona Press, 2019.

Loria, Kevin. "Trump Now Claims Migrant Children Will Be Reunited with Their Families: Here Are the Lifelong Psychological Consequences These Kids Face." *Business Insider*, June 21, 2018. http://uk.businessinsider.com/how-family-separation-and-detention-affect-children-2018-6.

Macchi, Victoria. "At US-Mexico Border, Africans Join Diversifying Migrant Community." *VOA*, August 31, 2019. www.voanews.com/usa/us-mexico-border-africans-join-diversifying-migrant-community.

Maduro, Renoldo J. "Curanderismo: Latin American Folk Healing." Ways of Healing, Ancient and Modern, Conference, San Francisco, CA, January 1976.

Maria, Dona. "Interview with Curandero_10." Recorded November 21, 1974. Audio, 57:02. https://cdm16775.contentdm.oclc.org/digital/collection/p16775coll3/id/55/rec/29.

Mindok, Clark. "Startling Increase in Physical and Sexual Abuse of Child Immigrants by US Border Patrol, New Report Alleges." *The Independent*, May 23, 2018. www.independent.co.uk/news/world/americas/child-sex-abuse-us-border-patrol-physical-central-america-trump-a8365966.html.

News Hour. "Detained Migrant Children Suffer 'Trauma After Trauma,' Say Pediatric Experts." *PBS*, September 17, 2019. www.pbs.org/newshour/show/detained-migrant-children-suffer-trauma-after-trauma-say-pediatric-experts.

Rappleye, Hannah, and Lisa Riordan Seville. "24 Immigrants Have Died in ICE Custody During the Trump Administration." *NBC News*, June 9, 2019. www.nbcnews.com/politics/immigration/24-immigrants-have-died-ice-custody-during-trump-administration-n1015291.

Romano, V., and O. Ignacio. "Charismatic Medicine, Folk-Healing, and Folk-Sainthood." *American Anthropologist* 67, no. 5 (October 1965): 1151–73.

Romero, Simon, Zolan Kanno-Youngs, Manny Fernandez, Daniel Borunda, Aaron Montes, and Caitlin Dickerson. "Hungry, Scared and Sick: Inside the Migrant Detention Center in Clint, Tex." *The New York Times*, July 9, 2019. www.nytimes.com/interactive/2019/07/06/us/migrants-border-patrol-clint.html.

Saldívar, José David. *Border Matters: Remapping American Cultural Studies*. Berkeley, CA: University of California Press, 1997.

Saldívar, Ramón. *The Borderlands of Culture: Américo Paredes and the Transnational Imaginary*. New Americanists, edited by Donald E. Pease. Durham, NC: Duke University Press, 2006.

Santhanam, Laura. "How Detention Causes Long-term Harm to Children." *PBS*, August 22, 2019. www.pbs.org/newshour/health/how-detention-causes-long-term-harm-to-children.

Seman, Jennifer Koshatka. "The Politics of Curanderismo: Santa Teresa Urrea, Don Pedrito Jaramillo, and Faith Healing in the U.S.-Mexico Borderlands at the Turn of the Twentieth Century." PhD diss., Southern Methodist University, 2015.

Smith, Matt, and Aura Bogado. "Immigrant Children Forcibly Injected with Drugs at Texas Shelter, Lawsuit Claims." *The Texas Tribune*, June 20, 2018. www.texastribune.org/2018/06/20/immigrant-children-forcibly-injected-drugs-lawsuit-claims/.

Solomon, Dan. "The Trump Administration Is Targeting Latino Texans Who Are U.S. Citizens." *Texas Monthly*, August 31, 2018. www.texasmonthly.com/politics/its-not-just-about-immigrants-anymore/.

Stillman, Sarah. "When Deportation Is a Death Sentence." *The New Yorker*, January 8, 2018. www.newyorker.com/magazine/2018/01/15/when-deportation-is-a-death-sentence.

Trotter, Robert T., and Juan Antonio Chavira. *Curanderismo: Mexican American Folk Healing*. Athens, GA: University of Georgia Press, 1997.

Uhlmann, Natascha Elena. "The US Government Deliberately Made the Desert Deadly for Migrants." *The Guardian*, December 29, 2018. www.theguardian.com/commentisfree/2018/dec/29/the-us-government-deliberately-made-the-desert-deadly-for-migrants.

The University of Texas Rio Grande Valley. *Curanderismo Collection*. Border Studies Archive. www.utrgv.edu/bsa/en-us/collections/traditional-mexican-american-folklore/curanderismo/index.htm.

———. "Los Que Curan." Published in 2012 at Border Studies Archive: *Curanderismo Collection*. Video, 40:15. www.utrgv.edu/bsa/en-us/collections/traditional-mexican-american-folklore/curanderismo/index.htm.

US Customs and Border Protection. "U.S. Border Patrol Nationwide Apprehensions by Citizenship and Sector in FY2007." www.cbp.gov/sites/default/files/assets/documents/2018-Jul/usbp-nationwide-apps-sector-citizenship-fy07-fy17.pdf.

6 Afterword

Humanitarian entrepreneurs of marketized migrant trauma

In putting forth a borderland hermeneutic that seeks to resacralize the migrant Other at the US-Mexico border,[1] it is necessary that I end this book with a discussion on the predatory desires of entrepreneurial humanitarians, particularly those lacking ethical currency. Framed as an afterword, I enter an unrestricted discursive space, albeit of my own making, in which I define the amorphous and complex phenomenon of humanitarian entrepreneurship at the intersections of migrant trauma and the US-Mexico border. Warranting this creative after flow of words is less about the causes of migrant suffering—for these concerns occupy much of the discursive energies earlier—than the commodification of migrant trauma for the professional advancement of humanitarian entrepreneurs.

For entrepreneurs investing in the field of humanitarianism, the Western intellectual marketplace—whether sacred or secular—provides an endless supply of theological and philosophical paradigms on the sanctity of humans. When compared to the State's low valuation of the migrant Other, any combination of liberal humanitarian discourses seems to suffice in providing humanitarian entrepreneurs with the needed ethical currency. Nevertheless, the entrepreneurial impulse undergirding their pursuit of ethical currency is likely to privilege humanitarian discourses that repel public suspicion of state collusion that at the same time do not jeopardize their relationships with credentialing actors. This interstitial domain lying between humanitarian entrepreneurship and the migrant Other points to an economy of professionalization that is radically different from the lived and hence embodied trauma of migrants, asylum seekers, and refugees at the US-Mexico border. In the latter context, migrant trauma emerges not from credentialing processes, but rather—for the migrant Other—trauma permeates their very being, as in a constant sapping of life from their daily strife against desacralizing forms of power. Whereas in the former context, humanitarian entrepreneurs relate to migrant trauma as bearers of credentialing processes that include state approval, financial sponsorship, educational training, and licensing networks, to name a few. In contrast to the traumatization of migrants at the US-Mexico border, humanitarian entrepreneurs negotiate their social positions by conceding to the demands of intellectual gatekeepers as well as plot their movements along a professional grid (notably, advancement in the latter domain can increase or decrease depending on their levels of white privilege). The residue of these entrepreneurial dealings is embedded into their humanitarian care of the migrant Other in ways that render their trauma a discourse primarily for professional consumption. The question therefore arises as to what sort of trauma is made present in this humanitarian entrepreneurial discourse? How is the trauma of the migrant Other represented in this discourse, and is their trauma recognizable to the migrants themselves? Do the credentialing processes of humanitarian entrepreneurs invariably redact migrant trauma for professional consumption, such that they privilege the dramatic over the mundane, the violent over the serene?

Moving through the credentialing process reveals an interlocking web of affiliations and plotted itineraries that humanitarian entrepreneurs are obliged to support in exchange for their professional prestige. Under these tentacles of influence, humanitarian entrepreneurs come to migrant trauma bearing a conceptual framework that is predisposed to diagnosing suffering rather than embodying it. This positivistic reflex is fostered by the credentialing process and as such values surveillance, inspection, and data collection when present with migrant trauma. Sifting further through these entanglements reveals a representation of migrant trauma defined by data points, percentages, scales, tables, and decontextualized snapshots for social media consumption. Here, the humanitarian entrepreneur's diagnosis of migrant trauma yields the initial phase of the marketization of trauma—a process that disembodies migrant sufferers from their suffering. As a collection of data, the lived traumas of migrant border crossers are distilled into malleable and transportable artifacts that then allow them a multiplicity of functions within the humanitarian's economy of professionalization. In this redacted form, however, would the migrants themselves recognize these artifacts of trauma as their own? To the detriment of the migrant Other, the communicability of their trauma within this context will inevitably privilege the cultural values of the humanitarian entrepreneurs and their sponsoring constituencies. In other words, humanitarian entrepreneurs often assume the position of spokesperson for migrant trauma, rather than the migrants themselves. In this way, migrants dispossessed of place are in turn dispossessed of their lived trauma, for it too is a profitable resource for those with professional privilege. There is therefore the manufacturing of migrant trauma by the State's desacralizing mission, of which serves to reproduce elite power, and the diagnosis of migrant trauma by humanitarian entrepreneurs, of which serves to elevate their professional prestige. Both of these economies desacralize the migrant Other—one by inflicting trauma and the other by way of extraction. What emerges is a double wounding process such that their otherness renders them a target for trauma and a resource of trauma. It is not that migrant border crossers are unable to speak, but rather that their desacralized otherness renders them speechless within these two economies of elite power.

With their material scarcity (i.e. traumatization) as an eradicating strategy of elite power, the commodification of their dispossessed traumas by humanitarian entrepreneurs introduces a commensurate eradicating force on migrants. Hence, by distilling certain traumas from migrants, the original composition of their traumas shifts from tormented personhood to humanitarian artifacts and, as such, the migrant's bodily existence recedes out of view, leaving behind that which the humanitarian entrepreneur has been championed to represent. Though forward looking, this commodification of migrant trauma should point us back to the question about the type of "presence" that humanitarian entrepreneurs embody with the migrant Other at the US-Mexico border. If the end product of their "presence" is solely the marketization of migrant trauma (double-wounding), then do we also need to cast a critical gaze on humanitarianism altogether? The difficulty, however, lies with the counterfeit nature of entrepreneurial humanitarianism, with its reliance on a liberating hermeneutic of the sacred and yet beholden to systems of professionalization that align it with colonizing power structures. Any extraction of lived traumas from migrant border crossers for public consumption is a very delicate matter and rife with ethical conundrums—from the personhoods of migrants to the subjectivities of humanitarian care. As for the notion of "presence," it is naïve to think that these conundrums are resolved simply by having two human bodies in close proximity to each other. In the end, who determines who is present in this encounter? Is it assumed in this encounter that the burden for making presence known lies with the migrant border crosser and not the humanitarian? Has the humanitarian engaged in a thorough enough assessment of self as to root out latent forms of racial bias or class superiority? Again, the credentialing processes for entrepreneurial humanitarians require close scrutiny, for they ensure that "presence" is predetermined prior to engaging the migrant Other. Employing liberal formulas of mainly European origin, humanitarian "presence" projects an ethic of care; yet this unidirectional approach anchors "presence" within a fixed dynamic that in turn makes migrant traumas a static template rather than a fluid dynamic that is profoundly personal. This is where humanitarian discourse defines migrant traumas rather than migrant traumas defining humanitarian discourse. In considering the subjectivity of entrepreneurial humanitarians (i.e. "presence"), are there traces of the humanitarian already present with the migrant border crosser even prior to being physically present? How have the received benefits of white privilege and professional prestige been made present to the migrant border crosser, such that entrepreneurial humanitarians operate as both manufacturers and extractors of migrant trauma? In other words, how have these social benefits wittingly or unwittingly contributed to abiding traumatization of migrant border crossers? Rather than "presence" defining the humanitarian entrepreneur's approach to migrant care, it more appropriately points to an intersection of subjectivities, composed of a multiplicity of presences that no one formula can completely identify. Hence the approach should not be how to reach out and communicate to migrant trauma (following a humanitarian-to-migrant trajectory), but how might migrant trauma communicate to humanitarians about what their social witness and participation has done to contribute to the abiding traumatization of migrants, asylum seekers, and refugees. The subjective nature of migrant trauma does not make it an extractable resource or a lived reality definable separate from the migrants themselves; instead, migrant trauma should reflect back the colluding presence of entrepreneurial humanitarians—that is their professional privilege, social investments, affiliations with white supremacy, and material assets.

What do humanitarian entrepreneurs gain professionally from their encounter with migrant trauma? And conversely, what do migrants gain from their lived trauma? Ultimately, who benefits the most from trauma: migrants or humanitarian entrepreneurs? These questions index another pivotal distinction between humanitarian entrepreneurs and migrant trauma that involves the accrual of status-changing benefits. Embodying the traumas of colonizing power and state desacralization suggests a visceral permanence that eats away at the livelihood of migrants, which is not a benefit but an indelible curse. The snippets of traumas carried away by humanitarian entrepreneurs, however, do provide significant social benefit within their economy of professionalization. Authenticating the trauma within this context are not the migrants themselves, but instead those comprising the humanitarians' credentialing network. Without any say in the matter, humanitarian entrepreneurs harness migrant trauma, a dynamic that replaces the embodied trauma with a representation of trauma that is disproportionally to their benefit than to the migrants. This marketized trauma severs migrant border crossers from their own lived suffering, which in turn allows it to work at its optimum as an extracted discourse among those investing in the humanitarian's credentialing processes and system of professionalization. This has the potential to have public spheres of influence expect the humanitarian to relay the trauma without ever demanding the migrant to be physically present. And even if migrants were to be physically present, the humanitarian spokesperson would still need to provide authentication for their presence to the audiences investing in the humanitarian's economy of prestige. In this way, humanitarian entrepreneurs exert enormous control over what is migrant trauma within the public sphere to the extent that their physical presence as spokesperson is indispensable to the presence of migrants. Conversely, what would it mean to reverse this economy of prestige such that the presence of migrants alone defines what is migrant trauma? Rather than extract the trauma from migrants in the form of data points, how can humanitarians be present with what is already present on the US-Mexico border? The aim here is not to redact migrant trauma for professional purposes but rather to accept it for what it already is: white supremacy, monopoly capitalism, state desacralization, etc.

On one end, the humanitarian can serve as a devastating counter force to state desacralization of migrant border crossers by privileging the migrants themselves in spaces of social and political influence. Yet on the other hand, commanding large quantities of material aid also affords humanitarian entrepreneurs access to an economy of prestige whereby their surplus provision of aid enables more their professional advancement than migrant presence. The monetary resources that accompany humanitarian's professional privilege also represent a redacting force over migrant trauma. This type of control stems from the overwhelmingly positive force of the initial humanitarian aid given to migrants such that the aid detracts from the long-term social benefits that the humanitarian receives from this exchange. To indict the very economic forces that have caused migrant trauma inevitably implicates the monetary resources that underwrite humanitarian entrepreneurship. In order not to jeopardize their funding support, humanitarian entrepreneurs will assign the causes of migrant trauma to chronic corruption and cartel violence in the migrants' homeland. This rhetorical move deflects from the broader US economic structures that have nefariously fostered the present violence in the migrants' homeland since the late nineteenth century.[2] By not scrutinizing these broader economic structures, which many migrants, asylum seekers, and refugees have embodied in the form of trauma since birth, humanitarian entrepreneurs make present a redacted form of migrant trauma that is palatable only for those providing monetary support. This form of migrant presence reinforces in part the State's desacralization of black- and brown-bodied people as innately criminal and culturally inferior. All the while, the economic structures that extract the natural resources from the migrants' homelands and subject them to sweat-shop jobs that pay a poverty wage continue to go uninterrogated.[3] The presence of migrant trauma should begin with making present the broader elite power structures that have contributed to it—like white supremacy, monopoly capitalism, and Western progress.

Artifacts of sensational violence

Although humanitarian entrepreneurs may use a liberal approach to migrant care, their credentialing process inevitably tames this approach in ways that make it more agreeable to the gatekeepers of professional prestige. Of central concern is less the tempering of a liberal activist approach to migrant trauma than the attenuation and hence fragmentation of the migrant's personhood. For humanitarian entrepreneurs, marketized migrant trauma—that is, trauma as a distinct collection of artifacts for professional consumption—prompts empathy through a macabre presentation of lived experiences.[4] As such, the humanitarian marketplace defaults to the spectacles of violence, torture, and rape over stories of the mundane, ordinary, and routine.⁵ These spectacles of sensational violence inevitably render migrants visible within the chaotic and uncivilized, thereby creating the necessary crisis moment for humanitarian entrepreneurial investment. By casting migrants as people destitute of agency, humanitarian entrepreneurs conveniently position themselves as the ideal caretakers, witnesses, and voices of migrant border crossers. These constructed narratives undergird the humanitarian entrepreneurs' economy of privilege such that they justify their operations. In contrast, the lack of sensational appeal in the mundane and routine of migrant trauma lessens the crisis moment, which in turn diminishes the relevancy of humanitarian entrepreneurs. Despite their nonsensational appeal, however, the mundane and routine do reveal an essential aspect of migrant trauma: their everyday will to live. By inspiring empathy through their everyday acts of agency, the result is not dependency—as to privilege humanitarian entrepreneurs—but rather independence as an act of freedom from colonizing power structures. In this way, the will of the everyday registers micro-revolutions against insidious actions that together wear on migrants' livelihood. On the other hand, investments in hyper-violent scenes of migrant vulnerability attest to strategies of control in which the dispensing of material aid to traumatized migrants fosters dependency, which then boosts the professional prestige of humanitarian entrepreneurs. This poses the following questions: Are there genuine ways that humanitarian aid can be given to migrants without entanglements to colonizing power structures? What sort of social arrangement does the provision of humanitarian aid set forth between migrants and humanitarians when the aid is inextricably tied to elite power? Linked to prestige are its material benefits, which humanitarian entrepreneurs are likely to enjoy in the form of higher wages, increased living spaces, or more "free" time. Yet for migrants deemed the black- and brown-bodied Other, this economy of privilege—an economy comprised of professional credentials and white privilege—is inaccessible, despite having been "present" with humanitarian entrepreneurs. In placing migrants within sensationalized narratives of hyper-violence, humanitarian entrepreneurs not only secure their role as humanitarians, they also ensure that the migrants themselves never benefit from their economy of privilege. At issue here is the framing of migrant personhood in such a way that they become preordained from settlements outside of the humanitarian's lived reality. Casted as dependent, vulnerable, and victims of homeland violence, they acquire a social profile that in turn is incompatible with the privileged social context of humanitarian entrepreneurs. For in the latter context, the expected social profile of its members correlates to preestablished criteria of hygiene, ownership, language, and whiteness. Hence, humanitarian aid that is tied to elite power structures has the potential to reinforce the containment of traumatized migrants within areas that are away from the privileged settlements of humanitarian entrepreneurs. The issue this raises is again about migrant presence. First of all, the plight of migrant border crossers serves as an automatic invitation to humanitarian entrepreneurs to be physically present with them where they are located; however, this invitation is rarely reciprocated in ways where migrant border crossers are able to settle in the neighborhoods of humanitarian entrepreneurs. How can the invitation of presence be reciprocated in the same automatic fashion to migrant border crossers? Can a requisite of their presence with migrant border crossers be the transformation of their own social locations, particularly in ways that allow for migrants to live among them (shop where they shop, attend the schools of their children, go to their churches, play in their parks, etc.)?

Although the mundane and the routine of migrant trauma also require urgent care, their value is how they bring into focus the migrants' agency within monopolistic economic practices, adverse consuming habits, and white supremacy. Through their everyday lives, they also expose the colonizing social context of humanitarian entrepreneurs and by association reveal their controlling tendencies and professional ambitions. Within the crisis moment of hyper-violence, it is the economy of prestige of humanitarian entrepreneurs that enjoys longevity versus the narrowly defined life span of migrant border crossers. The defined crisis moment not only sets limits on migrant personhood but also their exposure to the public—for once the crisis subsides, migrants are likely to fall out of the public eye. It also serves as the primary threshold for measuring the humanitarian's overall success and impact. By defining the crisis moment, humanitarian entrepreneurs also determine when it ends, which in turn affirms their professional expertise and hence increases their prestige. Ultimately, this finite crisis moment of migrants brings longevity to humanitarian entrepreneurs in the form of professional currency and renewed monetary support. One way to reverse this dynamic is to attend to their everyday acts of agency, thereby expanding the threshold of the crisis moment to include long-term systemic transformation to colonizing power structures. As indicated previously, the everyday acts of agency of migrants locates colonizing elite power at the microlevels of life—such as finding food, constructing provisional shelter, intuiting direction, turning to religious symbols, and crossing the border.

With sensationalized violence defining the crisis moment for migrant border crossers, the dispensing of humanitarian aid inevitably has a limited life span. This crisis moment does well in drawing in concentrated forms of material care yet falls short of contextualized care throughout the lives of migrants. By defining migrant trauma only within spectacles of sensationalized violence conversely, humanitarian entrepreneurs also set the parameters for the type of care migrants are to receive. In this way, violence marks a crisis which in turn calls for concentrated forms of human care to meet the crisis. Yet, does meeting the crisis also address permanently the routine lives of migrants—the fluctuations of their being, emotions, memories, and spiritualties, and the desire for a steadiness of place and belonging? Rather than setting the crisis narrative to hyper-violence, how can humanitarians broaden the narrative in ways that allow them to address the long-term systemic and cyclical conditions that produce migrant trauma? The form of care imagined here has in view a protracted commitment to the migrant Other, beyond the fluctuating currencies of professional prestige and the basic provisions of food, health supplies, shelter, and clothing. It is the type of care that seeks an abiding transformation to traumatizing socio-political conditions such that the will to live for migrants is no longer expended against the daily threats to their existence, but instead in the daily thriving in a system of equal distribution of wealth and privilege.

Though short-lived for the migrant Other, the crisis moment defined by humanitarian entrepreneurs is not void of a long-term mission, for the permanency it seeks lies within the humanitarian's economy of professional prestige. With the short-term mission of the crisis moment, addressing the migrants' basic needs, humanitarian entrepreneurs create a situation in which they alone become the ideal solution. As such, they intervene in the crisis moment with a confidence of its finality. All of this is set up by the humanitarian entrepreneurs' crisis narrative, for here sensationalized violence also points to a repertoire of care that they alone are able to dispense. In solving the crisis moment, humanitarian entrepreneurs emerge as agents of progress and migrants as the backward and dependent other. In this way, the short-term mission of the crisis moment renders permanent a perception of social roles: the progressive humanitarian (the social hero) versus the needy migrant other (understood in this dichotomy are incremental shifts in degree, depending on both groups' respective physiognomy, gender, sexuality, education, and class). Within the humanitarian entrepreneurs' economy of professional privilege, their progressive status yields long-lasting social benefits that not only affirms the credentialing processes but also helps to recruit future humanitarian entrepreneurs. Both the social benefits—like influence, prestige, and social mobility—and future recruits mark the long-term mission of the crisis moment, which is to reproduce the humanitarian entrepreneurial enterprise. The prestige that humanitarian entrepreneurs accrue after meeting a crisis moment that they have defined through narratives of sensationalized violence has in view permanent social benefits throughout their lives. Therefore, what would humanitarian care look like if it invested in the routine lives of migrants? Is it possible to have a protracted form of humanitarian care that attends to life span and the immediate need of migrants, one invested in permanent social change that affords access to elite economies of privilege in the routine lives of migrants?

Though the crisis narrative of sensationalized violence activates material aid for the migrant Other, it also formalizes their public profile as weak, primitive, and subservient. This raises an important ethical question: how does such a social profile invite further migrant traumatization? With the absence of the everyday acts of migrant agency from the crisis narrative, humanitarian entrepreneurs reinforce the reigning nativist argument that migrants at the US-Mexico border are socially and financially burdensome, low-skilled, unhygienic, and culturally taxing. In essence, when humanitarian entrepreneurs harness solely the violence associated with migrant trauma, they in turn create a permanent state of migrant dependency that grants permanency to both their professional prestige and the prevailing nativist ideology. Viewed differently, are the vulnerabilities associated with migrant trauma better understood not as an exploitable resource to bolster the prestige of humanitarians but rather as modes of resistance to the State's sacred apparatus of white supremacy, monopoly capitalism, and Western notions of progress? Moreover, do they point us more to what is malignant in the social milieu of humanitarian entrepreneurs than what is deficient in the migrants' personhoods? From this perspective, state-desacralized migrants at the US-Mexico border not only bear the wounds of humanitarian entrepreneurs' version of progress, but more importantly they also evidence a counter-will to live. Attached to their everyday lives is an indictment on Western notions of progress as well as an urge to us to abandon them for something different. Indeed, their trauma serves partly as an acute diagnosis of colonizing power such that the only viable remedy is an unprecedented social system with radically different investments in the sacred.

If migrant trauma offers us a critique on exclusionary social habits, consuming behaviors, and self-serving lifestyles, what sort of social system fosters migrant well-being and thriving? Though a necessary question for us to consider, the social critique that migrant trauma issues against the beneficiaries of the current system of Western progress should indeed delay our response. This is not to say that systemic remedies are unachievable; instead, it admits to the importance of lingering in the social critique as a pathway to social change. Yet as critical as it is to learn the particularities of the social critique that migrants embody, it is even more important not to make these disclosures define migrants' sole purpose. In part, their plight does represent the nefarious effects of the current system of progress; however, this is merely a preamble to a broader pathology of elite power (State's investments in the sacred) that requires the bulk of our critical energies. Moreover, to linger in the social critique should not negate the infinite modes of being to the migrant's personhood, for here we recognize that the social critique disclosed by migrant trauma is not an aspired mode. Migrant border crossers are not pursuing trauma as something essential to their livelihood, rather trauma is an imposition of the State. Trauma is forced upon them in concentrated forms and with eradicating force, all of which begins in their homelands and continues well after they have crossed the border. On the contrary, what migrant border crossers seek is transcendent value and its accompanying benefits, like settlement, education, social mobility, security, food access, leisure, vocation, friendships, and fellowship.

Ultimately, the social corrective that migrant trauma offers us should lead to their immediate good—that is, social correcting concomitant with an immediate material-changing social action. The more we linger in the social critique of power, institutions, epistemologies, and lifestyles, the more we perform social actions that help alleviate migrant trauma. Hence, the social critique does not end with a vast collection of data so as to boost professional prestige, but rather its results are daily transforming actions such that the will to live for migrants is expanded beyond just the struggle to survive. Accumulatively, this everyday praxis of social transformation marks a different ethical threshold in which life-giving treatment of migrants, asylum seekers, and refugees at the US-Mexico border define true civilizational progress. And conversely, their ill treatment admits to acute ethical and moral deficiencies in the social system—as is currently the case.

To prioritize the well-being of the migrant Other within a social system of settled people, it is essential that we view the exercise of human movement as intrinsic to our earthly existence. Different from settled people, those forced into geographical movement assumes a provisional human state of fluctuating social networks, limited supply of material goods, and irregular points for strength recovery. Yet settlement, which is equally intrinsic to our earthly existence, suggests a stationary social domain in which social networks, supplies, and shelter can be cultivated over a longer period of time and hence more predictable. Within this dynamic spectrum of human experience, migrants, asylum seekers, and refugees at the US-Mexico border are in forced movement toward settled people. Rather than deny their settlement upon arrival,[6] can provisions be made for them to join established US settlements? At issue here is less the lack of space than a malicious social system with abiding investments in the sacred that has desacralized migrant crossers beyond any human recognition. In this system, they are made into the nonsacred, the nonhuman, the criminalized other and as such only deserve death.

Migrant desire as an ethic of chosenness

Revealed in the multiple human migrations to the US-Mexico border is the desire for settled life. As many robust social critiques have shown,[7] these migrations are inextricably linked to the US's surplus accumulation of natural resources through colonizing systems like monopoly capitalism. In many ways, the desire for settled life in another country—particularly the kind incited by the innate will to survive—reveals a traumatizing preference because of what migrants are forced to leave behind. Yet how can such a preference inspire a new ethic of chosenness that is based not on divine selection, as advanced in US religious nationalism and the doctrine of Manifest Destiny, but rather on the migrants' desire for settlement? How would the definition of civilizational progress change if settled people based it on whether asylum seekers, refugees, and irregular migrants chose to settle in their society? In the US, notions of settlement (citizenship) have relied on religious nationalist narratives of divine chosenness (starting with the white Protestant heterosexual male landowner), which in turn has resulted in a traumatizing penal response against migrant border crossers. As the non-chosen other (most of whom are black- and brown-bodied people), migrants at the US-Mexico border constitute the undesirable settlers and as such are violently excluded from US society.[8] Here, white supremacist state agents who invest in religious narratives of divine chosenness are permanently antagonistic toward black- and brown-bodied migrants to the extent that their chosenness for settled life is permanently unattainable. Indeed, this excluding reflex marks a nefarious form of human desire that stems not from the will to survive but the will to conquer. Herein lies the value of religious narratives of divine chosenness for white supremacists in that they breed a form of desire that sanctions the violent removal of migrant border crossers from any meaningful form of settled life.[9] Thus, to be a settled person—that is, a desired person—the migrant Other must imitate white supremacist identity to the extent that the undesirable parts of their being (language, culture, and physiognomy) are effaced. Yet what would be the resulting society if its settled people determined their chosenness based on whether their settlement was chosen as a destination by asylum seekers, refugees, and irregular migrants? What would it mean to have the latter version of chosenness as part of the State's sacred apparatus?

For a settlement to be chosen by migrants as a destination introduces its settled people to a different calibrating ethic of chosenness, one grounded in the enablement and hence freedom of human movement. In contrast, a settlement/society of this nature would be deficient of progress (an outcome that both home society and host society would suffer) if those desiring to move are restricted from doing so. When settled people choose not to settle in their home society, are they freely able to express their will to live in the form of migratory movement? It would seem that for a home settlement to deny a person's recourse to migratory movement as a survival strategy it in turn contributes to a carceral state—which is a desire of the current forms of elite power. In securing migratory movement (the contours of which include the will to survive and desire for settled life) as an intrinsic freedom in both the home settlement and the host settlement, the migrant's desire emerges not only as a transformative calibrating ethic for both societies but as a principle of the sacred. For the home settlement, the choice to travel points to the desire to survive, while for the host settlement the choice to settle points to the migrant's desire for settled life elsewhere. Whether their desire is to move away from the home or host societies or move to the home or host societies, their migration constitutes a protected freedom with sacred status for both social contexts.

In designating migratory movement as the calibrating ethic of chosenness for a society, it has in view the will to live that permeates this mode of travel, which is different from privileged forms of travel that ensure the reproduction of elite power. Intrinsic to the current human migratory movements to the US-Mexico border is the raw desire to exist another day on the earth. As such, this form of forced movement admits to an alternative version of freedom that is informed by a migrant's will to live. From their will to live follow the acts of moving away and toward settled life, all of which comprises migrant chosenness. Thus, for a settlement/society (home or host) to measure its progress according to this ethic of migrant chosenness (a dynamic defined by migrant movement/migrant settlement), its settled people are destined to render migration as part of their sacred freedoms. In this way, migrants who settle in a host society introduce it to a version of freedom that protects the migrants' will to exist on earth, their choice to move, and desire for settled life elsewhere. For societies calibrated to Western doctrines of sovereignty and citizenship, particularly those informed by Protestant Christianity, among their protected freedoms are the movement of wealth to fixed centers of elite power and the recourse to extreme violence in order to exclude the movement of the people they have deemed undesirable. A society that determines its chosenness on whether migrants have chosen it as a destination for settled life does not restrict migratory movement, for such movement represents a fundamental privilege in its repertoire of sacred human freedoms. Different from the excluding response of many Western nation-states, a society calibrated according to migrant chosenness not only enjoys a version of freedom that is premised on the raw will to exist on earth (as registered in the migrant's forced movement away from and toward settled life) rather than on the will to conquer natural resources, monetary wealth, and people.

In casting human migration as an ethic of migrant chosenness rather than a social threat, the will to live/movement/settled life continuum comes to the fore as a set of governing freedoms for both the home society and host society. More specifically, migratory movement away from and then toward settled life reflect instinctual human actions, that when sanctioned to be the governing freedoms by both home and host society, the outcome is a dramatically different social system. In defining further migrant chosenness, there are first migrants in forced movement who have chosen not to stay in their home society; second, arriving to their destination marks the migrants' choice for the host society. To permit these choices—which are expressions of migrant desire—both societies affix their livelihoods, value systems, and reproducing schemes to proven life-giving modes of existence. Unlike the religious nationalist approach to the current state of mass migration, freedoms grounded in an ethic of migrant chosenness have in view modes of existence that can respond to natural disasters, war, and economic scarcity not with increased militarization of the border, mass detention, and deportation, but rather with strategies and instincts that enable all humans a viable chance at a meaningful earthly existence.

From here proceed the investments of both societies, particularly the kind that protect, sustain, and facilitate migratory movement as a basic human strategy for staying alive in an adverse world. Here, these societies define their respective notions of progress not according to monopoly capitalism and the mass movement of consumer products—a freedom that normalizes scarcity for a majority of the world's population—but instead according to migratory movements of humans as to ensure investments in their settled life. This proposed sacred freedom as gleaned from migrant chosenness has in view a form of settled life that begins with the migrants' raw desire for a meaningful earthly existence. The form of settled life imagined here has in view settlements that facilitate free movement of humans rather than wealth accumulation. In terms of their logistical layout, this may require for neighborhoods to utilize land more efficiently with smaller houses and less lawn space. In other words, the material reality of settled life privileges the proximity of human relationships and food nourishment outside of a hyper-consumerist framework.

The inflections of survival present within migration emanate from instinctual human impulses that creatively strive to extend life. Different from the will to conquer in hyper-consumerist based societies, the migrants' will to live registers a mode of being that aims to secure a meaningful form of settled life. When sacralized as a governing freedom, migratory movement has as its corresponding social system the furtherance of people's life spans instead of elite wealth. This way of ordering society is revealed in migrant chosenness, a society that facilitates movement because it is a necessary action to expand human life. The intermediary space in between the home and host societies is a fluid and multifarious reality of raw desire, extreme travel, and provisional rest points. In this fluid in-between lies the freedom of migratory movement. Yet migrant chosenness also reveals settlement as a governing freedom—the freedom to a settled life. Hence, for societies calibrated to an ethic of migrant chosenness, migrant settlement comes forth as an ancillary freedom to the sacred freedom of migratory movement. As with the freedom of migratory movement, the material reality that we can imagine accompanying the freedom of migrant settlement are living spaces that facilitate fellowship, plants, animals, and humans and nurtures physical longevity by harnessing the natural energies of the sun and wind.

By aligning a society's version of freedom with the notion of migrant chosenness, it ensures the freedom of a person's will to exist on Earth through migratory movement or migrant settlement. Rather than expanding bordering strategies as is typical in societies with a property-based ethic of chosenness, a society measuring its progress according to whether it has been chosen by migrants as a destination for settled life will inevitably seek to protect the forced movements of people seeking to live another day. For a society to deny migratory movements from entering a settled life destines it to an incarcerating state that solely benefits colonizing forms of power. For many anti-immigrant societies, land ownership is central to their versions of human freedom; yet such a framework assumes a permanent natural environment and access to human immortality. Here, the unsettled state of migratory movements is viewed as a social threat to the illusionary freedom of property ownership and as such requires an excessive border control apparatus of military personnel, surveillance technologies, prisons, and colossal fixed barriers across the natural landscape. Ultimately, societies calibrated to property-based freedoms function as carceral settlements in that they criminalize the most basic act in human survival—migration—while proffering an illusive ideal of earthly immortality through hyper-consumerism. On the other hand, to privilege migratory movement and migrant settlement as sacred freedoms with both home and host societies will have as an outcome a form of settled life in which migration is affirmed, protected, and facilitated. Such freedoms ascribe not to the illusive notion of life as a fixed state for both the natural environment and humans, but rather the notion that change, flux, and decay are inevitable and often require migratory movement as a response. Indeed, as sacred freedoms, they have the potential to displace colonizing power structures that depend on the fixity of life not as a way toward stability but as a necessary state for cultivating hyper-consumerism. For fixed lives are more susceptible to accumulating commodities, which in turn leads to an increase in financial debt, over-worked bodies, higher anxieties, and finally, shorter life spans. The resulting agencies of a society calibrated to an ethic of migrant chosenness begins from a disposition of gratitude toward migrants, asylum seekers, and refugees, and then acts to foster their settled life within that society in ways that extend their life spans. Here, gratitude is instantiated across the landscape, with guiding pathways, open bridges, and modes of transport that lead migrants easily to shelter, material goods, and social networks.

Gratitude as the response for a migrant-chosen settlement affirms the unfixed nature of life within this settlement. The ideal here is not a fictional state of human immortality, as offered in the current commodity-driven context, but instead a quality of life that stewards meaningful relationships with the earth, animals, and "Other" humans. This is where a migrant's desire for settlement can be liberating to a host settlement in that they set in motion modes of living that are meaningful and yet not permanent in the consumerist sense. They inspire living spaces that assemble easily with minimal damage to the environment while also disassembling quickly as to facilitate life-saving movements. Within societies that calibrate their freedoms according to sacralized notions of national sovereignty, the intrinsic human need to move is restricted or in some countries eliminated entirely. In being chosen by migrants as a place for settled life, the corresponding acts of gratitude are likely to include fellowship. Here, the penal system operates not against the migrants who are affirming the freedom of movement but on living spaces that restrict migratory movement. In other words, for those societies calibrated to an ethic of property ownership, the ensuing material reality looks much like what is found currently at the US-Mexico border. The sacralized notions of divine chosenness (Manifest Destiny/white supremacy) that undergird the freedoms of US property ownership have not only restricted migratory movement, but sadly they have normalized the genocide of land, animals, and people. Such a state measures its worth on the massacre of migrating people and the preservation of those divinely chosen to conquer. Yet through migrant chosenness, the corresponding action is not genocide but fellowship, for to be chosen by migrants sets in motion migratory movement and migrant settlement as sacred governing freedoms.

If the US-Mexico border offers us a haunting picture of a society calibrated to an ethic of property ownership, what would the quality of settled life be for US society if it was calibrated to an ethic of migrant chosenness? Though it is important for societies—whether in the homeland or host country—to have some level of predictability and systemization, the quality of its settled life is raised when those in migratory movement have desired it as a settlement destination. One way it does this is by synchronizing the rhythms and materiality of settled life to the governing freedom of human movement. As a governing freedom, migratory movement is then ascribed sacred status as an act of gratitude, thereby instituting the sacralization of the migrant border crosser. By sacralizing migratory movement as a basic human freedom, the result would indeed be a radically unprecedented society. Here, settled life is truly free—free from the fictional ideal of human immortality and its accompanying social habits; free from the mass genocide of migrants, asylum seekers, and refugees. For when a society determines its sacred worth based on whether it is desired as a place of settlement for those in migratory movement, what we will have is something entirely different from the current devastating state of affairs at the US-Mexico border. Denying migrants entry at the US-Mexico border excludes but also imprisons us within a constraining conceptualization of human existence, as this is a form of settled life without migratory movement as a governing freedom. This is the result of the State's abiding sacred apparatus of white supremacy, monopoly capitalism, and Western notions of progress, all of which desacralize migrant border crossers and set in motion a carceral state of existence under the argument that freedom needs to be protected with border walls, military weaponry, and surveillance technologies. On the other hand, being chosen by migrants, asylum seekers, and refugees will align society to a freedom that raises the quality of settled life but in time will be an indispensable freedom for all humans in the current world of rising water levels.

Migrant praxis of in-betweenness

The will to live that drives migrants, asylum seekers, and refugees away from and toward settled life (for many a cyclical process) is not an abstract life force but rather converts into self-initiated modes of food distribution, transcultural engagement, material resourcefulness, and border-crossing itineraries. Here, the forced movement of migrants constitutes an in-between position of unsettlement and as such they confront a continuous series of limited life options with an immense overflow of self-generated ingenuity, savvy, and spirituality. Framed as an in-between assemblage of life-giving desires, migration emerges as an ethic of migrant chosenness in which both home and host societies are chosen (e.g. home in terms of the hope of return or host in terms of a new destination). By formalizing their chosenness through governing procedures, home and host societies join a common social system that operates along the migrants' will to live/movement/settled life continuum. Among the progresses that such a social realignment would achieve is a value system that sacralizes migrants. Under an ethic of migrant chosenness, social institutions aimed at reproducing power would invest in the will to live rather than in the will to conquer. Here, the migrants' will to live provides settled people a more viable and life-saving response to a reality in which mass migration has become the norm in the face of accelerated environmental decline[10] and pervasive state-sanctioned violence.[11] By rendering the migrants' will to live/movement/settled life continuum a governing freedom, host and home societies draw upon a common repertoire of life-saving strategies that migrants, asylum seekers, and refugees themselves have modeled in their forced movements. For home and host societies to abandon their will to conquer for the migrants' will to live, the anticipated material reality is one that facilitates migratory movement in ways that alleviate the intensity of material scarcity in the home society. In contrast to the will to conquer, which creates permanent material scarcity, the aim here would be a shared scarcity as to minimize the loss of life in the home country.

In view of the current state of mass migration, this dynamic of shared scarcity should not function unilaterally but rather interchangeably in which home and host societies are able to switch positions depending on the intensity of the crisis situation. Yet with natural disasters and violence disrupting both home and host societies simultaneously, sharing scarcity may not be feasible from a fixed, settled position. Here, an ethic of migrant chosenness proves helpful in that settled people are resourced with life-giving strategies that emerge from an in-between position form unsettlement to settlement.

Apart from migratory movement indexing the migrants' will to live, this life-saving action unfolds across an in-between state of existence wherein migrant life is interstitial, liminal, and unsettled. With migration as an interstitial reality, from geographies to cultural identities to social systems, the will to live of migrants constitutes modes of in-betweenness that have materialized into a repertoire of life-saving strategies. In subscribing to an ethic of migrant chosenness, therefore, migratory movement is not only rendered a sacred governing freedom for both home and host societies—as to foster the will to live instead of the will to conquer—but also a life-saving praxis of in-betweenness for an increasingly unsettling world, from natural environment to social systems to economic regimes. In this way, the migrants' will to live reveals a way to live in a world dominated by the unsustainable will to conquer inherent of many property-based nation-states. Although forced upon migrants, asylum seekers, and refugees, their migratory movements are through an irregular in-betweenness that equips their instincts, spiritualties, and ways of knowing with a versatility of maneuvers for a multiplicity of power dynamics. Hence, migratory movement as a governing freedom enables home and host societies to share scarcity, and yet as a praxis of in-betweenness, migration also prepares both societies for a way of life that is commensurate with the current unsettled state of the world (nature, politics, societies, and economies).

Rather than stifle social bodies under illusions of life's permanence (property-based nation-states and hyper-consumerist societies), an ethic of migrant chosenness offers a praxis of in-betweenness that interchanges between identities, power positions, and ways of knowing throughout a migrant's lifetime. In a context of volatile climate change, fixed social bodies are poised to endure the brunt of the suffering that is set to unfold in the current age. Steady increases in sea levels across the globe have revealed the weakness of social systems with property-based or citizen-based value systems.[12] Moreover, with mass migration becoming more the norm—an irreversible product of decades of monopoly capitalism and Western notions of progress—fixed social identities are destined to revert to nationalist-driven violence against the migrant Other.[13]

Compatible with monopoly capitalism (the will to conquer) are fixed social identities, largely because their fixed state facilitates an object-collecting existence. Moreover, with fixed social identities comes the construction of stationary spaces that normalize hyper-consumerist habits along with their associated social anxieties. This fixity of social identities and commoditized spaces along with their ensuing object-collecting habits not only belie the mortality of all humans, but even more troubling, this social scheme reduces human life spans. By conflating civilizational progress with this scheme, fixed social bodies expend their labor energies producing and accumulating stationary gadgets that in their production instigate natural disasters and yet have little life-saving value in the face of them. Even more pressing is how this object-driven syndrome breeds a form of social anxiety that is a political resource for colonizing elite power and its manufacturing of violence.[14] Ultimately, the result of a syndrome subtended by the will to conquer is a chronic system of eradicating violence done to self, to nature, and to others.

Migrant subjectivity

From the perspective of fixed social identities (property ownership, citizenship, nationality, gender, ethnicity, able-bodied, sexuality, etc.), migratory movement not only admits to the will to live of migrants but also to the will to conquer of people in elite power. This spectrum of human willpower marks the contours of migration's subjectivity. Thus far, my exegesis of migration has sought to emphasize the will to live of migrants. As such, migration falls into a continuum of life-saving actions that span from the will to live (migrant desire) to forced movement to settled life. In keeping with this book's overall agenda of resacralizing the migrant Other at the US-Mexico border, my interrogations have sought to locate migrant desire, agency, and raw instinct, and doing so with the conviction that these life forces offer us more than sensational survival narratives but rather a way of being that can be life-saving for all humans. Hence, the migrants' subjectivity has led us to an ethic of migrant chosenness and its accompanying praxis of in-betweenness that as a social paradigm offers home and host societies life-giving strategies in an era of rapid environmental decline and nativist-driven violence. Beyond simply identifying the self-generated life forces that move migrants to settled life, does migrant desire point the way to an organic social system of life-giving modes of existence for the current age? Although forced into a life of migration, how does the will to live of migrants, asylum seekers, and refugees at the US-Mexico border prefigure a reality that all humans will inevitably face and therefore set forth ways to extend human life?

In contrast to migration as forced movement (will to live) is migration as manufactured violence (will to conquer). Here, migration signifies less migrant deficiency than Western social behaviors, habits, lifestyles, value-systems, and ways of knowing that together produce the conditions whereby people are forced into movement. In the current era, those manufacturing it can be traced to property-based nation-states that have normalized the fixity of social identities and spaces and their ensuing habits of object-collecting.[15] The manufacturing of this violence has ensured not only migration in mass but mass migration as the irreversible norm of the future. Soberly, the material resources needed to sustain the manufacturing process are rapidly decreasing and hence showing the unsustainability of Western hyper-consumerist societies. For this reason, redressing migrant trauma must include the host societies' resistance to fixed social identities and their ensuing object-collecting habits while also pivoting to an ethic of migrant chosenness and its praxis of in-betweenness. In this way, what is manufactured is not migration as violence but instead migration as a sacred life-saving freedom. Here, social bodies are invited to move interstitially, in between spaces, identities, and physical abilities, carrying along the way not mementos (object-collecting) but memories of kinship ties.

For object-collecting societies, the will to live translates into an insatiable ambition for immortality which in turn leads to the violent will to conquer. In contextualizing the migrants' praxis of in-betweenness, however, we see that their will to live pivots from an unsettling position that is brought about by the manufactured violence described earlier. Dislodged from settled life after multiple traumatic events in their home society, the forced movements of migrants instantiate life's transitory nature. Such forced awareness constitutes an abiding trauma as well as a catalytic force that propels them into a praxis of in-betweenness as a way to extend their lives. Closely attuned to life's transitory nature rather than to illusionary notions of life's permanence, the migrants' will to live pursues frugal investments that conserve and repurpose resources in ways that are counterintuitive to an object-collecting impulse. Such a praxis of in-betweenness learns to live creatively with scarcity by tempering over-consumption and rationing food supplies while nourishing rich kinship bonds.

In describing migrant praxis as interstitial maneuvers or in-betweenness, I understand migratory movement as a lived event occurring between home and host societies as well as an array of life-saving strategies that involve brokering between social identities, power positions, value systems, and ways of knowing. Included in the latter dynamic is the migrant's recourse to spiritual instincts in negotiating between multiple adverse power structures.[16] This mode of in-betweenness abandons Western systems of logic—as to reveal their inadequacy in confronting colonizing elite power—for a way of knowing that is spiritual in nature and hence operates subversively between the body and mind. Here, the will to live of migrants relies on a form of awareness that the Western scientific mind has discredited and yet for them effects real positive change in their material lives.[17] In assessing the nature of the migrants' spiritual in-betweenness (between body and mind and yet transcending time and space), it is crucial that we understand it as an integral part of their migration experience.

For the Western scientific mind, perception, awareness, and truth-making are inextricably linked to stationary systems of logic—that is, logics commensurate with fixed optic-positions as implied in the instruments of science (microscope, telescope, magnifying glass, etc.). As revealed in this book, these stationary logics have played a significant role in the manufacturing of migration, whether in terms of a criminalizing racial logic or an object-collecting impulse. Yet even as an outcome of stationary Western logics, the migration experience has a way of unseating them as primary sources for truth-making. Here, migrants, asylum seekers, and refugees turn more forcefully to a spiritual life force in between their bodies and minds and time and space as a reliable and trustworthy resource for extending their earthly existence. Such a spiritual phenomenon is indeed intrinsic to the mass migration experience and yet is overlooked in the dominant discourse of migration studies, largely due to the latent religious biases subtending the social sciences. For many migrants, their migration movement provides ample proof of their spiritual in-betweenness while at the same time revealing to them the ineffectiveness of Western systems of logics, largely because they inform the manufacturing of migration and its accompanying traumas. For home and host societies, the spiritual in-betweenness of migrant praxis is not an empty form of escapism but rather points to an abiding human practice that precedes the development of Western stationary logics. Beyond an activation of transcendent sensibilities, their spiritual in-betweenness points to a mode of critical awareness that intuits the operations of elite power, discerns the full depth of suffering, and more importantly diminishes object-collecting impulses.

By adopting the migrants' spiritual modes of presence as a truth-making resource, home and host societies displace object-driven logics and their accompanying manufacturing of violence—done to self, to nature, and to others. Implied in this proposed epistemological shift is not a ban on the laws of physics or practical knowledge but a divestment from Western systems of logic that, since the modern period, have proven destructive to all earthly life forms. Here, migrant spirituality bespeaks less religious practice than a fuller awareness of the sanctity of wounds and trauma as to engender deeper and more meaningful ties to life on earth. A form of spirituality in which the urgency of the will to live moves us not to the accumulation of objects or the reproduction of colonizing elite power, but rather closer to each "Other."

Notes

1 Caitlin Dickerson, "'There Is a Stench': Soiled Clothes and No Baths for Migrant Children at a Texas Center," *The New York Times*, June 21, 2019, www.nytimes.com/2019/06/21/us/migrant-children-border-soap.html.
2 Juan Gonzalez, *Harvest of Empire: A History of Latinos in America* (New York: Penguin Books, 2011), 58–80; Jason M. Colby, *The Business of Empire: United Fruit, Race, and U.S. Expansion in Central America* (Ithaca, NY: Cornell University Press, 2011), 19–78.
3 Tanya M. Kerssen, *Grabbing Power: The New Struggles for Land, Food and Democracy in Northern Honduras* (Oakland, CA: Food First Books, 2013), 22–27; Devon G. Peña, *The Terror of the Machine: Technology, Work, Gender, and Ecology on the U.S.-Mexico Border* (Austin, TX: The University of Texas Press, 1997), 3–102.
4 Jacey Fortin, "Drawings by Migrant Children in Texas Catch the Smithsonian's Eye," *The New York Times*, July 9, 2019, www.nytimes.com/2019/07/09/us/smithsonian-migrant-children-drawings.html; Rhina Guidos, "Smithsonian Inquiring About Drawings Made by Children at Catholic Center," *Catholic News Service*, July 9, 2019, www.catholicnews.com/services/englishnews/2019/smithsonian-inquiring-about-drawings-made-by-children-at-catholic-center.cfm.
5 Bailey Vogt, "Smithsonian Seeks Children's Drawings Depicting Time in Migrant Detainment Facilities," *The Washington Times*, July 8, 2019, www.washingtontimes.com/news/2019/jul/8/smithsonian-seeks-childrens-drawings-depicting-tim/.
6 Camilo Montoya-Galvez, "U.S. Says Asylum Seekers Encountered Along Entire Southern Border Can Now Be Returned to Mexico," *CBS News*, September 27, 2019, www.cbsnews.com/news/remain-in-mexico-u-s-says-it-can-now-return-asylum-seekers-to-mexico-along-entire-southern-border/.
7 Aviva Chomsky, *Undocumented: How Immigration Became Illegal* (Boston: Beacon Press, 2014); Gonzalez, *Harvest of Empire*; Tanya Maria Golash-Boza, *Deported: Immigrant Policing, Disposable Labor and Global Capitalism* (New York: New York University Press, 2015).
8 Nomaan Merchant and Verónica G. Cárdenas, "US Tells Migrant Woman 8 Months Pregnant to Wait in Mexico," *Associated Press*, September 6, 2019, www.brownsvilleherald.com/news/local/us-tells-migrant-woman-months-pregnant-to-wait-in-mexico/article_cdf9920c-d0e2–11e9–8802–73db0921b7e2.html?mode=print; Camilo Montoya-Galvez, "U.S. Is Returning Migrants to Places Similar to 'War Zones' in Mexico, Aid Worker Warns," *CBS News*, September 1, 2019, www.cbsnews.com/news/remain-in-mexico-us-returning-migrants-to-places-similar-to-war-zones-in-mexico-under-trump-policy/; Patrick J. McDonnell, "Pastor's Kidnapping Underscores Threat to Migrants Returned to Mexican Border Towns," *Los Angeles Times*, September 2, 2019, www.latimes.com/world-nation/story/2019-09-01/kidnapping-of-pastor-in-mexican-border-town-dramatizes-threats-to-migrants.

9 Miriam Jordan and Zolan Kanno-Youngs, "Trump's Latest Attempt to Bar Asylum Seekers Is Blocked After a Day of Dueling Rulings," *The New York Times*, July 24, 2019, www.nytimes.com/2019/07/24/us/asylum-ruling-tro.html; Audie Cornish and Georgette Gagnon, "U.N. Human Rights Office Says It's Concerned About Treatment of Migrants in the U.S.," *NPR*, July 8, 2019, www.npr.org/2019/07/08/739643751/u-n-human-rights-office-says-its-concerned-about-treatment-of-migrants-in-the-u-?t=1564740028411; César Cuauhtémoc García Hernández, "Locked Up Migrants and Fast-track Deportations: This Is What Trump Wants," *The Guardian*, July 30, 2019, www.theguardian.com/commentisfree/2019/jul/30/why-trump-attack-migrants-means-more-suffering-people-color.

10 Christopher Flavelle, "Climate Change Threatens the World's Food Supply, United Nations Warns," *The New York Times*, August 8, 2019, www.nytimes.com/2019/08/08/climate/climate-change-food-supply.html.

11 Angela Fritz and Luis Velarde, "ICE Arrested Hundreds of People in Raids: Now 'Devastated' Children Are Without Their Parents," *The Washington Post*, August 8, 2019, www.washingtonpost.com/immigration/2019/08/08/ice-arrested-hundreds-people-raids-now-devastated-children-are-without-their-parents/?noredirect=on.

12 NOAA, "Is Sea Level Rising? Yes, Sea Level Is Rising at an Increasing Rate," https://oceanservice.noaa.gov/facts/sealevel.html.

13 Zack Beauchamp, "The El Paso Shooting Isn't an Anomaly: It's American History Repeating Itself," *Vox*, August 6, 2019, www.vox.com/policy-and-politics/2019/8/6/20754828/el-paso-shooting-white-supremacy-rise.

14 Richard Davies, "UN—1995 to 2015, Flood Disasters Affected 2.3 Billion and Killed 157,000," *Floodlist*, January 11, 2016, http://floodlist.com/dealing-with-floods/flood-disaster-figures-1995-2015; Jennie Jacobs, "Report—Flood Losses in Europe to Increase Fivefold by 2050," *Floodlist*, February 17, 2016, http://floodlist.com/europe/report-floods-europe-increase-fivefold-2050; Amahia Mallea, "As Flood Risks Increase Across the US, It's Time to Recognize the Limits of Levees," *Floodlist*, July 19, 2019, http://floodlist.com/protection/limits-of-levees.

15 Mieke Bal, "Telling Objects: A Narrative Perspective on Collecting," in *The Cultures of Collecting*, eds. John Elsner and Roger Cardinal (Cambridge, MA: Harvard University Press, 1994), 105; Jean Baudrillard, "The System of Collecting," in *The Cultures of Collecting*, eds. John Elsner and Roger Cardinal (Cambridge, MA: Harvard University Press, 1994), 21; Susan Pearce, *On Collecting: An Investigation into Collecting in the European Tradition* (New York: Routledge, 1995), 178.

16 Cecilia Menjívar, *Enduring Violence: Ladina Women's Lives in Guatemala* (Berkeley, CA: University of California Press, 2011), 196–225. The recourse to religion appears integral to coping with the violence at home and on their journey to the United States; Robert Brenneman, *Homies and Hermanos: God and Gangs in Central America* (New York: Oxford University Press, 2012), 50–61; Timothy J. Steigenga, "Pentecostalization, Politics, and Religious Change in Guatemala: New Approaches to Old Questions," *PentecoStudies* 13, no. 1 (March 2014): 9–34, doi:10.1558/ptcs.v13i1.9; Jacqueline Hagan, "Religion and the Process of Migration: A Case Study of the Maya Transnational Community," in *Religion Across Borders: Transnational Religious Networks*, eds. Helen Rose Ebaugh and Janet Chafetz (Walnut Creek, CA: AltaMira Press, 2002), 72–92; Hagan, "Faith for the Journey: Religion as Resource for Migrants," in *A Promised Land, A Perilous Journey: Theological Perspectives on Migration*, eds. Daniel Groody and Gioacchino Campese (Notre Dame, IN: University of

Notre Dame Press, 2008), 3–19; Holly S. Eppsteiner and Jacqueline Hagan, "Religion as Psychological, Spiritual, and Social Support in the Migration Undertaking," in *Intersections of Religion and Migration: Issues at the Global Crossroads*, eds. Jennifer B. Saunders, Elena Fiddian-Qasmiyeh, and Susanna Snyder (New York: Palgrave MacMillan, 2016), 49–70; Daniel R. Reichman, *The Broken Village: Coffee, Migration, and Globalization in Honduras* (New York: Cornell University, 2011); Kevin Lewis O'Neill, *Secure the Soul: Christian Piety and Gang Prevention in Guatemala* (Berkeley, CA: University of California Press, 2015).

17 Gregory Lee Cuéllar, "Channeling the Biblical Exile as an Art Task for Central American Refugee Children on the Texas-Mexico Border," in *Latinxs, the Bible, and Migration*, eds. Efraín Agosto and Jacqueline M. Hidalgo (New York: Palgrave Macmillan, 2018), 76–84; Gregory Lee Cuéllar, "Deportation as a Sacrament of the State: The Religious Instruction of Contracted Chaplains in US Detention Facilities," *Journal of Ethnic and Migration Studies* 25, no. 2 (February 2019): 8–14.

Bibliography

Bal, Mieke. "Telling Objects: A Narrative Perspective on Collecting." In *The Cultures of Collecting*, edited by John Elsner and Roger Cardinal, 97–115. Cambridge, MA: Harvard University Press, 1994.

Baudrillard, Jean. "The System of Collecting." In *The Cultures of Collecting*, edited by John Elsner and Roger Cardinal, 7–24. Cambridge, MA: Harvard University Press, 1994.

Beauchamp, Zack. "The El Paso Shooting Isn't an Anomaly: It's American History Repeating Itself." *Vox*, August 6, 2019. www.vox.com/policy-and-politics/2019/8/6/20754828/el-paso-shooting-white-supremacy-rise.

Brenneman, Robert. *Homies and Hermanos: God and Gangs in Central America*. New York: Oxford University Press, 2012.

Chomsky, Aviva. *Undocumented: How Immigration Became Illegal*. Boston: Beacon Press, 2014.

Colby, Jason M. *The Business of Empire: United Fruit, Race, and U.S. Expansion in Central America*. Ithaca, NY: Cornell University Press, 2011.

Cornish, Audie, and Georgette Gagnon. "U.N. Human Rights Office Says It's Concerned About Treatment of Migrants in the U.S." *NPR*, July 8, 2019. www.npr.org/2019/07/08/739643751/u-n-human-rights-office-says-its-concerned-about-treatment-of-migrants-in-the-u-?t=1564740028411.

Cuéllar, Gregory Lee. "Channeling the Biblical Exile as an Art Task for Central American Refugee Children on the Texas- Mexico Border." In *Latinxs, the Bible, and Migration*, edited by Efraín Agosto and Jacqueline M. Hidalgo, 67–88. New York: Palgrave Macmillan, 2018.

———. "Deportation as a Sacrament of the State: The Religious Instruction of Contracted Chaplains in US Detention Facilities." *Journal of Ethnic and Migration Studies* 25, no. 2 (February 2019): 1–20.

Davies, Richard. "UN—1995 to 2015, Flood Disasters Affected 2.3 Billion and Killed 157,000." *Floodlist*, January 11, 2016. http://floodlist.com/dealing-with-floods/flood-disaster-figures-1995-2015.

Dickerson, Caitlin. "'There Is a Stench': Soiled Clothes and No Baths for Migrant Children at a Texas Center." *The New York Times*, June 21, 2019. www.nytimes.com/2019/06/21/us/migrant-children-border-soap.html.

Eppsteiner, Holly S., and Jacqueline Hagan. "Religion as Psychological, Spiritual, and Social Support in the Migration Undertaking." In *Intersections of Religion and Migration: Issues at the Global Crossroads*, edited by Jennifer B. Saunders, Elena Fiddian-Qasmiyeh, and Susanna Snyder, 49–70. New York: Palgrave Macmillan, 2016.

Flavelle, Christopher. "Climate Change Threatens the World's Food Supply, United Nations Warns." *The New York Times*, August 8, 2019. www.nytimes.com/2019/08/08/climate/climate-change-food-supply.html.

Fortin, Jacey. "Drawings by Migrant Children in Texas Catch the Smithsonian's Eye." *The New York Times*, July 9, 2019. www.nytimes.com/2019/07/09/us/smithsonian-migrant-children-drawings.html.

Fritz, Angela, and Luis Velarde. "ICE Arrested Hundreds of People in Raids: Now 'Devastated' Children Are Without Their Parents." *The Washington Post*, August 8, 2019. www.washingtonpost.com/immigration/2019/08/08/ice-arrested-hundreds-people-raids-now-devastated-children-are-without-their-parents/?noredirect=on.

Golash-Boza, Tanya Maria. *Deported: Immigrant Policing, Disposable Labor and Global Capitalism*. New York: New York University Press, 2015.

Gonzalez, Juan. *Harvest of Empire: A History of Latinos in America*. New York: Penguin Publishing Group, 2011.

Guidos, Rhina. "Smithsonian Inquiring About Drawings Made by Children at Catholic Center." *Catholic News Service*, July 9, 2019. www.catholicnews.com/services/englishnews/2019/smithsonian-inquiring-about-drawings-made-by-children-at-catholic-center.cfm.

Hagan, Jacqueline. "Faith for the Journey: Religion as Resource for Migrants." In *A Promised Land, A Perilous Journey: Theological Perspectives on Migration*, edited by Daniel Groody and Gioacchino Campese, 3–19. Notre Dame, IN: University of Notre Dame Press, 2008.

———. "Religion and the Process of Migration: A Case Study of the Maya Transnational Community." In *Religion Across Borders: Transnational Religious Networks*, edited by Helen Rose Ebaugh and Janet Chafetz, 75–92. Walnut Creek, CA: Altamira Press, 2002.

Hernández, César Cuauhtémoc García. "Locked Up Migrants and Fast-track Deportations: This Is What Trump Wants." *The Guardian*, July 30, 2019. www.theguardian.com/commentisfree/2019/jul/30/why-trump-attack-migrants-means-more-suffering-people-color.

Jacobs, Jennie. "Report—Flood Losses in Europe to Increase Fivefold by 2050." *Floodlist*, February 17, 2016. http://floodlist.com/europe/report-floods-europe-increase-fivefold-2050.

Jordan, Miriam, and Zolan Kanno-Youngs. "Trump's Latest Attempt to Bar Asylum Seekers Is Blocked After a Day of Dueling Rulings." *The New York Times*, July 24, 2019. www.nytimes.com/2019/07/24/us/asylum-ruling-tro.html.

Kerssen, Tanya M. *Grabbing Power: The New Struggles for Land, Food and Democracy in Northern Honduras*. Oakland, CA: Food First Books, 2013.

Mallea, Amahia. "As Flood Risks Increase Across the US, It's Time to Recognize the Limits of Levees." *Floodlist*, July 19, 2019. http://floodlist.com/protection/limits-of-levees.

McDonnell, Patrick J. "Pastor's Kidnapping Underscores Threat to Migrants Returned to Mexican Border Towns." *Los Angeles Times*, September 2, 2019. www.latimes.com/world-nation/story/2019-09-01/kidnapping-of-pastor-in-mexican-border-town-dramatizes-threats-to-migrants.

Menjívar, Cecilia. *Enduring Violence: Ladina Women's Lives in Guatemala*. Berkeley, CA: University of California Press, 2011.

Merchant, Nomaan, and Verónica G. Cárdenas. "US Tells Migrant Woman 8 Months Pregnant to Wait in Mexico." *Associated Press*, September 6, 2019. www.brownsvilleherald.com/news/local/us-tells-migrant-woman-months-pregnant-to-wait-in-mexico/article_cdf9920c-d0e2-11e9-8802-73db0921b7e2.html?mode=print.

Montoya-Galvez, Camilo. "U.S. Is Returning Migrants to Places Similar to 'War Zones' in Mexico, Aid Worker Warns," *CBS News*, September 1, 2019. www.cbsnews.com/news/remain-in-mexico-us-returning-migrants-to-places-similar-to-war-zones-in-mexico-under-trump-policy/.

———. "U.S. Says Asylum Seekers Encountered Along Entire Southern Border Can Now Be Returned to Mexico." *CBS News*, September 27, 2019. www.cbsnews.com/news/remain-in-mexico-u-s-says-it-can-now-return-asylum-seekers-to-mexico-along-entire-southern-border/.

NOAA. "Is Sea Level Rising? Yes, Sea Level Is Rising at an Increasing Rate." https://oceanservice.noaa.gov/facts/sealevel.html.

O'Neill, Kevin Lewis. *Secure the Soul: Christian Piety and Gang Prevention in Guatemala*. Berkeley, CA: University of California Press, 2015.

Pearce, Susan. *On Collecting: An Investigation into Collecting in the European Tradition*. New York: Routledge, 1995.

Peña, Devon G. *The Terror of the Machine: Technology, Work, Gender, and Ecology on the U.S.-Mexico Border*. Austin, TX: The University of Texas Press, 1997.

Reichman, Daniel R. *The Broken Village: Coffee, Migration, and Globalization in Honduras*. New York: Cornell University, 2011.

Steigenga, Timothy J. "Pentecostalization, Politics, and Religious Change in Guatemala: New Approaches to Old Questions." *PentecoStudies* 13, no. 1 (March 2014): 9–34. doi:10.1558/ptcs.v13i1.9.

Vogt, Bailey. "Smithsonian Seeks Children's Drawings Depicting Time in Migrant Detainment Facilities." *The Washington Times*, July 8, 2019. www.washingtontimes.com/news/2019/jul/8/smithsonian-seeks-childrens-drawings-depicting-tim/.

Index

Anglo-American 4–5, 28, 46
Anzaldúa, Gloria 11–19, 58–9, 113, 124
archive 3, 21, 27, 55, 97; master 20–1, 27–8, 30, 42; trespassing on 27
art 58–9, 71
Austin Daily Statesman 34, 37–8

barrida 125–6
Bible 21, 29, 65–73, 83–4
black- and brown-bodied 2, 18, 46, 56, 82, 84, 86, 110, 112, 124, 127–8, 145
Blunt, W.F. 37–40, 42–4
border: border-crossed 4, 11–12, 27–8, 143; border crosser 14, 137; border crossing 17, 56; bordering violence 82–6, 110–11; border security 2–3, 14, 16, 35–6, 38, 39–40, 73, 82–5, 89, 97, 115

carceral mission 94
chaplain 5–6, 21, 83, 94–7
clergy 1, 32, 97, 115, 128
colonization 6–8, 11–13, 15, 46, 60, 90, 110, 123
CoreCivic 88–9, 92–6
corpo-reality 122–4, 126
corrido 21, 55, 57
counter archive 20–1, 55, 97
C.P. Diaz, Mexico 35
criminality 6, 20, 45, 64, 73, 85, 111–12, 122, 126, 128
criminalized 9, 16, 87, 89, 111–12, 122; racially 3, 9, 16, 65, 87, 112, 125
curandera 22, 112–13, 116–28; praxis 116–23, 125–8
curanderismo 16–17, 19, 21, 112–18, 121, 128
curing space 119–20, 126–8

Daniel 66–72
Department of Homeland Security (DHS) 87, 89, 93
desacralize 8–9, 11, 15, 18–20, 27, 37, 46, 73, 81–97, 115, 144, 149
detention 21–2, 40, 81–97, 146
disease 34–47, 85, 111–12
Dubose, Sergeant C. 43–4
Duval County 87–8

elite 1–16, 28–9, 55–6, 110–24, 127–8, 139–47, 151–4
emasculate 20, 58, 62, 64
empire 4, 12, 22, 27, 47, 90
ethnic Mexican 5–6, 11, 20–1, 28, 32–47, 55–66, 73
evangelical 3, 16, 65–70, 81–6, 90–2, 97, 115, 123

Foucault, Michel 27, 47, 119

GEO Group 88–9, 92–4
Grassroots Leadership 88
Grupo Juda 65–8

Hamilton, H.J. 37, 45
Hartman, Saidiya V. 31, 34, 46
healing 9, 12–14, 17–22, 30, 41, 58, 62, 111–28
hermeneutic 1, 3, 9, 11–22, 28–9, 41, 45–7, 62, 72–3, 82, 85–7, 92–7, 110–16, 135, 137; of the sacred 3, 11–20, 29, 41, 45–6, 111–12, 116, 137
hero-underdog 69–72
Holley, Mary Austin 32
Hume, Lea 35–40

Index

ideology 60–1, 94–5, 143
immigrant 21, 32, 68, 70, 73, 81–97, 147
Immigration and Customs Enforcement (ICE) 68, 85–7
inspection 15, 20, 27–30, 35–7, 39–42, 45–7, 136

Laredo, Texas 20, 28, 34, 37–47
legitimating power 4
Léon, Luis D. 110, 116, 120

male 4, 13–14, 19–21, 30–1, 34, 36, 39–42, 44, 57–68, 82, 84, 86–7, 93, 116–17, 144
masculinity 30, 60, 62–5, 82, 122
master-narrative 20, 27–8, 30
McCarty, Rev. John 5–7, 9, 11–12, 33–4, 45
Mckiernan-González, John 37
McKnight, J.M. 38
medical care 28–30, 95
meta-narrative 20, 55–6
Mexican male 20–1, 57–66
Mexican poor 35–7, 40, 45
migration 4, 35, 38, 65, 68, 70, 82–97, 144–54
minoritized 116–29
Montejano, David 42
Morín, José López 55, 72

nonsacred 2–3, 5, 7, 11, 17–19, 56, 73, 86–7, 94–5, 112, 127, 144

Paredes, Américo 28, 47, 55, 59, 73
Peña, Manuel 57–8, 69
postcolonial 4, 11–14, 18–19, 21–2, 58, 60, 64, 84, 90
Poulantzas, Nicos 81
public health 35–45

quarantine 5, 37–8, 40, 42, 45

racialize 27, 31, 82, 85, 90, 111, 124, 128
racial logic 15–16, 20, 28, 30, 41, 121, 153
Rankin, Melinda 33–4, 119
religious care 21, 82–3, 90–4
religious right 81, 84
Río Grande (Rio Grande) 7, 19, 35–6

sacralization 3, 5–6, 11–12, 14–15, 18–21, 28–47, 55–6, 60, 65–73, 85–97, 110–28, 138–9, 149
sacred apparatus 3–4, 14, 18–19, 36, 41, 45–6, 55, 84–6, 89–91, 111, 115, 124, 128, 143–5, 149
sacred Other 11–21, 95, 110–29
sacred-to-human 115
Saldívar, Ramón 57
Saunders, Bacon 28–9
Sayers, Joseph D. 37–40, 42, 44
scientific 2–3, 12, 15, 20, 27–30, 37, 39–41, 45–7, 55, 70–3, 116–17, 153
Serco 87–8
smallpox 20, 28, 34–41, 43, 45–6
social wound 56–8, 64, 119–20, 122, 124
State: archive 36; -sanctioned 2, 4, 9, 11, 28, 34, 39–40, 47, 56, 62, 64, 82, 86, 128, 146, 150
susto 11, 118, 123–6

Texas: Rangers 20–1, 28, 42–66, 73, 97; State Medical Association 48
Texas-Mexico borderlands 20, 30, 34
Treaty of Guadalupe Hidalgo 7, 9, 11, 12
Treviño, Jacinto 61, 63–4, 69
Trump, Donald 21–2, 68, 73, 81–91, 94–7

US-Mexico borderlands 1–5, 9, 12, 14, 16, 28, 35, 47, 55, 65–8, 73, 82–6, 92, 95

vaccination 37–8, 40–1

Webb County 38–9, 42
Western 1, 3–4, 8, 14–18, 27–9, 41, 46–7, 55, 70–3, 116–17, 139, 143, 149, 151–3
white supremacist 15, 30, 41, 46–7, 71, 73, 85, 96, 145; white superiority 32
wounded 12–13, 15, 22, 44, 56, 58, 62–4, 112, 117–20, 125, 127–8

Zacate Creek 37, 40–7, 96

Printed in the United States
by Baker & Taylor Publisher Services